W9-BMB-188

The Voice of Experience

To Stir a Magick Cauldron is a bold experiment in teaching what were once secrets of the Craft. Modern Witchcraft practices are presented in a straightforward manner by an acknowledged Craft elder. *To Stir a Magick Cauldron* is the sequel to the enormously popular *To Ride a Silver Broomstick: New Generation Witchcraft*.

Written for today's Witch, *To Stir a Magick Cauldron* is filled with dozens of techniques—many never before published—that unite Divinity with magick and knowledge. Take a fresh look at the Old Ways packed with insights and teachings drawn from a variety of backgrounds. Not structured for any particular tradition, the lessons and exercises in *To Stir a Magick Cauldron* are presented in a solitary format. Explore the exciting world of the working Witch through daily devotions, advanced circles, and a full and wide-ranging course of magickal study. There is even a Wicca 101 Test of Modern Craft Knowledge based upon the teachings offered in this book and its companion volume, *To Ride a Silver Broomstick*.

To Stir a Magick Cauldron is an upbeat and down-to-earth guide to intermediate-level magickal practices based upon the personal experience and success of a third-degree working Witch. Silver RavenWolf has worked long and hard to build bridges of understanding and harmony within the Craft community.

The land and our people are meant to prosper. The destiny of the working Witch is to emerge in strength and talent as we assist with the rebirth of balance in our culture. That's what this book is all about: the never-ending process of self-study and spiritual transformation.

Whatever your path, *To Stir a Magick Cauldron* presents a challenging and stimulating course of advanced magickal study that is unique within the Craft. Let Silver RavenWolf lead you beyond the mundane world into the mysteries and magick of New Generation Witchcraft.

About the Author

"My dedication to the world of alternative publishing and the rights of individuals to practice their chosen religious beliefs is more than a conditioned response," says Silver RavenWolf, Director of the International WPPA. The International Wiccan/Pagan Press Alliance is a network of Pagan newsletters, publishers, and writers. "The written word of the people of this century is vitally important in the realm of alternative religious practices and theologies," she explains. "Without these publications and writers, with their unceasing dedication to the people of the new generation in spirituality, we would be once again under persecution."

Silver is a Witch with many cloaks. "A woman once asked me what I do for a living," she chuckles. "I couldn't answer her. I do so many things that she would get bored or insulted with my list of 'I am's.'" Born on September 11, 1956, Silver is a true Virgo; she adores making lists and arranging things in order. "I hate housework, but I can't stand a messy house. I have determined a robot/nanny would be useful. If anyone can build one for me, let me know."

To Write to the Author

If you wish to contact the author, write to:

Silver RavenWolf
P.O. Box 1392
Mechanicsburg, PA 17055-1392, USA

Please enclose a legal-sized self-addressed, stamped envelope for reply, or $1.00 to cover costs. The author will not reply unless this guideline is met.

If you wish more information about this book or other Llewellyn titles, please write to:

Llewellyn Worldwide
P.O. Box 64383, Dept. K424-2
St. Paul MN 55164-0383, USA

Both the author and publisher enjoy hearing from you and learning of your enjoyment of this book and how it has helped you. Llewellyn Worldwide cannot guarantee that every letter written to the author will be answered.

To Stir a Magick Cauldron

A Witch's Guide to Casting and Conjuring

Silver RavenWolf

1999
Llewellyn Publications
St. Paul, MN 55164-0383, USA

To Stir a Magick Cauldron © 1995 by Silver RavenWolf. All rights reserved. No part of this book may be used or reproduced in any manner whatsoever, including Internet usage, without written permission from Llewellyn Publications, except in the case of brief quotations embodied in critical articles and reviews.

FIRST EDITION
Ninth printing, 1999

Cover art: Sally J. Smith
Cover design: Anne Marie Garrison
Interior illustrations: Silver RavenWolf, pages 2, 24, 46, 66, 94, 122, 154, 198, 234; Tom Grewe; symbols on pages 281-284 from *Living Wicca* © 1993 by Scott Cunningham
Book design and layout: Jessica Thoreson

Cataloging-in-Publication Data
RavenWolf, Silver, 1956 -
    To stir a magick cauldron: a witch's guide to casting and conjuring /
    Silver RavenWolf -- 1st ed.
        p.   cm.
    Includes bibliographical references (p. xxx) and index.
    ISBN 1-56718-424-3 (trade pbk.)
    1. Witchcraft. 2. Paganism. 3. Magic.   I. Title.
    BF1571.R388   1995
    133.4'3--dc20   95-45595
                                                                          CIP

Llewellyn Worldwide does not participate in, endorse, or have any authority or responsibility concerning private business transactions between our authors and the public.
    All mail addressed to the author is forwarded but the publisher cannot, unless specifically instructed by the author, give out an address or phone number.

Llewellyn Publications
A Division of Llewellyn Worldwide, Ltd.
P.O. Box 64383, St. Paul, MN 55164-0383
www.llewellyn.com

Printed in the United States of America

This one's for the Morrigan

May all Her people
live long and prosperous lives . . . .

Morrigan Book Blessing

Hearken as the Witch's Word
calls the Lady and the Lord
Moon above and Earth below
Sky's cool blue and sun's hot glow,
in this right and ready hour,
fill these pages with thy power.
May no unprepared eye see
the secrets which entrusted be
to I who walk this hidden road
to find the Hearthstone's calm abode
Guardians from the Four Directions,
hear me and lend Thy protection:
may these truths of Earth and skies
shielded be from prying eyes.
But to the Witches whose map this be
may the way be plain to see;
and, through all the coming Ages,
may we find home in these pages.
So mote it be!

—Jack Veasey

Other Books by the Author

To Ride a Silver Broomstick
Beneath a Mountain Moon (fiction)
Angels: Companions in Magick
American Folk Magick—Charms, Spells & Herbals
Teen Witch
Witches Runes (formerly *The Rune Oracle)* (with Nigel Jackson)
To Light a Sacred Flame
Silver's Spells for Prosperity
Halloween—Customs, Recipes & Spells

Forthcoming

Silver's Spells for Protection

Table of Contents

Acknowledgements

A good book is never, ever written alone. Friends and family listen to you prattle about it for an eternity, until in their opinion, it is finally out of their hair. To my family, thanks for bearing with me as I glued myself morning, noon, and night to the computer. Yes, the keyboard is detachable from my hands. See? Now we can go bowling, swimming, and (shudder) school shopping.

To Bried FoxSong: The strength and support you have given over these many years has not gone unappreciated or unnoticed. You were always the first, and the best, teacher.

To Lord Serphant of Serphant Stone: You accommodated your world to help me in mine. Not many people would do that. I honor you as well.

To Lord Ariel Morgan: You provided an opportunity for advancement. I will be forever grateful.

To the men and women of the Black Forest Clan: Together, we have made a wonderful temple. May our people live long and prosper, as the saying goes.

Special thanks to: Lady Diane McDonough, my friend and confidante. Lady MorningStar of MorningStar Farms, whose contributions to this book and stable personality uplifted my sense of self. Cynthia, for reading through the manuscript and offering special insights that only a new student to the Craft could provide. I love your many questions. They keep me on my toes. Lord Tim Zidik, for being indispensible to the Clan, and providing his own twist of information for this book. Lady Black Isis, for sharing her friendship with me. Lady Bats for circling always, in good form.

Finally, to my husband of fifteen years—hang on for the next fifteen, it will most certainly be grand. I've never met anyone with such stubborn determination to make something work. I admire you.

To wrap up these thank-you's, I don't want to forget the Llewellyn staff, who most assuredly work hard on every author's book, right down to the switchboard operator, who is always pleasant and helpful. Sometimes I think we pen-in-hand-people don't give you the credit you deserve. Special to my heart are Nancy Mostad, Acquisitions Manager—my friend and an excellent author in her own right—and Jessica Thoreson, for her editing expertise and dynamite personality.

Preface: Lifting the Veil

It is ten minutes till midnight on Samhain Eve, the last harvest of the year and the time of the Feast of the Dead. The world fills with pulsating energies, straining beyond the veil to touch humankind, to remember, and to return the gift of memory.

You find yourself standing in a large, secluded clearing. Some call it a grove, others the Nemeton. The tall firs flanking three sides of this magickal place continue to stand firm and regal, their dark shrouded limbs beckoning secrecy and protection. Behind you lies the midnight-white stubble of a corn field, its bounty given to the people so that they may prosper during the harsh, cold months to come. The vile poison of humankind smokes in the background—the cities overflow with crime and despair, corruption and greed. No longer are you a person of centuries past, but of the present.

A mist creeps upon the ground. Light, silvery, it tickles the hems of pant legs and long, heavy gowns, then caresses cloaks and capes of many hues. The moon begins its arduous journey across the heavens, casting rippling beams of ivory magick upon all below. As before, you are one among many—young and old, robust and slender. A sea of faces, each barely masking taut anticipation, wavers before you. Eyes of all ages examine the grove carefully. Are they satisfied that all is ready? Whispers undulate in the mist, weaving the threads of unity among the people. You can feel it. They strive for oneness with the Universe, drifting close, then separating. With relief, you know you are finally a part of those around you, searching for a common goal.

You glance at a lone woman who stares at the poisoned heavens, her lips set in a determined line. Her gray cloak swirls about her in a breath of chill, evening air. She pads gracefully to the center of the circle, moving through deep flickering shadows of the surrounding torchlight. Your attention draws to the whispers among the people.

"What shall we do?" mouths an old woman to her companion.

"Don't think tonight will change anything," the young man whispers.

"All has not been well for the people since your last visit," says the woman beside you. "Though the elders are doing a good job at hiding it."

The group mind touches you. It is a fleeting thought, a stab of pain. Despair snakes through their energy.

Perhaps it is hope that spurs the others on, or fear that cloaks their minds. Maybe it is sheer determination. With graceful, practiced hands, the woman in gray prepares the need-fire, bowing reverently as the flames take hold.

A hush envelops the grove as the flames rise to the heavens, licking and spitting sparks that refuse to die. Every man, woman, and child draws closer to the fire. They clasp hands. An old woman puts her booted foot next to the instep of the man beside her, and he does the same to the person beside him. The entire circle links and becomes one. You are one with the heartbeat of the Universe.

In silence, the woman lays her hands upon a mound of dirt near the need-fire. Eyes closed, she speaks softly. She utters words only the Gods can hear. Moving to a bowl of water, she repeats the procedure. From a pocket in her gray woolen cloak she withdraws a handful of powdered herbs. With a delicate flick of her wrist, she throws the powder into the jaws of the flames, murmuring with the hiss and spit of the wood. Arms outstretched, she steps back. Mist and fragrance rise in a voluminous cloud above the sanctuary.

Many around you inhale the sacred breath of the elements. Shutting your eyes, you too breathe slowly. A warm sense of love encircles you. The burdens of life lift away, layer upon layer. Your heart is free, your soul purified. All breathe in unison. You are one.

The creeping mists and rising fragrance coalesce above the need-fire. You sense there are a few in the sacred grove who wish to break and run. The minds of the elders hold them firm—this must not happen. You can feel the mental touch of the strong and pure as they pull together the scattered energies attempting to free themselves.

"The circle has not yet been cast," sputters a young female.

"Hush!" hisses the old woman who first drew the people together. "You do not yet know all the mysteries!"

The form above the need-fire tightens. The woman in the circle kneels beside the mound of dirt, digging her hands deep, cupping the soft loam in her palms. She rises, lifting her cupped hands to her breast.

"As the sands of time dissolve into the oneness of the Universe, I call forth the Ancient Ones to protect us and impart their wisdom. Ancestors of old, arise now and join the human bridge that awaits you." So saying, she opens her arms slowly, then parts her fingers, allowing the dirt to patter to the ground. From the shadows cast by the flickering need-fire, wraiths of those beloved pass among the living.

Suddenly you know why you are here. It is so simple, yet so complex. It doesn't matter whether you have been practicing alone, or with a group. It doesn't matter if you have dedicated yourself, or someone assisted you. What matters is the Great Mystery.

With anticipation, you understand that everyone here surges toward the same purpose. Together, you will wake the Mother from her sleep of two thousand years. The reign of Her Son draws to a close. Under the tutelage of the Son, the Children of the Mother learned to love, work, and develop on the earth plane—much like the Son himself. It is time to reunite with Her, and bring balance back to the planet. Only at Samhain can the Mother awaken from her deep slumber among the dead. Then new legends will grow from Her people; legends of prosperity, peace, and love.

The woman in the circle raises her arms and clasps her hands together, index fingers extended, pointing to the need-fire.

Mother Wise and Mother Strong
Wake to meet your mighty throng
From the vortex now give birth
A magick circle round our girth.

A blue dot appears in the center of the need-fire; it expands into a brilliant blue circle. Rushing out and encompassing all present, it forms a protective bubble around the entire company, above and below.

"As above, so below!" shouts the Witch. "This circle is sealed!" The howl of wind and wolves rings in the ears of all, yet nothing physically moves.

"She is coming!" shouts an excited child. "She is coming!"

Your heart pounds in anticipation.

The woman again points to the center of the need-fire.

Mother Wise and Mother Strong
Wake to meet your mighty throng
From the element of air
Bring our Mother, wise and fair.
From the element of fire
Bring the Mother we desire.
From the element of earth
Form Her essence, give Her birth
From the element of water
Bring to us the Sacred Daughter.

The crowd begins to stamp the ground as they chant the words of the woman. The hair on the back of your neck begins to rise.

A scream.

A crack.

The God stands in the center of the circle, his muscles rippling in the fire-light, his mighty head tossing golden sparks from the tips of his antlered rack.

Silence, sweet and dark, descends upon the circle.

He raises his ebony eyes to the heavens. "Wake now, my Lady, for Our time has come. As you bid so long ago, I have guarded your children. My duty is now fulfilled. Together, your children and I await your return. Wake, my Lady, to the new Aeon."

The ground rumbles, the trees shudder, but the people hold firm. From beneath the earth the cries of birth sound, cutting the air with a living frenzy, pouring forth into the circle. The center of the need-fire pulses and expands. Electrified air fills your nostrils. The Goddess arises, She-phoenix of the flames. Ravens swoop from the west, hovering and screaming in the air above her illuminated head. Smiling, She floats from the fire and embraces the God.

She has risen!

The veil lifts.

Introduction

We Pagans and Witches have an interesting statement that goes something like this: "Merry meet, and merry part, until we merry meet again." If this is the first time you are picking up one of my books, then merry meet! I'm sure you and I have much in common. Together, we will explore the realms of the religion and magick of the Craft to enhance your life. If you have read some of my other books, then merry meet again! I'm honored to spend time with you. I hope that you too, learn some new things and have fun with a little of the old.

With information designed for solitaries, coveners, and traditionalists alike, we will explore both new and old aspects of the Craft. I have had the pleasure to walk in all three types of worship: solitary, eclectic circle, and tradition. Interestingly enough, I don't prefer one over another. Each is different, yet similar in their intentions. Each has its own set of activities designed to enhance the spiritual, mental, and physical parts of our lives. As before, I'm going to stay out of Craft politics. It is a queen I do not serve. This has occasionally gotten me into difficulties here and there, but the God and Goddess have always been by my side, showing me the possible paths I could take, and assisting me in the decisions I have chosen.

That, my friend, is the basis of the Craft: Each individual is free to make choices for him or herself that will improve his or her environment, family, career, and spirituality. People of the Craft also have the power to remove things from their lives that impede their growth or cause danger to their well-being. In essence, all Witches have control over their own lives, and are responsible for their actions.

This material focuses on solitary practice. My reasoning is simple—you can be in all the groups and traditions you like. When it comes down to it, some of the most powerful magick you will ever work and the most personal spiritual experiences you will ever have will come when you are working alone. I do not imply that magnificent magick from group workings is irrelevant; no indeed. Those things closest to your heart, however, will be done on your own. You came into this world by yourself and you will leave in the same way. It is the cycle of life, after all. It doesn't matter if you are a self-dedicated Witch or an elder of a large tradition—your individuality makes you important. Your unique flavor molds your magick into a caliber that no one else can match.

The text you are about to read describes a very important part of my life, and like *To Ride a Silver Broomstick,* speaks plainly and simply about living a life of a Witch. It is also a testimony to magick and my religious beliefs. *To Ride a Silver Broomstick* beat the odds in getting published in the first place. It beat them again by becoming one of the top sellers for the company. If that isn't magick and belief, I don't know what is! What I wish most to stress is this: If I can capture my dreams and hold on to them, so can you. Of course, we are all expected to work and grow to continue the life of these dreams. Who says you can't have a career as an artist? Who says you can't have a stable and happy home? It is going to take a lot of work on your part, because as you work, you learn. Isn't that what life is all about—learning, challenging, and bringing ideas and dreams into form?

The Craft is a natural way of life and a natural way of living. When practiced with honor and within ethical bounds, it is harmonious and breeds harmony, just like any other religion on the face of this planet over the span of its wise years. The Craft is exciting. It allows you to mix religion, science, and individuality, making the best possible you, and the best possible world around you.

It can happen!
It happened to me.

May You Never Thirst,
Jenine E. Trayer
aka Silver RavenWolf
October 31, 1994

To Stir a
Magick Cauldron

Transformation of the Witch

Conjuring Your Courage

Of Frogs and Ponds

You are the foundation of your religious practices and your magick. You can learn the various religious theologies, but it takes your courage to put them into motion. Advances in psychology and medicine confirm the connection between our spiritual, mental, and physical bodies. What affects one, affects the others. Alternative health care enthusiasts have been screaming for years that bodily healing and the mind are connected. During my research on Pow-Wow[1] magick and faith-healing, I discovered some of the intricate links between mind, healing, body, and Divinity. Astounded at my own successes, I immediately taught my children and friends everything I could lay my hands on to improve the quality of their lives.

Spirituality is the hub of the Wiccan religion. Without it, magickal achievements quickly degenerate in the face of the intricacies of everyday life. Magick without Divinity has been the reason for many downfalls, such as the decline of the Hexmeister Doctors in south-central Pennsylvania during the early twentieth century. Success in Witchcraft requires serious application of the mind guided by the spirituality of the soul. In other words, don't mess with magick if your heart isn't into positive stuff. Eventually, you will fail. A good Wiccan group focuses on spirituality, not egocentricity. It is the same for

---

1. Pow-Wow is Pennsylvania Dutch German Witchcraft. See *HexCraft* by Silver RavenWolf, Llewellyn Publications, if you are interested in this topic.

a solitary practitioner. When spirituality is forgotten or pushed aside for the purpose of widening personal ponds, ritual becomes empty and the matrix of the group is permanently damaged.

We are all like the proverbial frog who strives to be comfortable in his/her own pond. If we allow our pond to become stagnant, we lose. If we drain the spirituality from our pond, we lose. If we try to drag negative energies into our pond, upsetting its balance, we lose. If we try to mess around in someone else's pond, we are subject to death by drowning. If we insist someone else share our pond with us, demanding our pond be widened to satisfy only ourselves and not the needs of others, the floods of destruction will come—no more pond.

Every human loses when spiritual balance is no longer important.

Those Nifty Tools

Every religious structure has tools designed to assist the seeker. If you don't believe me, take a trip to the library or turn on TLC (The Learning Channel) or the Discovery Channel and check out some of the major religions of our times (and of times long ago). Most of these religions have colorful tools and props to lift the psychological spirits of the participants. Wicca is no different. I find it amusing that those religions that seek to oppress do not use many props or colorful applications these days. To me, it is a sick person who can find no humor or beauty in religion or gaiety in the celebration of God. To be serious all the time is a mental drag—forcing religion to become a boring and tedious set of motions. These forms of religion condone the repression of the people they were originally designed to serve. In my mind, religion should be more than a book from which everyone can twist the words. It should be built on personal acts of joy, laughter, pleasant thoughts, high self-esteem, and the satisfaction of assisting others in their time of need.

However, a tool, whether it be the wand, cup, pentacle, athame, broom, censor, or whatever, cannot express joy. It cannot laugh. It does not have high self-esteem. It does not feel the satisfaction of helping others when the job is done. It takes the person activating the appropriate energies of the Universe to do these things. Yes, tools can become filled with your energy, but they do not direct the energy on their own. They need you to do that. To be honest, if tools were necessary for your heightened spirituality, they would have taken the trip through the birth canal with you. That would be an interesting experience! "Yes, Joan, I gave birth to a twenty-pound baby today. He came with a chalice, a wand, a beautiful silver pentacle, and oh yes, the athame. I believe he is going to be a Wiccan!" Ouch!

The working Witch has his or her view on tools, their need, and their uses in perspective. You don't have to have them, but they are nice, fun, and assist in the various applications of your work. I've gotten far too many letters and phone calls from people who tell me, "I have to wait until I collect all my tools to take my dedication." Bull! I never told anyone they have to have an entire room stocked with magickal gizmos to practice the Craft. You and Divinity are all that's necessary—the rest of the stuff is fluff. It's great if you have it, but you're not going to fail if you don't. In essence, you don't have to have tools to conjure spirituality. Instead, you've got to have guts.

✿ Your Work ✿

For one full month, put away all your tools. Work both religiously and magickally without them. Record your experiences, including psychic, mundane, physical, mental, and spiritual reactions.

Harmony Without Harm

I once read a tarot book by Sasha Fenton in which she was describing how to do a particular tarot spread. As she wrote, she realized her sample spread explained a phone call she had received an hour earlier. As the reader, I thought this was interesting. For some reason, how the event occurred during her writing process stuck in my mind. Now I know why.

Today was an interesting day for me. I wrote for two hours, met with a student, took care of my family, talked to my editor, answered some letters, did my school crossing guard routine, did six loads of laundry (I do have four kids, you know), got a call from a close friend in New York, and finally plopped myself back at the computer around 11:00 P.M. Tonight was the second evening of the full moon, hence somewhere along the line, work needed to be done. Today was also the anniversary of Scott Cunningham's passing, and that too, was on my mind. I went to the altar and lit a candle for him.

Back to my desk I went. My husband was watching television, trying to ascertain when the Susquehanna River would crest. He was attempting to read the stock market at the same time. I turned on my computer and got ready to rock—my CRT[2] and me.

Wrong.

The phone rang. I looked at the clock. Who could be calling me at this hour of the night? Normally, I leave the answering machine on and wait for the message. If it is an emergency, I'll pick up. I didn't wait for the machine to come on, I simply grabbed the receiver.

The individual on the other end of the line was a stranger to me. He'd been given my number by a local shopkeeper. I'm still a little mystified as to

---

2. CRT is an abbreviation for Cathode Ray Tube—generally used in referencing one's computer.

why I was the lucky recipient of this call, other than the fact that the caller said he was a Wiccan, after a while.

Okay, I thought. At least it wasn't someone who wanted me to scare "boogies" out of his house. (Hey, it was a full moon; you get all kinds, you know.) I assumed I was on firm ground. I was talking to a strange person at 11:30 at night who said he was a Wiccan and believed—never mind, you wouldn't believe me if I told you. It might as well have been a boogie haunting by the time I'd spent twenty minutes in the conversation.

Very carefully I began asking questions here and there, trying to help him with his problem. At one point I closed my eyes and asked the Goddess for support and to allow the right words to come out of my mouth. (It was a full moon, after all.) Setting the individual's problems aside for the moment, I discovered that the person had never done any ritual, had never heard that Wiccans do any type of religious devotions, nor had even attempted to cast a circle. He did say he burned candles and told me jokes about coming out of the broom closet. A half an hour into the conversation, I was more confused than my caller—who never did give me his name, but informed me he was highly intelligent (didn't I realize this?) and had many, many books.

Uh-oh.

Here was precisely the example I was trying to explain, not but—oh my stars—an hour before. Time certainly flies under a full moon.

And here was a message for me to pass on to you. *Magick does travel the path of the least resistance.* This time it was through my phone line. The message? Oh, sorry. Books are great, networking is great, phone conversations are great, but none of them will do you any good unless you put what you learn into practice and experience life and religion for yourself. To be a Wiccan or a Witch, whichever handle you deem most appropriate, you have got to live the structure. Wearing a pentacle and cracking jokes about "closet time" doesn't cut it.

Did I say this to the fellow on the line? No. Granted, there are people who need a slap upside the head, but not this guy. He needed me to keep my mouth shut and my ego in check. Explaining how magnificent my pond is and bragging about what I know would not have been an act of service to this individual. Basically, he needed someone to listen, and with luck, create harmony without harm.

Daily Devotions

One of the things I covered with our caller (I say "our" because you are sharing this experience with me) was to explain the concept of daily devotions. The individual was a stranger to me, and the time was limited. There was no way I could educate him on the structure of Wicca in a forty-five-minute phone call. Remember that all individuals are seekers—each looks for harmony and balance in his or her own way. Each person is struggling with the ecosystem of his or her own pond. Don't feel bad if your efforts don't go well, as long as you know in your heart you did what you could. Perhaps your job was to open a mental door. It is not your responsibility to walk the person through it.

When people come to you with their problems, whether they be religious or mundane, listen first to determine what you can do to help them, and learn to compartmentalize issues. That's what a Witch at work does. Use your wisdom to determine what is beyond your scope of assistance. This process will allow you to give the seeker the most service possible in a short time. If you get off-track with the individual, he or she may be parked in your dining room for several hours.

Daily devotions are very important to the working Witch. You can throw the bones and celebrate all the holidays you want, but when it comes to choosing which way to go and how to get there, daily devotions are the key to success. Witchcraft is not simply a set of magickal operations—it is, indeed, a religion. It is based on holy precepts that have a basic rule of order, including petitions to divinity in the form of daily devotions. When you are up to your eyeballs in goop (that you most likely created yourself with the help of your personal, built-in goop maker) you can dump it all at the feet of the God and Goddess and say, "Help! I've created a monster, and I don't know what to do with it. Save me before it eats me up!" The difference between Craft prayer and other religious prayer is in the focus and control of energy.

Before I analyze devotions for you, let's do some work.

Many religions have sacred hours where prayers are intoned or acts of honor are practiced. The Craft is no exception. Many of us say grace before meals, prayers before bedtime, etc., as in any other religion. Devotions have a purpose—they calm the mind, open the spirit, and allow one to look beyond the present events that keep us occupied and open us to the positive forces of the Universe. The most common times to perform sacred devotions are:

Upon rising
Noon
Sunset
Before sleep
Before meals
Before a magickal working
Before a ritual

A daily devotion isn't kneel, blab, run off to the shower. It is a testimony of faith and can be an act of intricate beauty, leaving one fulfilled if done correctly. It is an act of personal empowerment.

The biggest drawback with devotions is remembering to do them. Later in this chapter I will walk you through a few devotions I've written, but such devotions need to speak to you on a personal level. You will get a chance to write both informal and formal devotions.

❀ Your Work ✿

Project 1: Write five simple devotions for the following times: Upon rising, noon, sunset, before sleep, and before meals. Keep them short and to the point so you can memorize them.

Project 2: Practice these devotions for at least thirty days, then stop for one week. Can you tell the difference in yourself? These devotions will allow your spirit to grow and teach your mind to calm itself when calm is most needed. When you have mastered the simple devotions, you could choose one sacred hour to be a little more elaborate then the others. Your decision may rest on timing (you know you won't be disturbed before bedtime) or because you enjoy a particular hour of the day (such as sunset).

A daily devotion fits into any positive, religious structure. Although this is a text on the religious and magickal applications of Witchcraft, there is no reason why anyone of any positive faith could not use its teachings in other religious formats. If you have a friend who is going through a bad time, why not suggest the idea of a devotion to him or her? The devotion is not unique to any one religious structure, it is for everyone.

A devotion may be as long or short as you like; however, it must encompass enough linear time for you to ground, center, perform the devotion, then ground and center again.

To ground means to make yourself stable. This can be done in a variety of ways. I teach my students to envision their legs as tree trunks, rooted to the Earth Mother. Other people like to begin by putting their hands on the ground, the altar, or a table top. If you are into gems, you can hold a piece of hematite. Take several deep breaths and exhale slowly. Shut your eyes and feel your connection to the earth.

Centering is the process of pulling your energy to a central point in your body, normally at your navel, or slightly above or below. Try all three to determine which is the most comfortable for you. Almost every meditation or Craft book on the market today talks a little bit about centering. Your center is the seat of your power, and in an emergency you will need to access it. (We will get to that later.) For now, practice is important. If you use your devotions every day, at least morning and night, you will also be practicing your magickal skills.

Centering is normally done after the grounding process. To get the feel of centering, imagine that your energy is a big sheet stuffed in a little box (you). Let the sheet expand past your body. Let it flap in the breeze for awhile, then suck it back in. Let it out again, this time half way, then pull it in again. Now let it out a little bit, and bring it back. Do this at least ten times a day until you get used to the "feeling."

One of the most important things I have discovered when teaching others is that they must learn to ascertain for themselves what various spiritual, healing, and magickal activities feel like to them. For example, you know by now how you feel when you are coming down with a cold or the flu. With every person, the energy balances in the body register differently to the conscious mind. It is vital the student realize how that energy manifests symptoms or signals that will be processed by their conscious mind. To do this, you must take your time and register the feeling when it occurs. Allow your mind to catalogue it for future reference.

This is how the High Priestess or group leader learns to manipulate energy, both her or his own, and that of the group. Some work on instinct, others by feeling, and still others by sight. It is also how the working Witch knows when the time is right to let go of building power or to focus on something specific. Anyone can do it, it simply takes practice and belief in yourself. If someone says to me, "I've been trying and trying to raise energy, but nothing happens," I know they haven't walked themselves slowly enough through the process.

After any type of meditation or magickal exercise, you should ground yourself again. There are several ways to do this:

1. Run cold water over your hands.
2. Hold a piece of hematite in your hand. (You choose the hand in which it feels best.)
3. Imagine energy draining from your body, through your feet, into the earth.
4. Send the excess energy into the Universe for peace, healing, etc.
5. Send the excess energy into your tools or into your altar.

A devotion should always raise your energy level and leave you feeling refreshed. A very wise elder once said to me, "No, no dear, you never use *your* energy, you manipulate the energies around you." Now, here is where the grounding and centering part comes in. To show you exactly what he meant, practice the grounding and centering exercise below.

The Tapestry Meditation

Steady, Even Breathing

Take a deep breath and relax all the muscles in your body. Take another deep breath and relax your mind; think of a positive place. Take another deep breath and imagine you are floating freely in a positive Universe. Continue until you are completely relaxed and calm.

Pull in your personal energy to your navel. Count down from ten to one, slowly.

The Energy of the Sacred Horn

Visualize the God above you, glowing gold, reaching out to touch you. A beam of golden light leaves his hands and spirals downward to kiss your head. Your head fills with the light, which continues downward through your body, traveling deep into the womb of the Goddess.

The Energy of the Sacred Cauldron

Visualize the Goddess below you, now connected to the God by the gold light. Her aura glows silver. She is reaching out to touch you. A jet of silver steam leaves Her hands and spirals upward to kiss your feet. Your feet fill with the magnetic steam of the earth, and this steam continues to spiral upward through your body.

The Sacred Tapestry

The rising earth power weaves around the descending golden light, and circulates through your body. The sun power flows down to connect with the belly of the earth. The cauldron/earth power rises to connect to the sun.

Your Sacred Center

Feel yourself now glowing with the energies of the Universe. Center the energy given to you. Direct this energy into personal healing, healing for others, or for some other positive goal.

The Sacred Return

Return the gold energy to the God with thanks. Return the silver energy to the Goddess with thanks. Center yourself once again. Let any excess energy drain off into the ground or toward a positive goal, such as healing the earth.

Count slowly from one to ten. Open your eyes and breathe deeply. You should feel relaxed and wide awake.

In basic Wiccan belief (although this may differ from trad[3] to trad or group to group), it is said that the God emanates the power and the Goddess directs and disperses it wisely. In this way, balance in the Universe is created. This devotion meditation isn't easy. If you are not up to par with your visualization work, you will have to practice it a bit until you can get the images

---

3. Trad means tradition or traditional Witch; one who belongs to a specific branch of Wicca. See Chapter 9 for a full discussion of traditional Witches.

focused and moving in the required manner. However, if you work with it long enough, you will be delighted at the benefits.

A devotion should be focused on positive energies. As you have seen with the previous example, your intent and focus should be on thoughts of happiness, joy, reverence, honor, etc. When you are finished, you should feel refreshed, cleansed, and at peace with the world.

Not all devotions are meditations. For example, every morning I go to my altar, ground, center, say a small prayer, then anoint myself. When I began doing devotions, the feeling of peace and calm came to me when I had finished. Now, all I need do is touch my altar stone to begin my devotion and my pattern of "peace with myself and the world" immediately kicks in.

A devotion can be spontaneous or you can write one in advance. There are two kinds of devotions—impromptu (when you say what is on your mind) and rehearsed (a set of memorized words or motions). Both work well. Both will reach the same desired end. For the most part, I do not recommend reading a devotion, though you could read a favorite passage in the middle of a devotion, if you so choose. A long reading, whether it is in ritual or in devotion, takes away from the focus as we are apt to blab off words rather than live them. I've noticed participants in group ritual tend to become bored during long readings. They shift their feet, look around, and are not spiritually moved by the piece. (Hint: If you are visiting a group ritual where long readings are the norm, close your eyes and meld with the spirit of the words—the purpose can touch you through visualization.) Rehearsed words, if said at the right pace, can provide you with a profound experience, or can be used as a springboard for impromptu speech.

A devotion is a ritual of energy. Seekers are always striving toward learning the Wiccan mysteries. Although I am a traditional Witch myself, I clench my teeth every time a magickal person alludes to "the mysteries." After many years of personal and group training, I have discovered that those who spout about "the mysteries" in vague terms are merely trying to impress others, or hide the fact that they never figured the mystery out. The mystery is not hard to comprehend. We are all one. That's it—that's the mystery. How you meld with the collective unconscious is your set of mysteries. How you feel in meditation is your set of mysteries. How you participate in group energy and ritual is your set of "mysteries." How you do magick is your set of "mysteries." How you raise your spirituality and commune with God/Goddess is how well you understand "the mysteries."

When you work with the combined energy of yourself and the Divine, you have accomplished, understood, and interacted with a Wiccan mystery. A devotion then, is a Wiecan mystery.

A devotion should be done in private or in a group ritual environment where the practice is understood and respected. Religion and magick are both private affairs. If there are people around who are going to make fun of you, look down at you because they think you've chosen a second-rate religion, or disapprove of the actions you've chosen to honor Divinity, it will only cause stress on your part and inhibit your performance.

I receive many letters from people who either are interested in practicing Wicca or have begun recently, and are having difficulty with parents or partners who will not accept their choice. In most cases, this opinion comes from one of four sources:

1. The partner or parent is uneducated about our religion. This is not an insurmountable problem and can be solved by time, patience, educational materials, as well as the partner observing how you live, the positive changes that come about in your personality, and the fact that you have not grown another head.

2. The partner or parent has been educated, but is selfish. "How will it affect me?" he or she thinks. "What if the neighbors, our family, or my business partners find out—what will they think of me?"

3. The Wiccan doesn't really want to share his or her religion. After all, it makes the person special and can be something reserved for self. This too, in its own way, is a selfish act. As the partner is shut out, it hurts his or her feelings and makes him or her think the worst.

4. Intensified brainwashing from other structured religions or friends. This is a hard one to deal with. If the mind is truly closed, you will have to come to grips and make a choice. Either it is what you want, or what the world wants. If you cannot compromise, something has to give.

It's been a long time since I've had to fight the battle on the home front for my religion. First, I educated my partner. Fine, but that doesn't mean we didn't swing into #2 or #3. We did. We had several verbal rows over the subject. However, our story has a happy ending. (Although I'll admit that a bizarre set of circumstances guided my spouse and me closer together.)

When two elders of the Craft were scheduled to visit me to confer my third degree, I was really worried. My husband no longer objected to my religious choice and had been working with me in the magickal community for quite some time, but I knew in my heart that he was very uneasy about the entire situation in general. We vacillated between #2 and #3 on that list. I can still remember sitting at the dining room table, waiting for the elders to arrive. My husband was standing at the window, then walked outside on the patio. Two car doors banged and my husband stuck his head in the door, "They're here," he whispered. "And you'd better prepare yourself." I later found out my husband was talking about Lord Serphant, who looks the equivalent of Gandalf in Lord of the Rings, staff, beard, and all.

A friend of mine was with me, and we looked at each other in terror. How my husband accepted these people would determine whether or not my weekend was going to go in the toilet. Let's face it, if your spouse is miserable, it is going to affect you, one way or another. My husband is a Leo, so guess how effective he can be. Ahem.

The first evening was non-commital. *Well, one down, two to go,* I thought.

The second day was absolutely bizarre. To begin with, my husband helped Lord Serphant take all the furniture out of my dining room. Together, they made a ritual area, complete with many stones from the yard, as well as constructing a stone altar. I was in shock. Not only was my husband extremely amiable to these people, he was helping them rip the house apart. Did anyone have a camera?

On the second night, the ceremony commenced. Because my husband would continue to work with me and assist in my training and rituals of other individuals, it was determined that he would be allowed to participate in my third-degree initiation. Yes, I know this is practically unheard of in traditional circles—but wait until I tell you what happened, and how I know it was the right thing to do.

As with all Wiccan ceremonies, there is a time when the God and the Goddess are invoked. This isn't a secret, and I'm not telling you the entire ritual so I'm not going to get batted on the head for giving out private information. Anyway, this was done, the work finished, and the circle closed. The degree had been conferred. I remember sitting in the middle of my dining room floor and saying to Serphant, "We've done this before, you know."

He smiled, patted me on the head and said, "Welcome home."

Then, we turned right around and initiated five of the women who had been working with me. To put it bluntly, it was a night of magick, mystery, and exhaustion.

We were all busy the next day, seeing our guests off and all the things that go with entertaining, so I didn't really notice much. Besides, degree ceremonies have a way of opening things, changing attitudes, etc., so I doubt I would have noticed Lady Godiva riding naked on a horse down the street.

It was two days later that I realized something very strange had indeed occurred. Actually, I didn't notice it, the children did.

"What's happened to Daddy?" They were all lined up in front of me— one, two, three, four—and the dog was sitting at the end of the line.

"What do you mean? He's out in the backyard, isn't he?" I asked.

They all looked at each other the way children do when they are sure that you aren't going to want to hear what they have to say, but one of them will have the guts to blurt it out. It was the oldest who finally took the plunge. "Daddy is different."

This was starting to sound like a B-rated horror movie. If I remembered correctly, my house is not situated in Amityville, nor was I recently involved in the remake of *The Body Snatchers.* "Different how?" I asked.

Child number two: "Well, different, that's all—but different nice."

"That's right!" said child number three.

Child number four nodded solemnly, which is unheard of—he's a Sagittarius and I don't think he ever stops smiling.

"I'm glad you all think Daddy is different in a good way," I said lamely. Come to think of it, my husband had been acting differently ever since the night of my ceremony. He was calmer, happier, and very nurturing to everyone, even strangers. (Leos don't particularly care for strangers on their turf.) Now, let me make it clear that my husband was a nice guy before the ceremony; that's why I married him in the first place. But, to be sure, he was different somehow … but different good.

Today, my husband functions as an elder in the tradition. We work as a team on many things. With others, he leaves me my space to do what I need, and I leave him space to do what he needs. It is my firm belief, and the belief of the elders present that night, the belief of my children, and the belief of all those who were connected to the work here at that time, that something strange and wonderful blessed our home that night. From that moment on, we have never argued about the Craft. She truly does change every thing She touches, and everything She touches changes immensely.

I debated on whether I should tell you this story or not. It is rather unbelievable. At first, I was going to fictionalize it and put it in *Beneath a Mountain Moon*. It occurred to me that in a fictionalized version, no one would really believe it, but hope that something like it could happen—that's what fiction is for, after all, to explore alternative realities. At the last minute, I took it out of that book. It happened. It's real. And you should have the advantage of that knowledge in a book about my reality.

A devotion does not require ritual tools, although they can be added if you so desire. Devotions can be performed with wands, chalices, bowls, athames, or your hands. You do not need a big collection of items to become one with Divinity. Part of my personal morning devotion is to light a candle that burns until mid-afternoon. At sunset, I light another that burns till about my bedtime. What makes the devotion special is how you tailor it so it gives you the most benefit.

A devotion can be done anywhere, at any time, depending upon the focus, of course. Most of us lead busy, active lives, and it is not possible to perform a lengthy devotional several times during the day. Most of the working Witches I know reserve at least one time a day for a complete devotional, such as morning or before bed, and the remainder of the day perform "quickies." (Don't get funny.)

Fast devotionals can be a walk outside at lunch time where you breathe deeply, relax, and link yourself with Divinity, or when you simply shut your office door, lean back, and meditate for five or ten minutes. If you are constantly surrounded by people, go to the bathroom. Hopefully no one knows what you are doing in there, anyway.

A devotion does not need to be done in sacred space, but you can make it so. Sacred space is a purified area, a specific place you have cleansed and consecrated for a specific function. We will cover sacred space, cleansing, and consecration in detail in Chapter Two.

A devotion does not need to be done in a cast circle, but you can make it so. A cast circle is called a magick circle, where energy is erected to pocket the energy you raise until it is ready to be released. (See Chapter Five.)

The mystery of the devotion is becoming one with the Universe.

Daily Devotionals for You to Try

I wait to do my morning devotion until after I am fully awake and walking around the house. I figure if I'm bleary-eyed and unsteady, I'm not giving my full attention to the matter at hand. I don't know about you, but my focus upon rising is lousy. Also, you will find a house full of tumbling people at 6:30 AM, charging around each other to muscle into the bathroom, my postage-stamp-sized kitchen, and out the door. The first thing I do is drink something warm, then get dressed and awake enough to deal with the day. At night, I wait until everyone—I mean everyone, including the dog—has settled down for the evening. I take a long shower or ritual bath (so I will not be bleary-eyed again, this time with exhaustion) before the devotional. The evening devotional is my favorite. I can take time with it and relax, with the cares and worries of the day long past and laid to rest. I play favorite music on my stereo and sit by my altar, soaking up the peaceful energies of Divinity.

The following devotionals are those I practice myself. You'll not find them in any book. I wrote them, and have been performing them for many years. Some have words, some do not. They are often simple, sometimes complex, patterns to connect with spirituality.

Devotion to the Lady and Lord

Stand at a window that faces the rising sun (moon). Ground and center. Stand in the Goddess Position (feet apart, arms out from either side, palms tilted toward the sunrise). Breathe deeply again.

Lift your chin. Balance your energy by turning one palm down, and leaving the other up.

Continue to breathe deeply. Turn your palms the opposite way, turning the palm that was down up, and the palm that was up, down. Continue reversing your palms, allowing the energy to flow through your body.

Focus on the energy of the Lady moving up from the ground. Focus on the energy of the Lord in the sunlight that touches you through the window. Say:

> *I am one with Universal perfection.*
> *I invoke the positive energies of the Lord and Lady to cleanse and*
>   *bless my body and spirit*
> *So that I may perform this day in love and honor*

> *(Sleep this night in peace and wisdom)*
> *As is befit a member of the Craft of the Wise.*
> *So mote it be.*

Put your arms down. Breathe deeply again, then ground and center.

In the evening, stand where you can see the moonlight, and rework the words a bit for blissful sleep and dreams of wisdom, as in the example above.

Devotion of the Elements

This is an excellent devotion for outside, but can be done inside, if you have something to represent the four elements on a dresser top, your altar, etc. Get dressed properly for the weather (of course) and step outside.

This is a type of devotional that can be done "down and dirty." For example, let's say you are busy in the morning and don't have much time to spend on your devotion. This one could be done at a bus stop in a very obtuse manner. Simply turn in the appropriate direction and shut your eyes, or look upward. No one will know what you are doing.

Face East, toward the rising sun, and breathe deeply. Ground and center yourself. Put your hands out in front of you, palms facing East. Feel the energies of the East moving beyond your fingertips. Say (or think):

> *Element of the East,*
> *I greet thee this morning (afternoon/evening) in perfect peace and*
> *perfect trust*
> *Bless me this day (afternoon/evening) with patience, wit, and*
> *mental harmony.*

Turn to the South, or take a walk in that direction till it feels right, then stop. Ground and center yourself. Put your hands out in front of you as before, palms facing the South. Feel the energies of that direction moving at your fingertips. Say (or think):

> *Element of the South,*
> *I greet thee this morning (afternoon/evening) in perfect love and*
> *perfect trust*
> *Bless me this day (afternoon/evening) with passion and healing.*

Take a walk to the West, or simply turn in that direction. Ground and center as before, then put your hands out before you. Say (or think):

> *Element of the West,*
> *I greet thee this morning (afternoon/evening) in perfect love and*
> *perfect trust*
> *Bless me this day (afternoon/evening) with healthy transformation*
> *and love.*

Take a walk to the North, or simply turn in that direction. Follow the previous steps of grounding and centering, then put your hands out before you. Say (or think):

> Element of the North,
> I greet thee this morning (afternoon/evening) in perfect love and
>   perfect trust
> Bless me this day (afternoon/evening) with stability and prosperity.

Walk to a place you feel is center, and ground and center again. Cross your arms in the "God" position (arms folded across your chest, legs spread apart). Say (or think):

> Guardians of the Spirit,
> I greet thee this morning (afternoon/evening) in perfect love and
>   perfect trust
> Bless me this day (afternoon/evening) with wisdom.
> Cleanse my body and spirit, so that I may be strong among the ranks
>   of the Craft of the Wise.

Ground and center.

This devotion can be repeated at noon and sunset, beginning with the direction of the sun. For example, at noon, the sun is overhead, so begin with the South, the element of fire and midday. At sunset, the sun is in the west, so you would face the West and begin your devotional there. Finally, before you retire, begin at the North, in honor of home (magnetic North). You are traveling clockwise around the wheel of elements.

Devotion of Ancestral Fire

This is one of my favorites, since Pow-Wow, a mixture of Heathenism, Celtic Witchcraft, and Native American Indian energies, is part of my genetic heritage. In Pow-Wow, fire (representing the South) and ice (representing the North) are the main elements used for magick and healing. I perform this devotion around mid-morning, but it can be done as soon as you awaken, if you like. If you must leave for work in the morning (as most people do), use a birthday candle. If you work at home, then use a tea candle, as it will burn until about noon. Consider the size of your candle and the amount of time you have available. I also perform this devotion before I retire each night.

Although you can simply use the Lord and Lady for this devotional, it is best tailored to the divinity you have chosen as your patron Goddess or God. If you have not chosen one, keep in mind that archetypes have many faces, yet the energies attributed to each remain the same. This devotional would be excellent for Sekhmet (the Egyptian Lion-Headed Goddess), Bried (as she is seen as a Celtic Fire Goddess of healing and has a cauldron in some myths), Igaehindvo (Amerindian Sun Goddess), Vesta (Roman Goddess of Fire), Agni

(Hindu Fire God), Nusku (Babylonian Fire God), or Taranis (Continental Celtic God of Lightning and Shrines). If you are a traditional Witch, by all means use the deities most familiar to you.

This is a simple devotion, but heavy in energy. As it pulls in ancestral worship, you may wish to call upon one of the Ladies of the Gates of Death (such as the Morrigan, Gubba, Hella, or the Calliech) to allow ancestral knowledge to reach you. I believe in working with Gods and Goddesses who are part of your personal, genetic mythology, especially in the beginning of Craft practice. I think a lot of seekers disregard these archetypes because they are looking for something new. If you like working with archetypes outside your cultural lineage, by all means do so, but give your history a chance at some point in your studies. In this ritual, I move between Continental Celtic deities and a few of the Heathen deities later absorbed into the Germanic culture.

Before you begin this devotion, keep in mind that all work is to be done with cleansed and consecrated items. This means that each item has been passed through the energies of the four elements, relieved of their negative energies, and blessed in the name of Divinity. If you use your working items only for magick and devotion, then cleansing, consecrating, and empowering need only be done once a month (preferably at a full or new moon, inside a cast circle). Personally, my magickal things are only that—magickal, religious items. I don't use them for cooking, cleaning, or other mundane employment. There are working Witches who use their magickal items for mundane chores as well. The choice is yours.

Supplies: An empty table or altar, a small cauldron (or fire-safe bowl), a candle cup or small holder that will fit inside the cauldron, a small handful of ice chips, one candle, a lighter.

Preparation: Set the cauldron in the middle of the table. If you can, make sure your body is facing either North or South, as these are the energies you will employ. Place the candle cup inside the cauldron. Sprinkle the ice chips around the outside of the candle cup, inside the cauldron.

Breathe deeply, then ground and center. Hold your hands over the ice and say:

> *I greet this day in love and trust*
> *I call my Ancestors from the dust*
> *Steadfast energies from the North*
> *Wisdom now, come ye forth.*

Light the candle and place it in the candle cup. Ground and center. Hold your hands over the flame (not too close, of course), and say:

> *I greet this day in love and trust*
> *I honor my Ancestors, gone to dust*
> *South brings harmony, passion and gain*
> *In service doth the working Witch reign.*

Ground and center. Put both hands around the cauldron and meditate on connecting with Divinity. You should feel your energy level rising now. If it helps, mix the energies of fire and ice together by moving your hand in a clockwise direction over the cauldron.

> *In honor burns this candle bright*
> *Of those gone long before*
> *To thee, O _____ I call your light (I call this night)*
> *To guide me ever more.*

Ground and center, leaving your work area with a smile on your face.

The Meal Devotional

The blessing of food and drink is older than our modern calendar. People of many cultures and religions have called upon Divinity to bless the food and drink set before them, and used the food and drink as representations of Divinity, long before the advent of Christianity. In ritual ceremony, this is called the blessing of the cakes and ale.

If you are at a table with several people, suggest they hold hands while the blessing is said. The mixture of energy helps small ones to focus and keep their hands off the food before it is served. Big people settle down, and are not apt to crack as many jokes once hands have been linked, especially if you are at the head of the table, monitoring the energy flow.

This particular blessing was designed to include the weather patterns in which we live. For example, the weather fronts move across our area from west to east.

> *From the East the sun rays shine*
> *From the South the gentle rain*
> *From the West blow winds divine*
> *From the North the gifts of gain.*
>
> *We gather now to bless this food*
> *In perfect peace and love*
> *Lord and Lady touch this meal*
> *With magick from above.*

Altar Devotion (by Jack Veasey)

> *Let what I feel fill me*
> *but not consume me;*
> *let me follow what I feel,*
> *but not be forced;*
> *let me become the kind of soul*
> *who never clings too hard,*
> *who lets go and yet loves;*

let me imagine better worlds,
yet work in this one;
let me touch, and treasure, even
people I can never hold,
and let me learn from all my losses;
let me out and let me in,
and let me see, and let me be
a window—maybe broken— but through which
a bit of air and sunlight comes.

The Devotion of the Altar

This is, by far, my favorite devotional. I wrote it three years ago for my study group and we have been using it ever since as an integral part of both our outer circle and traditional teachings. It is a result of watching several traditional Witches performing their opening ceremonies. It can be used by anyone, whether solitary or traditionalist. The altar devotion serves several purposes:

1. It allows the Witch to ground and center before any magickal working.
2. It sets the tone of the ritual.
3. It prepares your mind for spiritual and magickal pursuits, blocking out the mundane.
4. It focuses your mind and body on the energies embodied at the altar.
5. It mixes the energies of the four elements on the altar and melds them to spirit.

Supplies: Salt (place at compass North); water (place at compass West); stick incense (place at compass East); one candle, preferably red (place at compass South); illuminator candles or lamps, if you so desire.

Timing: Any time, whether before ritual or as a daily devotional.

Tools: None are required, though some individuals prefer to use a wand or athame. These days, I use my hands for most of the devotion, save when making holy water. Then, I use my athame.

Recitation: The altar devotion can be said out loud, or you can do it in your head. Wicca, unlike ceremonial magick, does not entirely depend on the precise blend of words or syllables to create a specific energy.

With all your supplies on the altar, take a few moments to relax and consider the task at hand. Shut out offending noises; become the center of your focus. Music helps to enhance the mood.

Breathe deeply; ground and center. Raise your hands before you, above your head in the Goddess position. Slowly pull them down and in at eye level and envision touching Divinity. Draw them slowly down and in toward your heart chakra,[4] then cross your wrists on your chest in the God position. You are now ready to begin.

Light the illuminator candles, envisioning the light of Divinity shining upon yourself, the altar, and the work that is to be performed.

Begin at the East. Light the incense; clap your hands sharply over the flame to extinguish it. Hold your hand over the incense and say:

> *Creature of Air*
> *I cleanse and consecrate thee by the Ancient Energies of the East*
> *I remove all negativity in this world and in the world of phantasm.*
> *Blessings of the Ancient Ones be on you now.*
> *So mote it be.*

Pass your hand over the incense three times (some Witches prefer to do a banishing pentagram[5]) to banish, then imagine a sparkling light around the incense.

(Because of my Pow-Wow heritage, the element of fire is of great importance to me. Therefore, you will find this incantation a little longer.) Light the candle, then hold it up at eye level and say:

> *O Creature of Fire*
> *Work my will by my desire.*
> *Black Forest ancestor, light my way*
> *Aid the magick cast this day.*

Set the candle down in the South, then say:

> *O Creature of Fire*
> *I cleanse and consecrate thee by the ancient energies of the South.*
> *I remove all negativity in this world and in the world of phantasm.*
> *Blessings of the Ancient Ones be on you now.*
> *So mote it be.*

Pass your hand over the flame three times (or do the banishing pentagram) to banish, then hold your hand steady to bless, imagining a sparkling light surrounding the candle.

At the West is water. Say:

> *Creature of Water*
> *I cleanse and consecrate thee in the names of the Ancient energies*

---

4. The chakras are seven energy vortexes in the body. These vortexes are located at specific points all in a row, which makes them easy to remember. Their locations and colors are: crown of the head (white), third eye or forehead (purple), throat (blue); heart (green); navel (yellow); below the navel (orange); groin (red). Individuals working in healing or meditational exercises often refer to the opening and closing of chakra centers to clear out negativity, promote self-healing, and bring protective and positive energy into the body.

5. See Chapter Seven for complete instructions on the banishing pentagram.

of the West
I cast out all negativity in this world and in the world of phantasm
Blessings of the Ancient Ones on you now.
So mote it be.

Pass your hand over the water three times (or do the banishing pentagram) to banish, then hold your hand steady to bless, imagining a sparkling light surrounding and infusing the water.

At the North is salt. Say:

Creature of Earth
I cleanse and consecrate thee in the names of the ancient energies of
the North
I cast out all negativity in this world and in the world of phantasm
Blessings of the Ancient Ones on you now.
So mote it be.

Pass your hand over the salt three times (or do the banishing pentagram) to banish, then hold your hand steady to bless, imagining a sparkling light surrounding and infusing the salt.

Hold the bowl of water in your hands and raise it before you, silently, in communion with the Gods. Move the water bowl to the center of the altar. [6]

Place three pinches of salt in the water (or balance a little salt on the athame blade and sprinkle it into the water three times—this takes practice, by the way). Stir thrice with your finger (or the blade). Pick up the athame, and say:

As the rod is to the God
So is the chalice to the Goddess

Begin to lower the knife into the water. As the knife is inserted into the water, say:

And together, they are One.

At this point, envision the water exploding with Divine energy. Make this energy colored, if you like.

---

6. Some traditions prefer a flat pantacle (not pentacle) in the center of the altar, or a wheel, pentacle, or in our case, a cauldron. This serves as a focal point of what the tradition represents or what the solitary works with, and gives you a hint of the type of magick performed. For example, if the pantacle is in the center, most of the ritual formats revolve around the mixture of Witchcraft and ceremonial magick. If a wheel, then a great deal of the work hinges on cycles, such as the wheel of the year, the seasonal changes, the eight paths of raising power, or the phases of the sun or moon. If there is an astrological symbol, or symbols, a great deal of the work follows the path of the heavens. If a cauldron, you are dealing with transformational change, where a great deal of ritual is focused on the betterment of self in the spiritual planes and the protection of the land and its people. If a stone, you are touching natural magicks of earth, air, water, fire, and the unity of the spirit. None of the focus listed are right or wrong—simply different, designed to meet the various needs of the group mind.

Remove the knife. Imagine that the altar is a giant cauldron. You have cleansed and blessed each element on the altar. Now, you are going to mix them together—meld them, if you will—into a vortex of positive, Divine energy. Beginning at the North (as all things come from the North for me, but some Witches prefer the East) in a clockwise, spiral motion, stir your hand over the altar five times, imagining the energies mixing together.

Tap the hilt of the knife, or your fingers, soundly five times (one for each element, plus Spirit) at the right, lower corner (the corner closest to your right hand if you are right-handed, the corner closest to your left hand if you are left-handed) to seal the power of the altar.

The devotion is done. Ground and center.

At this point, you can quit (if you are performing a daily devotional) or continue with your working. Throughout the text, I will refer to this devotional as a starting point for the Witch at work. Keep in mind that there is no single, right way to do anything in the Craft. There are a variety of actions, words, and patterns to complete any task. This way is simply one way to do it.

Before we go further, I'd like to talk a little bit about "feelings." During any magickal act, such as the previous devotional, you may experience a variety of sensations. Some individuals get hot flashes, feel a tingling in their fingers, or an all-out zap of energy throughout their bodies. Intuition and feelings are important in the Craft when it comes to spirituality and magickal workings. If it feels right, keep going. If it doesn't, stop and consider what may be wrong. Sometimes we are too tired to work magick, or we are sick, etc. In these instances, relax and feel the energy of Divinity, ground and center, and utter a short prayer. There are times when we are not physically capable of much of anything and that is okay. No one expects you to be super Witch. Do your best, and feel at peace. That is all anyone can ask for, and it is all you can ask of yourself.

❀ Your Work ✿

Project 1: Write a set of your own daily devotionals.

Project 2: Practice them for thirty days, preferably from new moon to new moon or full moon to full moon.

Project 3: Perform some or all of the devotions in this chapter.

Project 4: Conduct a favorite ritual, adding a new devotional written by yourself.

Angel
Incense

Conjuring Sacred Space

I n the past several years of writing and teaching, the topic of sacred space always managed to fall in my lap. "Oh, Silver, we need an article on sacred space. Would you mind doing it for us?" It got to where I would groan internally when the topic was mentioned. I forgot one of my favorite quotes from Richard Bach's *Illusions:* "You teach best what you most need to learn."

Sacred space and a cast, magick circle are two entirely different principles that meet during ritual and magick to become one. You don't have to cast a circle in sacred space; likewise, you don't need physical sacred space to cast a circle. Notice the words I use here: *don't have to* and *don't need.* Calling Divinity works regardless of where you are or in what circumstances you find yourself. However, simply because you don't need to cast a circle doesn't mean you shouldn't do it.

Many Witches complain that there are few advanced Wicca texts on the market. To find intermediate and advanced techniques, they turn to ceremonial magick, which provides more steps, more toys, more words, and more energy work. There is nothing wrong with this (I have many ceremonial friends and both admire and respect them), but there has to be a way for Wiccans to grow within our own religion, as well as study techniques relating to magick from other sources without giving up the practical power of the religion.

Part of the problem stems from our society in general. In a hurry-up world that provides unlimited information at our fingertips, it is difficult for the new student of the occult to understand that many Wiccan mysteries hinge on the maturation process and personal cycle. In short, most humans look for the easy way to do things. The media and marketing strategies support this limited view of the world. Unfortunately, there is no way to make a low-fat, five-minute meal in the occult, whether you are practicing alone or in a group.

When an individual becomes interested in Witchcraft, he or she is taking the first step in the reformatting of his or her life. It is a total make-over that reaches down into the very soul of the person. Habits, patterns, thought processes, and beliefs all need to be assessed, then tailored, enhanced, or trashed as the situation dictates. This does not happen overnight. It does not happen in one year's time. It is a process that never stops, because the Craft is a religion that urges its practitioners to be their best in this lifetime. To be exceptional at any activity is to build skill and faith. Building anything requires positive reinforcement, patience, and practice.

Many Wiccan mysteries begin with intuition, supported by actions that bring positive and life-affirming results, allowing you to reach further into self and outward toward Divinity. Logic and negative thoughts stifle intuition, twisting it away from the truth, resulting in self-doubt and destruction of self-esteem. Mind you, logic is not a bad thing, but it shouldn't control your life.

Learning the basics of sacred space is important when studying both the religious and scientific aspects of the Craft. Although tools, furniture, and other decorations can go in a sacred place, they are not required, nor does their presence create sacred space. Finally, no matter how long your involvement in occult studies, keep in mind that there is more to learn. What you may have thought to be a simple concept (such as sacred space) when you began your studies, can take on a mystery of its own as you journey further into an enlightened state. Witchcraft is unique in its presentation. If it fits, doesn't hurt anyone, and the result is favorable, develop it. There is no one right way to practice the Craft or be a religious person in general; everyone views sacred space differently. Here are some Craft theologies and examples on the subject.

The Universe is sacred space. In essence, all life and all places are sacred. To defile the air we breathe and the ground upon which we walk is to defile ourselves and our planet. Our planet is a sacred space in the Universe, as are the other planets and heavenly bodies. Therefore, sacred space can be a natural reservoir of energy, such as a stream, a mountain, a field, and so on. This type of sacred space belongs to everyone and to no one. Along your way, you will find people who call themselves self-appointed guardians of natural sacred space. Some of these guardians are megalomaniacs, trying to impress you with their importance. Use your common sense and don't fall for double-talk.

To appreciate Universal sacred space, we must look beyond modern religions and move into a place and time where the Earth and all upon it were honored by Shamanistic peoples. Because their survival depended on the land, not the dollar, they became linked with the world around them. Although superstition is not acceptable, intuition is. When our society destroyed what it considered superstition and replaced it with logic, it weakened our intuition.

The native people of the Americas and the clans of Europe felt strong ties to the land. As the land prospered, so did the people. As the people prospered, they reciprocated through their care of the land. Many times, deity names were not given to a particular stream, field, or pond. However, to protect the area, the people would call upon a guardian whose energies carried an association with prosperity or protection. For example, in one Celtic custom, the God Tarranis protected the hearth, home, and property. A shrine erected to that God (often beside or near running water) guarded the homestead. Offerings of milk or honey were left at the shrine by those living on the land. Sometimes, the people would name the energy of a natural sacred place, creating a thought-form from it to protect the energies located there.

Not all natural places are immediately useful as sacred spaces. Over the years, the land has become grumpy with humankind. Circumstances, such as wars, slaughter, and hatred created by people can eat away at the delicate balance and positive energy normally found there.

As an example, during the spring of 1994, the father of one of my students requested that I come out and bless his property. A recent visit from a monk, who had the odd talent of predicting family events caused by the energies of the land on which people lived, gave them a scare. The monk had excellent prediction gifts, but these gifts did not include solving proposed problems. For example, he visited a potential property investment for a young gentleman who was also considering marriage. The monk warned the man that the terrain had an unusual split. The energies there would not be conducive to family life, and if the young man bought the property and lived there, he was sure to find divorce at his front door within one year. The prospective buyer did not heed the monk's warning, bought the property, and subsequently divorced his bride nine months later. On another occasion, the monk told a family that as long as they lived in their home, money would be an illusive dream, as the slant of the property allowed water to run to the West. The owners went bankrupt.

This is the background they gave me. My student's father, by the way, is a psychologist, and reads voraciously on various religions. Although not a practitioner of the Craft, he was well-versed enough to know what his daughter was involved with and respected her beliefs. I like parents like him!

When I arrived at the home (magickal paraphernalia in tow), I discovered another predictive gem from the monk. He informed the owners that any adult woman who filled the reigning female roll of the family would sicken and die if she remained on this property. How pleasant. The house owner's first wife had died of cancer several years before. His second wife now had an odd affliction in her right leg that the doctors could not diagnose. Could I do something for her? And, could I do something about the land?

First, we went over the mundane stuff. Had they had a radon check? Were there any power lines about (those evil EMFs,[1] you know), and had they had the water checked? Had they sprayed any pesticides recently or regularly over the years? The owner promised to investigate these things. In the meantime, my job was to figure out what the heck to do about the property. As this was a

---

1. EMF stands for Electro-Magnetic Fields. Scientists are currently studying the effects of these fields on human beings.

residential area, I also asked about neighbors, and found that most did not stay for long periods. The street was a relator's dream of musical residences. I asked about the history of the land. It was a new development, thrust onto land accustomed to a combination of forest and cornfields for over a hundred years.

Having a famous predictive monk preceding you with a story about how this land hated women does not put one into a comfortable position. Last time I took a shower, I believe I was still inhabiting a woman's body. I'd thought it odd that the land would take a patriarchal view, as to me, the land is feminine. You know, Earth Mother, and all those teachings? It didn't make any sense to me at all. Unless, of course, as one of my friends (Bried FoxSong) suggested, the land did carry female tendencies and was jealous of any other adult females sharing space with her. Now, if we were talking about a Deva, that was entirely possible.

I'd blessed houses and land before, but never tackled such an ominous task. I decided to take consecrated stones from my property, as well as fashion a stang to erect as an altar, decorated with beaded leather thongs made by myself and my children. I also brought along an Eye of Horus I'd made over the winter to turn away any evil generated by neighbors. You never know what the trigger may be until you start digging around and eliminating possibilities.

I picked a Saturn day to do the job as I wanted to transmute those energies, bind negative energies and dismiss others, neutralize the situation, provide protection for the residents, and manifest prosperity for both the land and its people. I also checked to make sure the moon wasn't void of course. (We'll get to the reasoning on that later.) The weather had been nasty that March, but I lucked out. It was sunny and enough warmth danced about to get the blood running. What more could I ask?

My first order of business included walking the boundaries of the owner's land. The property was pentagon-shaped. At the top of the pentagon stood a lifeless peach tree. We were near the heart of the original farm family nucleus, as the barn stood to the right (by the point) and the old farmhouse nestled beyond, off the current owner's property. The land where my student lived now may have been a barnyard or even a slaughter area. However, with peach trees in the yard, it very well could have been the family orchard. In its agricultural heyday, most farms in this area had their own private apple, pear, and peach trees away from the slaughter house.

My next task was to sit in the middle of the yard and have a little meditative chat with whatever was living there. In sacred space, constructed to house only my body, I sat back and let the impressions come in. Very carefully I checked for feelings of animosity, hatred, sickness, etc. I got none of that. I even expected a screaming earth spirit to shake its finger at me and tell me where I could go, and what I could do when I got there.

Not a thing.

What I discovered was loneliness, pure and simple, and confusion. Land energies are not on a time schedule as humans understand it. To this land, people came here, tore out the trees, and created death. They dug, moved, and damaged everything. I looked around me. Houses were everywhere. There were swimming pools, metal sheds, patios—all the things that humans feel they need to survive. I saw fancy decks and elaborate fire pits. Ribbons of macadam snaked up and down the land, weighing down the precious soil beneath. Soil accustomed to plenty of rain, growing things, and the pitter-patter of animal paws now dealt with humans' play toys, hatreds, and selfish desires. People forgot about the land, and all the junk they stuck into and on it. The torn natural ground cover, the murder of the trees, and destruction of natural habitats, were still fresh on its mind, as if it happened yesterday, not twenty or thirty years ago. Like a little child who loses all that is important, it had feelings of frustration and pain. It also carried a very feminine, and feline, personality.

I told the land what I wanted to do—bless it, relieve some of its pain, and make it a sacred place the owners would love and honor. The choice of where to put a shrine is more a matter of intuition, rather than one of compass points and regimentation. As I came out of my meditation, I looked in front of me to see two forsythia bushes at the end of the yard, arched toward each other—to me, this was a perfect place for a shrine. Later, I discovered compass-wise, these bushes were fairly near East. I dug a hole, erected the stang, and supported it with stones, finally placing a flat stone before it to serve as an altar. I later explained to the owner that he would have to sink the stang further into the ground, as his own gesture of good will toward the land.

With my student, we went to each corner of the property (beginning clockwise and at the point of the pentagon) and placed a fertilized egg in the ground. My student said the following at each corner:

Blessings of the Gods on you
As this egg returns to the ground
So will health and prosperity grow for this land and my family.

We then placed a consecrated stone from my property over each egg. In the future, should my student wish to repeat what we did that day as a daily ritual, she can find our magickal markers without difficulty.

Back at the altar I began digging in my bag of magickal goodies. Out came salt, water, beer, incense, my cauldron, oil, and a tea candle. I set up shop, performed the altar devotion, and blessed the stone with oil. I then poured the beer as an offering around the altar and stang in a clockwise motion. I took the now holy water, and poured it before the altar in the shape of a crescent moon. No grass would grow there that summer, leaving the mark of the Goddess on the land.

In this case, I did not close down the energies I had called because my intention was to make a permanent, sacred space. It would take a while, about the cycle of one full moon, for the energies and the people on the land to harmonize. I also explained to both the owner and the female head of household that they should leave offerings of milk and honey at least once a month. I then suggested cultivating a flower garden around the altar, and keeping the forsythia trimmed back so when one looked out the kitchen window, the altar would be within view. As the female head of household also believed in the power of Buddha, I suggested His statue become a part of the shrine. The visit ended with some healing instructions and energy work for the woman's leg.

What I did that day at the home of my student is what working Witches do. You respond to a need and harmonize the situation with the skills you possess. When you realize that all religions are from a single source and you can work within any structure's parameters, then you have indeed mastered the most important Wiccan mystery, that of blending images, beliefs, and energy into one positive force—the harmony of the All.

Ancients Witches hearken nigh
Earth and Wind, Water and Sky
Stars above and core below
Peace and prosperity, energy flow.

I suppose you want to know the outcome of this story. The woman of the household got better. The physicians finally came up with a diagnosis and did whatever physicians do. In fact, she felt so much better, she eventually got outside and planted some of her favorite flowers.

Did the father of my student believe in anything we had done? You'll get a kick out of this. Although he was pretty quiet about it, his true feelings came out about three months later. The family went on vacation. When they returned, there was no sign of the shrine. The father panicked, running around the yard, shouting that some awful thief had stolen his shrine. What were they going to do? It was okay. Remember, I placed the shrine between two forsythia bushes. While the family vacationed, the bushes grew completely over the shrine, like a giant, flowering waterfall, and protected it from any intruders. Upon lifting the boughs, there stood the shrine, as peaceful and strong as ever.

I believe the land is most comfortable with its owners. Of course, should they ever move—well, that's another story.

Where the Witch is, the place is sacred. This follows the premise that if you are living a life of harmony and following the Wiccan Rede of "an it harm none," you are operating in sacred space.

❀ Your Work ❧

Project 1: If you own land where you live, design a shrine and a ritual to go with its erection. Perform it.

Project 2: If you do not own land where you live, take a walk outside and connect with the earth energies around you. Talk to them. Introduce yourself and have a great conversation.

Project 3: In meditation, greet the nature spirits (or Devas) of your property. Devas can assist in both your health and spiritual growth. You only need ask them.

In my hometown, I'm known as the Pow-Wow Witch. Trads are not understood here, Pow-Wow is. Pow-Wow energy is something that you carry with you, all the time. This energy is foreign to many Witches in the United States because there aren't that many of us practicing these days. It's unusual because it carries its own "beat." Like Craft, the power is passed from one generation to the next, or from expert to student. Sometimes, the energy lies dormant through several generations before it is activated again. Unlike general, modern magicians, Pow-Wows learn to create immediate sacred space without the use of tools. They make it by weaving words, sacred breath, and Divine energy together. There is no beginning, no trigger, no devotion— although all these things can assist in the performance if the Pow-Wow so desires. Pow-Wow is the last vestige of European Craft found in this country. To survive, it instinctively linked itself to the magick of the land here, that which is compatible with the indigenous peoples of the Americas.

My study and practice of Pow-Wow was an important milestone in my life. I had always believed there was Craft before Gardner. (No offense to Gardnerians intended, I assure you, as my Craft lineage comes partially from that direction.) I wanted to know the mysteries as they applied to the area in which I live and my heritage. It was through the practice of Pow-Wow that I began to understand that the Witch is the Magick (an observation made by Marion Weinstein), and that he or she is sacred—indeed, all humans are sacred. I also got to touch what it may have been like to practice as a solitary Witch hundreds of years ago, as Pow-Wows operate alone (unless extreme nasties are about). Finally, it dawned on me that for any Witch to successfully work in the Americas, he or she must make the effort to meld with the land and its energies where he or she is living or working. As much as I adore trad work and the history of the magickal religions, I realized that to touch the ancient mysteries, one must touch sacred space alone. In the process, one must learn to *be* sacred space, a harmonious vehicle internally, to work successful magick externally.

> *Sacred space within myself*
> *Earth and sky, light and health*
> *Blessings of the Goddess shine*
> *Bring to me thy love Divine*
> *As above, it is below*
> *Now peace and love around me grow.*
> *Be I Witch, Faery, or Elf*
> *Sacred space I call myself.*

Sacred space is an area, whether tangible or intangible, where people meet in perfect love and perfect peace. Such a space would be the environment of an open circle or a study group where there is balance and harmony. Study groups work best in sacred space prepared with burning sage combined with a blessing. If there is greed, jealousy, or power-tripping taking place (to name a few possibilities), the space remains defiled and unfit for acts of ritual or magick. In traditional practices, none may enter the magick circle if they carry a grudge against another group member. The High Priestess carries the responsibility to ensure differences are resolved before a ritual begins. If the argument or unfortunate feelings cannot find another outlet or resolution, one or both of the participants may be asked to leave. To carry this thought further, one should not enter sacred space if permanent hard feelings have developed between two or more people.

❀ Your Work ❁

Project 1: Make a list of what you feel makes you sacred. Make another list of what you feel makes you not so sacred. Can you improve upon yourself?

Project 2: Practice centering yourself by expanding your sacred self outside your human body, then pulling it back in. Do it slowly, snap it like a rubber band, make it move out in waves and coil back in. Think of the many ways you can expand and contract your center. Practice this every evening for one moon, and at least once a week thereafter.

The Salute of the Cauldron

Creating sacred space for several people, whether it be family members at a special holiday or an open study group, does not require a full-blown ritual format. Our family designed a salute that each member participates in equally. The only tools for this act of honor are a small cauldron and a candle that fits inside in a candle cup (you can also use a tea candle). Whether we are sitting on the floor, standing, or around the table, we all gather together in a rough circle. Going clockwise and starting with the person in the North, each performs the salute, utters a silent prayer, and passes the cauldron to the next person. Two things are necessary:

1. That the cauldron not grow too hot to hold.
2. That the individual be old enough so he or she won't drop the pot.

Light the candle and say:

> *Ancient Ones I now impart*
> *By candle flame remove the dark*

Hold the cauldron with both hands, chest level, at arm's length and say:

> *Blessings of the Goddess upon us.*

With the entire cauldron, make the sign of the banishing pentagram and say:

Blessings of the God upon us.

Then pass the cauldron right through the center of the imaginary pentagram. Visualize the cauldron filling with Universal love and peace. Pull the blessings of the Universe back through the pentagram (toward you). Utter a soft prayer over the cauldron:

Love and joy, peace and trust
I conjure thee among the Clan

Pass the cauldron to the next person in a clockwise direction.

There can be many variations to this salute. On occasion, each person stands at a specific quarter and says something special for that direction and its representative energies:

Blessings of the North upon us
Winds of strength
Bring us perfect peace and perfect trust.

Blessings of the East upon us
Winds of intellect
I conjure harmony, love, and trust.

Blessings of the South with trust
Winds of creativity
Gently touch each among us.

Blessings of the West draw nigh
Winds of love
Through the Universe, hear my cry.

When the last person receives and blesses the cauldron, return it to the person who began the salute. He or she is to hold the cauldron out at eye level and add the final blessings:

The mysteries now rise
For the children of the wise.

Shining daughters
Shining sons
Ancient ones of forest.

Perfect love and perfect peace
Enter here before us.

Depending upon the nature of the night, whether it be an Esbat, a Sabbat, or a simple meal, you can fill the cauldron with something other than a candle. We have blessed seeds to disperse among those present for blessings of prosperity in their home, small jewelry for them to wear, or hard candies for them to eat after a specific working.

In some Craft circles, an end salute when the work or celebration concludes is standard procedure. It need not be done by everyone. You can choose someone ahead of time, or the leader of the group or family may wish to perform this function.

> *Eve of work and night of pleasure*
> *Happiness circles now full measure*
> *Earth and Fire, Air and Water*
> *Heaven's Queen and Moonlight's Daughter*
> *Bless this company as we leave*
> *Carry His protective seed.*
> *Blessings of (your patron God and Goddess) upon you.*

❁ Your Work ❁

Project 1: Practice the Cauldron Salute.

Project 2: Write your own Cauldron Salute to match your tradition or personal practices.

Sacred space is where you live. Where the Witch is, is sacred. However, remember that your everyday environment soaks up the energies you raise, cast off, pull in, or manipulate. There are all sorts of things bouncing around your house at any given time.

I consider my home and my property sacred space. It is important to me to honor the land on which I live, as it is providing a place for me on the planet in this incarnation. Over the years, I have learned to command my environment to ensure it remains a sacred space. This is an important lesson for every one of us to learn. Sometimes it is difficult to maintain in the face of the needs of others, where you must learn the delicate balance of serving versus being overrun and mauled. It also requires faith. We would like every act with others to end or pass in a harmonious manner, but humans are not willing to allow this environment to exist to fulfill a personal need of their own. When the desires of others threaten the stability of your environment, you must have faith and courage to hold the balance necessary for harmonious interactions with other people. This requires work on your part, and should be one of the first areas of your life that you learn to perfect. In doing so, you will develop several skills that will be useful to assist others in their time of need in the future. Moving your environment toward harmony and retaining it is not a selfish act, but an act of Universal love.

Witches at work must remember that magick follows the path of least resistance. Many dabblers, when they learn this mystery of energy movement, hesitate to continue their studies. Why? Simply because they fear the change that positive forces may bring into their lives. A sad example of this situation I can think of are women who are currently living in an abusive environment and refuse to make positive movements toward release, due to their fears and repressive programming. Subconsciously, they know their present environment is dangerous, yet they are not willing to move beyond their fear to escape the situation. If you think I'm talking through my Witch's hat here, think again. I too suffered through an abusive marriage many years ago. Fought, left, and lived to tell the tale. It did not end there, however. I cannot count the women who have walked through my door for readings, or who have come to my open circles for a short time, never to return, as they are embroiled in these unfortunate life experiences and can not find the courage or the faith in themselves to change the situation. Using magick here to rectify the situation may result in one of the following difficult scenarios:

1. The abusive spouse may end up in jail.
2. The abused individual may find that he or she has to move to another environment.
3. Due to circumstances, the abused spouse may have to deal with the reality of getting a job.

In these cases, the individual may see change as loss. Until the person moves far enough away from the negative environment to assess logically what was (or is) happening, he or she is denying change and is not ready to make the journey. This change does not happen overnight, hence the frustration a non-trained individual feels. Thoughts of failure loom too close for logical consideration of the whole problem.

On a milder level, but no less important, are individuals who hate their jobs (your work environment is important, too), but for any number of reasons, refuse to look beyond their present situation for something new. With the use of magick, the person may very well lose their job, simply because the Universe is trying to right the situation, the individual is too stubborn to do much on the mundane level to change it, and the path of least resistance is—you guessed it—no more job. Of course, this is a bland statement, ignoring many factors a working Witch might use, such as:

Being focused
Looking at all angles of a situation fairly
Being willing to accept change
Being willing to work harmoniously with his or her chosen environment
Being specific on the level of need for change

It is up to the working Witch to be responsible for his or her own environment and ensure that it, above all else, remains sacred and harmonious. Naturally, there are mundane things you can do to secure harmony and sacredness, like working with the land, remodeling, or keeping your home in good repair. You don't have to be rich to have a pleasant, clean environment in which to live and work. Keeping things fairly in order helps, as chaos breeds contempt for self and others. Screen phone calls with an answering machine, set rules on times you are available for visiting, etc. These are all things which are rightfully in your control and should work for you in the way you feel most comfortable.

The working Witch also must learn to practice harmoniously with others to create a sacred environment. Learning to control your behavior without losing your identity is also important. Skilled Witches know when to speak, when to back down and let others voice their needs and opinions, when to quietly fold, when to work toward a harmonious solution, or when to stand out from a crowd to provide a role model for others to see. The way we affect people is the message we send before us, both in this lifetime and in times to come. If each working Witch considers carefully the results of his or her actions, the world indeed will be a better place.

The Eternal Flame House Shrine

You have progressed to a point where combining your altar for work and as a shrine is no longer feasible. Grab an end table where you can load some of your treasures and choose deity energy that is protective in nature for your home and family. Place the table in the direction attributed to that deity. The center focal point of your shrine should be a candle or oil lamp. Do not use an electric lamp, as part of the purpose of the shrine is its need for maintenance. By caring for and guarding the eternal flame, you expend positive energy and connect with Deity. Flicking a light switch simply will not fill the need, nor will it heighten your skills. Choose something that is inexpensive to supply, such as a miniature lamp or a holder for a tea candle. Your task is to create sacred, pulsating energy, whether or not the flame is actually burning.

After you arrange and decorate the shrine, take a few minutes to visualize the eternal flame of wisdom and protection in your mind. Do not light the candle or lamp yet. In the astral, build a replica of your shrine and light the sacred flame with holy breath.

Wiccans, along with many other magickal people, believe there are many planes of being. The Earth, our touchable world, resides on one of these planes. The astral can be defined as another dimension, a place where many planes of being are available (or not) to the human. The astral can be reached through the process of meditation or other mental exercises. In this exercise, you are accessing the astral through a meditation sequence. In this mental sequence, build a room with an altar that matches your physical area on which you will mentally put a candle. It will be ever-burning. Every time you go back to this safe and sacred mental place, the candle will be burning.

In the mundane world, light the candle.

> *Eternal flame*
> *Light Divine*
> *Enter here*
> *This sacred shrine.*

Eternal flame
Pulsate bright
Burn for me
Day and night.

Eternal flame
From ancient song
Bless this house
All life long.

This sacred shrine is dedicated to _____
Who in His/Her infinite wisdom
Will shelter, protect, and provide
Harmony and enlightenment for the Children of the Wise.

Let the candle burn until it is no more. Each evening for one cycle of the moon, light the candle first in the astral (the mental sacred place you have created in meditation), then in the mundane. Watch the energy grow around the shrine and flow out into the room, then encompass your entire home or apartment and all that is inside. Repeat the invocation above, or create one.

When the cycle is over, light the candle or lamp whenever you can. Repeat the entire blessing, both in the astral and in the mundane, each full or new moon.

✿ Your Work ✿

Project 1: Make a pact with yourself that you are willing to be responsible for your environment. Do this in ritual and support with nightly meditations and affirmations. Do the latter for one moon cycle.

Project 2: Design and erect your house shrine. Follow the directions for the Eternal Flame.

Sacred space can be ritually created for a long-term or short-term purpose. Creating longterm sacred space would be the act of building a home shrine (indoors or outdoors), a hearthstone altar, or a mini-altar that remains intact for as long as is deemed useful. Dedicate altars to Universal energies. Construct household shrines to honor a particular deity, as outlined above. Most working Witches have a hearthstone altar (the central altar of the property, whether indoors or out) and at least one shrine. This allows the hearthstone altar to be free of unnecessary clutter when the Witch is at work. Ritually cleanse physical sacred spaces, then consecrate and empower them for positive use, as shown previously with the house shrine.

Create short-term sacred space to encompass a ritual circle or yourself while you are meditating. It can be a short distance around your body, or cover an entire room of people. This is referred to as technical sacred space as it is created for a short-term purpose. Trigger this type of space by a call to the four quarters, four watchtowers, four elements, four angels, four winds, four totem animals, etc. It is up to the Witch on who or what to call, how, and why. There is no one right way to call quarters. What is right, is what gets the job done for you.

When the intention is to create a sacred space for the purpose of melding it to a magick circle, I have seen it constructed in three ways:

1. Before casting the circle, where the quarter/element call is first. This theology involves making an area of perfect love and perfect peace before casting the magick circle. Here, you are asking the energies you have focused on to join you in the celebration and to assist you in the work you plan to do, rather than stand there like He-Man with arms crossed and teeth bared to protect the circle.

For example, a friend of yours wants to get pregnant. She and her husband have been trying for a long time without success. They have done all the appropriate mundane motions, like medical tests and trying at the optimum times for her chemistry. Alas, alack—no baby. At this point, she comes to you for help. "I'm ready for Divine intervention," she says, "will you please help me?"

Unless you are stupid enough to ask for Damien, you don't need those menacing quarter guards to do a fairy Godmother/Godfather-type thing. While you are at it, you may not wish to use the athame (cutting and all). Maybe a wand or your hands would be better to create sacred space and draw a circle. In this sacred space, you are looking for assistance in bringing something sacred into form—what is more special and sacred than a baby? Like the fairy Godmother/Godfather, you will work for insemination, protection, and gifts from the elements to assist in carrying the baby full-term and giving it Divine attributes. I look at it this way: if a couple comes to me to help them conceive, then the Universe is looking to produce a special child. Don't get me wrong, all children are special, but if you call a Witch, something mysterious and beautiful is afoot.

Initiations are another time when sacred space is important. In several traditions, the performance of initiations takes place in sacred space only and the magick circle is never cast, as somewhere, someone wrote that only those initiated into the mysteries may enter the magick circle. Here, you are looking for a witness to the events. You are seeking acceptance from the Ancients for this candidate and asking for any gifts they might like to bestow on the seeker. The elders present are responsible for the protection of all present. If they can't handle it, they shouldn't be elders. Of course, there are many traditions in which much of the initiation procedure takes place outside a magick circle that is erected (complete with quarter calls) before the candidate enters the ritual area. Traditionalists also may ask guests to wait out of view during the circle casting and quarter calls at all of their rituals, as these two actions are secret and therefore privy only to the initiates of that tradition. Also, it is difficult to create astral sacred space or cast a circle when there are many people in a small room, especially if the procedure requires you to walk the perimeter.

Finally, in larger groups, there simply is too much consternation floating around to call quarters or cast a decent circle unless you are highly skilled in energy work. People are full of excitement, chatter, laughter, etc., and it can be difficult to get them to settle down. An example of this is at a festival site, where there may be up to five hundred people present.

Why am I giving you all this group information? To show you there are a variety of ways magickal people operate, no one set of procedures is the right way for everyone, and that you do have a choice in the way you practice your religion. A good teacher says to the student: "This is the way I do it, and it is the way we will do it together for the sake of building your skills in an area of mutual understanding. However, feel free to experiment. In the end, you will use what is best for you."

2. After a circle casting. The magick circle is cast first to create an area of perfect peace and perfect trust (see the difference?), and creates a house or boundary for the quarter energies to guard. These are the energies with big muscles and flashing teeth. They can't guard if they don't know where to stand—hence, the circle first and then the quarters. This is helpful when you have designed a ritual for a specific purpose (called a rite).

3. Sacred space and the circle are created all in one shot. This is a more advanced technique, because it requires good visualization techniques, an understanding of energy flow, and control. This is best done while working in a solitary capacity, since students or inexperienced guests will not understand that it has taken years of building your skills and going through the physical motions to complete this type of procedure with accuracy. They will not see the nuances that go on in your mind, and will therefore assume you have attempted a shake-'n-bake creation. It is also valuable in an emergency, where you need all the energies you can muster at that given moment. However, there is personal pleasure in creating sacred space and casting a magick circle where time is not an issue. This is why you will find Witches who have been practicing for many years still participating in group ritual, or setting aside several hours to complete a project of their own. Taking your time enhances skill and cleanses the spirit. It also unites and builds power among group participants.

We will cover all three types of technical sacred space later in this book, including various circle conjurations to enhance your studies.

Sacred space is created on the astral plane, during meditation. Most adept magickal individuals work well on the astral plane or planes of the astral. Once you have learned to meditate, the next step is to use this technique to enhance your skills, such as healing or divination. In the astral, you can go forward and backward in time, gain wisdom from a variety of oracles and teachers long gone from the mundane world, and increase your self-esteem and potential for success. Problem-solving and wellness programs are enhanced through working in the astral. I can not impress enough on any student of the occult the benefits of meditation—mentally, physically, and spiritually.

It takes a few journeys into the meditative state to fully design sacred space. If it helps, draw it on paper first. Include power items, such as a special altar, an unusual cauldron, a specific type of tree, etc., that will be with you. After designing the space, call Divinity into it, as you would in the mundane world. You can fill the space with the presence of a particular archetype or Universal, positive energies. It doesn't matter what or whom you choose. What matters is that it is comfortable for you and is a safe, peaceful place.

❁ Your Work ❧

Project 1: Design, on paper, your perfect sacred space. Use colored pencils, crayons, paints, or pastels. You can even create a nice needlework or banner if you like.

Project 2: For one full cycle of the moon, create your ultimate astral sacred space in meditation and visit it every evening, if only for a few moments.

Sacred space created by magickal people before you. Finally, there is physical, sacred space cultivated by humans before you. Examples here would be sacred areas blocked off by indigenous peoples (Native American Indians), Witches and Pagans who have set up nemetons at groves, campsites, and sanctuaries; hearthstone sanctuaries designed by a Mother Coven; historical sites cultivated and preserved in both the Americas and Europe; etc. When visiting these places, it is appropriate to leave an offering, such as a favorite bracelet, gemstone, necklace, or an item that is biodegradable, such as rice, water from your altar, or an acorn from your favorite oak tree. The gifts are limitless; the intent is focused—one of honor and harmony. As you give the offering, utter a prayer that fits the site and the occasion.

Guardians of this sacred space
Blessed energies great and small
Strength and protection for this place
And blessings on us all.

Meditation of the Five Winds

Indian Peg is a historical figure in my hometown. She is long gone to the Summerland, but her legend lives on. Indian Peg, goes the story, was a powerful conjurer and magick woman. Around here, lots of people consulted her for her healing skills. My grandfather Baker often spoke of her to both me and my father. She lived deep in the woods, at the top of a dirt lane. They even named the road after her—The Indian Peg Road. At a local historical society meeting a few years ago, one of the attendees suggested I go out to her old place. There was a leering dare in his voice. Sometimes people have such silly notions about Witches, you know.

At the time, I didn't think much about it. Life goes on and I had other things to keep me busy. Years passed and here I am, writing this chapter for you. You will find that most working Witches are also learning Witches. We are constantly honing our skills, trying to unearth new data or attempting to create positive ideas to assist both humankind and ourselves. No one ever stops learning, although we do reach plateaus in our progress.

I meditate every day for a variety of purposes, including relieving stress, staying healthy, gathering information, creating solutions to problems, and coming up with ideas to write about. During one evening's sequence, I found myself on a dirt road. Who do you think my meditative self put there? You guessed it—Indian Peg. The following meditation is one she showed me to share with you. I have tried it both as a meditation and then as a procedure for quarter calls. The first sequence of meditation is best if done in five parts— one gift for each day. If you do it in the morning, record both the meditation and the events of the day of the meditation. If you do it at night, record the meditation, any dreams you may have during the night, and the events of the next day. Work with the gift given each day, visualizing it in your life and using its energies. After you have completed the entire meditation sequence, you can put the parts together and do them in one meditation for reinforcement and further learning.

The Gifts of Indian Peg

Close your eyes and take several deep breaths. Use a familiar relaxing exercise, and ground and center.

Create an astral sacred space, such as a mountain clearing. Imagine you are sitting cross-legged at a campfire. Breathe deeply and enjoy the mountain scenery. Focus that you are here to receive the gift of the four winds from Indian Peg. She joins you at the campfire and you exchange pleasantries. She will sit across from you, about a foot away. After a time, she will tell you she has a gift for you and that you are to hold out your hand. Watch closely as she deposits her special treasure.

This is the first gift, the gift of the East Wind. In your hand, you will see a tiny, golden, spiraling wind. Watch as it swirls and sparkles in your hand. This is the wind of intellect, the gift of the mind. Relax and feel how this wind affects your inner being. How does it feel in your hand? How does it relate to your life now? How can you use it to help others? When you are through, let it go and thank Indian Peg.

The second gift is the gift of the South Wind. She will pass a tiny, ruby wind to you. Watch as it swirls in your hand. This is the wind of creativity and

41

passion—the gift of sparks and light. Relax and feel how this wind affects your inner being. How does it feel physically in your palm, compared to the East Wind you previously experienced? It is lighter, heavier, thicker, thinner, dryer? How does it relate to your life now? How can you use it to assist others? When you are through, let it go and thank Indian Peg for her gift.

The third gift is the gift of the West Wind. Indian Peg will hand you a tiny, sapphire wind. Watch it swirl and undulate. This is the wind of rebirth and transformation—the gift of wisdom from the ancients, as the West is their sacred direction. What is its consistency? How does it compare to the East or the South Wind? How does it differ? How can you use this wind in your life? When you are through, pass it back to Indian Peg and thank her. She will put it carefully in her pocket.

The fourth gift is the Wind of the North. Indian Peg will tell you "everything comes from the North," then place the wind carefully in your palm. This is an emerald wind, the gift of stability and the energy of the Mother. How does this wind affect you? How can it help you on your life path? When you are through, let this wind go and be sure to thank Indian Peg.

The fifth gift is the Wind of the Spirit. A raven circles the clearing, swooping lower and lower, until it lands on the shoulder of Indian Peg. In its mouth is the Gift of Spirit. Hold out your arm and let the raven alight there. Open your palm. It will walk down your arm and delicately deposit a silver wind with tiny stars interspersed, as if caught in cotton candy. The raven fades away, encompassing you in its magickal wake. The wind grows from your palm, swirling around you. How does it feel? How can you use this wind in your life? When finished, imagine the wind in your palm again. Summon the raven and it will retrieve the wind for others to share. Thank Indian Peg and offer her a gift. She will take it, give you parting words of wisdom, then disappear.

Breathe deeply now. Count from one to five and open your eyes.

Ground and center. Record your experiences.

After you have completed this first sequence of meditations, you can move on to a more complicated method of working with the five winds.

The next step is to work with them individually throughout the day. Use the sacred winds in problem-solving situations, healing, and creative opportunities. Try them in spell casting and rituals. Finally, written below is a concept that is marvelous for family rites, to teach children and students about sacred winds and sacred space. There are no words to memorize, although you must memorize the concept of the Five Winds.

Call of the Five Winds

Supplies: Your breath; five tubes of glitter (gold, red, blue, green, and silver); five candles (gold, red, blue, green, and silver); a one-foot by one-foot flat stone; a pair of soft cloth gloves.

Choose an area where you will not be disturbed, don't mind glitter on the floor, and will feel at peace.

Put on the gloves. Set the stone in the center of where you will be working, and place the silver candle in the middle of the stone. Set the candles around the stone in the appropriate quarters:

> East: Gold
> South: Red
> West: Blue
> North: Green

Cleanse, consecrate, and empower the stone. Bless it with oil and holy water if you like. Do the same with the candles. Place the glitter tubes within easy reach.

Play gentle music, if you like. Relax in the center of the room, beside your stone. This simple sacred space alignment requires that you be seated.

Do the altar devotion (or something similar) to begin your alignment.

Sit facing the East. Light the gold candle. Take a small amount of gold glitter in your hand and close your eyes. Concentrate on what the energies of the East represent to you and what you need in your life that coincides with these energies. You also can consider what you would like to honor. What gifts have you received recently from the energies of the East? Once you have contemplated long enough, open your eyes and blow the glitter off your gloved hand. Imagine the energies of the East wind blessing you, your sacred area, and any tasks you wish to perform that use that energy. As the glitter descends, remember what the small winds looked like in the previous meditation and envision them before you, touching you gently and bringing gifts of love and unity.

Repeat this procedure with each quarter, moving around the stone like the cycle of the seasons. Meditate on the blessings of this life and use this time to find solutions to problems, inspire creativity, etc.

After you finish, thank the energies you have called and bid them farewell. Extinguish the candles in a counterclockwise motion.

Ground and center.

Clean up and record your experiences.

After you have used all the props (candles, glitter, gloves) a few times, try the procedure using only the center stone. Take it outside if the weather is fine, and do the entire ritual in your head, as you did it in the physical realm before. What are the differences? Which do you prefer? For the record, traditional wind color associations were:

East: White
South: Red
West: Black
North: Yellow

If you like, try these and see what changes come about—or does the meditation remain the same? The Five Winds represent energies unique to themselves as well as those energies that coincide with the standard directions, sometimes called quarters. Quarter energy not only assists you in creating and protecting sacred space, it is also there to help you. These are very real energies that work. They don't stand there while you do your Witchie thing with their thumbs stuck in their mouths. They will work with you and assist you for as long as you need them. In that respect, then, quarter energies are not billowing entities that are to be summoned from the deep by a command from an egocentric human who wishes to have power over all. They are graceful and potent energies, to be sure, not minions to be squashed under your magickal heel.

Five Winds Cord

Finally, here is a bit of self-esteem magick using the Five Sacred Winds and a thirteen-inch cord of ⅛-inch thickness.

Supplies: A white or black cord, thirteen inches long; your center stone; five candles, as before.

Follow the directions for calling the winds given before. As you call each wind, ask it to empower the cord, except this time, begin with the Center (lighting the candle first), then move to East, South, West, and finally, North. As each wind is called and an appropriate time is given for request and energy exchange, put a knot in the cord in the following manner:

End -----7------5------3------1------2-----4-----6------ End

1=Center	2=East	3=South	
4=West	5=North	6=Goddess	7=God

At this point, there are two things you can do with the cord: Leave it, and during the next week or month, untie the knots when you need the energy represented; or tie the two ends of the cord together to make a sacred circle, and hang it by the North knot over your bed, over your altar, or put it in your pocket or purse.

At this time, you may wish to meditate for a while, or simply relax. When you are finished, say farewell to the Sacred Winds.

Ground and center.

Clean up.

❁ Your Work ✿

Project 1: Go to your local library or historical society and investigate historical sites in your area. Find three that may represent sacred space. Visit these areas and perform a meditation there. Write down your experiences. Later, you may wish to visit these sites in the astral or return in the physical.

Project 2: Practice the Meditation of the Five Winds for one full moon cycle. Keep a record of your experiences both in the astral and in the physical world.

Project 3: Practice the Call of the Five Winds for one full moon cycle. Keep a record of your experiences both in the astral and in the physical world.

Project 4: Try the Five Winds Cord experience. Keep a record of your experience.

As you can see by the examples in this chapter, the possibilities of sacred space are not only unlimited but varied through your perception. Throughout the life of a working Witch, the need and practicality for cultivating and maintaining sacred space is extremely important for success. How you maintain the present affects both yourself and others in the future. Your personal interaction with sacred space is a valuable Wiccan mystery.

Conjuring Laughter, Focus, Triggers, and Salutes

I guess you've gotten the hint by now that practicing the Craft is a lot of work. Granted, it is work you should enjoy (if you don't, catch the next religion to find something you do like). Magick requires patience and skill-building techniques. Religion requires an integration, a willingness to work toward the growth of self and spirit. Both instill great joy and unity when practiced correctly. Correctly here does not mean a specific set of motions or words, but rather the ultimate association with Divinity. I've seen a fair number of salutes and circle castings from diverse individuals and traditions in the last twelve years. None of them have been incorrect. Execution of some is better than others, but that doesn't make them any less religious or magickal in nature. All of them have one important aspect in common—the art of tuning body, mind, soul, and surroundings in harmony with the Universe.

Conjuring Laughter

I tell my students, "It must be fun. It is okay to laugh at your own mistakes and relax in the circle of magick. Laughter is magick, after all." Stuffy rituals where everything must be politically correct are fine, too, if that is what you prefer. Personally, I think life is too solemn for most folks. Seek the Craft for both enlightenment and stress reduction in your life, but don't forget laughter and fun. We should reach into ritual and find joy, not condemnation for calling the West quarter twice by mistake. It can happen!

It has certainly happened to me. Laughter can be a trigger to spirituality. When I started working in the tradition, there were many more people involved. The High Priestess (ahem) isn't supposed to make mistakes. At least that's what I thought. I assumed it was my position to be as perfect as possible to be a fine role model. Unlike many traditions, we all take turns to make sure everyone gets a chance to work with others and perform rituals in key positions. On this particular evening, it was my job to present the dedicant[1] to the God and Goddess. The night before, I practiced my lines diligently in the bathtub (the only place in my house where I will not be disturbed). The others could read their pieces out of books, but I was going to know my part my heart. This was a serious ritual and only once in a lifetime does an individual receive a dedication into our tradition. It should be special, said with feeling.

I breezed through the Goddess portion of the presentation. The words "Queen of Heaven, Queen of Hell" always give me trouble. Halfway there, I thought. This was going to be a piece of cake. I began my bit about the God: "Oh Father, Son, and Potent Gun!" rang my words throughout a room of thirteen stunned people. I turned to our female, twenty-two-year-old dedicant and said, "Considering your age, I hope he shoots blanks for the time being!" Witches howled that night. Don't let anyone tell you they don't.

Of course, my greatest horror was during the presentation of a third-degree priestess to the service of the Lord and Lady. It was my first time in conferring such a degree and I was nervous. It went well, till near the end. I took her hands in mine and slowly raised them above our heads. I proceeded to ram our hands into the chandelier. It swung like hell. This time, I was mortified. I looked straight in her eyes and said, "Oh, and I give you the gift of humor; as a third-degree priestess, you're going to need it!" The woman was a lawyer. Guess the Goddess was trying to tell us something.

We all make mistakes in ritual and the cosmos is not going to collapse due to an error of your making. I think the God and Goddess force humor upon us if we are not open enough to let laughter in our lives. A friend of mine in North Carolina told me his most embarrassing ritual snafu was when his athame got caught in the altar cloth. He turned from the altar to raise his hands above his head and pulled the entire altar set up with him, incense, candles, statues—the whole works went plummeting to the ground. "I was absolutely mortified!" he wailed. I loved it.

The individuals who work here, in my home, at our Sisters of the Cauldron healing circles, founded the group on laughter. We have discovered that if the group is getting tired, a little laughter perks everyone up and gets us going again. We've done some of our best healing in the throes of laughter. Of course there is a time to be serious, but never, ever stop conjuring laughter for

---

1. A dedicant is an individual wishing to pledge him or herself to the Craft for a year and a day, in a sort of trial run. See Chapter 9 for a more complete description of a dedicant.

the sake of religion. Laughter, after all, is an excellent tool of focus. You are all laughing at the same thing, focused on the same idea. The longer you laugh, the more quips you add, the longer and more directed the focus. And you thought magick was all book work, where every single act of magick had to be planned for eighty days and eighty nights to succeed—pah!

How does laughter help a solitary? My, my, I thought you would never ask! If you are feeling overly stressed but would like to do that special ritual anyway, watch something amusing on television to lighten yourself up a bit. You know, something like Rush Limbaugh or the Three Stooges, whatever you are into. Read a funny book, or talk to your next-door neighbor—whatever makes you hoot. Finally, learn to laugh at yourself. If you flub in your ritual, laugh at yourself. It won't hurt anything. Laughter always lightens any emotional wet blanket.

❁ Your Work ✿

Project 1: Write a complete ritual using your favorite comedy character. Make it as humorous as possible. Keep it in your Book of Shadows to refer to when you are down or gloomy.

Project 2: When you make a mistake in the Craft, whether it is the performance of magick or a religious function, tell yourself it is okay to laugh, then do it.

Focus From the Heart

I find the reading of long passages in solitary ritual to be boring. You know what you are there for. You really don't need someone else's words to relay your feelings. Unlike other religions, Witchcraft does not require someone over you to call the shots with Divinity. It only needs you and your willingness to interact. Reading diminishes your focus on what you are doing because you are spending too much energy honing in on the task of reading, rather than meaning of the words. If you try to do a dramatic reading for yourself, you may lose your focus. You should center on the intent, rather than flair. If you like a particular passage, then memorize it. That's right (sigh, groan, ho-hum), take the effort to commit the words to memory. Start with something small and work into larger passages, if you like. Great things can happen in personal ritual when you take the time to express a memorized piece. These favorite passages can act as triggers to retrieval of higher wisdom.

✿ Your Work ✿

Project 1: Before you go further in your studies, find one piece that appeals to you and memorize it. It can be the Charge of the Goddess (either in poetry form or soliloquy) by Doreen Valiente, or a poem by Starhawk. Ed Fitch has some excellent collections of verse in his book *Magickal Rites From the Crystal Well.* Many American continental Witches use Valiente's Witches' Rune. It doesn't matter, as long as it means something to you.

Use memorized pieces at any point in the ritual. In some traditions, the group focuses on a familiar recitation as soon as everyone enters the magick circle. The anointing can occur either before or after the recitation. Consider it a pep rally, where everyone gets their magickal motors going before the planned ritual actually commences. In other circles, group recitation snuggles close to a key aspect, such as the invocation to the God/dess, before raising power for the work, or sets the stage for the cakes and wine. As a solitary, you can put the recitation wherever you like—before, during, after, it doesn't matter. Take the piece you have learned and place it where it fits best for you. There is no wrong way to add a memorized piece to your work.

Of course, while we are on the subject, there is nothing wrong with writing your own poem or soliloquy. Be creative and adventurous!

Project 2: Perform a ritual with your memorized piece.

Project 3: Write your own special piece that can fall within any type of ritual. Use it faithfully.

Many working Witches, whether they be solitary or traditional/group, use a short poem, rhyme, or speech to ground themselves before they do anything religious or magickal. This act serves as a trigger—the first step toward melding with positive, Universal energies. For example, if you decided to do a full ritual, there may be much to do, depending on your style. Before you gather or set up anything, step up to your altar, say the piece you have memorized (or part of it), then ground and center. You don't even have to say it out loud if you don't want to. Keep in mind its purpose—the one you have designed for yourself.

Dying to know what I use, aren't you? Okay, I'll give, but the credit goes to someone else—Marion Weinstein in her book *Earth Magick.* This passage has always meant a lot to me:

There is One Power
Which is the God and Goddess
Which is perfect in truth, order, clarity, and mutual good.

With this simple passage, I'm ready to zap. We have a poster in our living room that says:

WARNING!
YOU ARE LOOKING AT A
HIGH PERFORMANCE HOUSEHOLD
WE CAN GO FROM
ZERO TO WITCH
IN 2.1 SECONDS

Get my drift?

Triggers

Any action, motion, word, or thought falls into the category of triggers. They need not be elaborate or complicated. In the occult, triggers are meant to allow you to quickly turn mundane circumstances into magickal ones, whether they are scientific or religious in nature. Triggers, as the word indicates, encompass actions, words, or thoughts that quickly set practices into motion and create affirmative mental programming. How fast should triggers work? By the time it takes you to think one, two, three. The desired result happens about ninety percent of the time, leaving ten percent to error due to your level of energy, circumstances, and intent. The more you work at perfecting personal triggers, the better you will get at them.

Why bother with triggers? Actually, triggers come naturally. The longer you work at anything, whether it be occult in nature or some other skill, the faster things fall into place. Results will gather speed. Triggers are positive in nature, save for instances of physical self-defense, which is another set of circumstances entirely. Later in this book, I will teach you triggers for physical and psychic self-defense that have worked both for myself and my students.

If triggers are a natural phenomena with the progression of the level of skill, why bother to enhance their growth? Think of triggers as devices for expansion and doors to new realms. The more doors you open, the more information and experiences you will cultivate. The more experiences you have logged in your quest for religion, the better prepared you are to take on the challenges and joys of this lifetime. So far, we have covered several triggers, such as meditation, written or memorized passages that cultivate inspiration, the altar devotion, and the action of creating sacred space. All these can be triggers to both inner knowledge and the act of ritual, should you so desire.

One of the easiest triggers to cultivate is one you invent yourself, using your hands. This trigger can be for any occult endeavor, but I will give you a specified task to begin with, then you take it from there.

51

✿ Your Work ✤

Your main objective is to design a set of hand motions that will trigger tranquillity within yourself.

Project 1: Begin by designing three separate patterns, and experiment with each pattern twice a day for a week. Be sure you write them down so you can repeat them precisely the way you initially designed them. Which pattern do you prefer? Perhaps you would like to fine-tune one of the patterns or meld portions of the three patterns together.

Project 2: Write down precisely what single pattern you feel will be the trigger for providing calm and tranquillity within yourself. Practice this pattern for one week. Do you have noticeable results? If not, redesign the pattern and continue your practice.

When you have settled on a specific pattern of hand motions, use them during periods of stress. If you have designed something rather elaborate, it may not serve your purpose. For example, imagine your boss is acting like an idiot, causing you to feel stressed. You would look stupid if you went back to your desk in the center of a technological sweat-shop and began waving your hands around in the air like Chicken Little. It would be wiser to take a trip to the bathroom to do your hand motions. Keep track of your successes and failures. Naturally, given the variety of circumstances in life, simple hand motions may not work every time. However, they will greatly reduce stress activators and assist you in living with more joy, patience, and pleasure.

Once you have gotten a handle on this type of trigger, consider how you could develop other triggers for yourself. For example, the Lesser Banishing Ritual, as found in Donald Michael Kraig's *Modern Magick,* is an excellent way to bring peace into your life before a ritual, conjuring sacred space, devotional prayers, or an altar devotion. Perhaps you are a card reader or an astrologer. Design a trigger that will assist you in opening the lines of communication you will need before a performance. This would apply to any of the arts as well, such as dancing, writing, painting, or music. Don't forget other tasks, such studying for an exam, memorizing information—the examples are unlimited. Remember, in the end, the trigger should cause a reaction as quickly as you can say one, two, three.

Even when you are in a hurry, there are ways to put yourself "between worlds" by using triggers. For example, teach yourself to make sacred space by physically walking an area, envisioning a blue flame boundary between yourself and the rest of the world. (Some people like to visualize a green circular hedge, rather than the blue flame.) Later, no matter where you are or what you are doing, you can take a little walk to create the sacred space. You can calm your nerves or do a magickal action in your head.

The Robe of Stars

Working Witches never stop growing in their spirituality. They never cease searching for better methods of life interaction. They do, however, adopt specific triggers that they may use during an entire lifetime. One such trigger is the Robe of Stars, designed to bring peace and spirituality before an important event in your life. This event can range from a business meeting in which you wish to be successful to performing an initiation of another into the Craft of the Wise, celebrating a specific holiday, or honoring God/dess energy. The Robe of Stars is a mental trigger, supported by props, if you desire. The object is to complete the trigger enough times so that in a few months or weeks, you will need only the words "the Robe of Stars" to trigger the energies. This does not mean you should never perform the devotion again. All mental pursuits need reinforcement by physical actions at intervals to keep them fresh in your mind.

Provide enough time to perform this trigger before the actual event.

Focus on the event you are about to encounter.

Take a bath or shower. Lay the clothes (including your shoes, jewelry, and any accessories) you will be wearing at this event by your altar. Relax and breathe deeply. Imagine that you are sacred space.

Mix holy water and a dash of the herb of your choice (you will have to consult a magickal herbal for this, such as *Cunningham's Encyclopedia of Magickal Herbs*). I use one from this book, or a mixture of lavender, angelica, rosemary, hyssop, and cinquefoil.

Empower the mixture in tune with the event and what you desire to manifest as a result of your attendance. If you like to use candles and their corresponding colors, choose the candles that best suit the occasion. Cleanse, consecrate, and empower them. Light the candles. Focus on your desires.

Hold your hands (or prop, such as a wand or athame) over the clothing and accessories. Draw a banishing pentagram in the air. If you do not like using the pentagram, choose another sacred symbol. I do not advise using the Christian cross, as originally it was a symbol for attack. If you want to use a cross, use an equal-armed one.

Sprinkle (lightly, to avoid stains) all your clothing and accessories with the mixture. Keep your desires focused, but don't strain yourself. This is an act of affirmation. You are not summoning the avenging Morrigan (hopefully).

Breathe deeply and relax. Hold your hands over the clothing and accessories (or use a wand or other prop). Close your eyes and visualize the most beautiful robe of stars you can muster. The robe is one of power, purity, protection—

any number of positive energies you wish to instill in it. You can envision any color robe you like. After all, it is your personal star robe, tailored for you. Astrally place that robe over your clothes and envision it melding to the fibers of the physical material. Take your time.

If you like, you can say something like the following:

> *By the positive powers of the Ancient Ones*
> *I clothe myself in the Star Robe of peace, power, and honor*
> *That I may walk the path of both protection and enlightenment*
> *That I may greet any situation with grace and clarity*
> *That I may behave in a positive manner*
> *In the names of the God and the Goddess*
> *May my destiny be the affirmation of life*
> *I have made it so.*

If you have chosen a particular God or Goddess archetype, you may like to put their names in place of "God" and "Goddess." In the Black Forest Clan, we honor the Morrigan and Herne. You may also like to say, "In the name of the All" or "In the name of Universal Divinity." It doesn't matter. All positive God/dess forms lead to the same source. Again, as with much of the Wiccan philosophy and religion, the choice is yours.

Let the candle burn while you get dressed. Continue focusing on positive manifestations for the event at hand. When you are finished, extinguish the candle. You may like to utter a special devotion or use a particular hand pattern. Then go about your normal business.

After the event, when it is time to disrobe, mentally pack away or return the star robe to a special astral trunk where you know it will be cleansed and empowered. You need not perform a special devotion for this. A mental storing and a word of thanks to Deity will do. If you like, you can relight the candle you used to perform the devotion. As you light it, envision any loose ends created as a result of your attendance at the event. Tie them neatly and attach one end to a positive thoughtform. Now relax, watch television, read a book, or go to sleep.

Pieces of jewelry can serve as triggers, too. Many traditional, clerical Wiccans have an empowered necklace. This jewelry stands for spiritual and magickal pursuits, or accomplishments on their path. Some use torques (a type of necklace), a set of bracelets, a pin, or other items to pull in specific energies. The necklace symbolizes the never-ending cycle of humanity as well as Universal concerns.

For our Clan, I designed a woven cord for first-degree initiations. This cord goes everywhere, no matter what the function. It is very personal to me. The cord links everyone initiated by our Clan. When I touch the cord, I think of the bond between our brothers and sisters, and how we all came together.

❀ Your Work ❀

Project 1: Record your findings when using the stress-reduction triggers. When you feel you are ready, teach a friend or family member a stress-reduction trigger.

Project 2: Develop new triggers for ritual purposes. Keep a record of your experiences.

Project 3: Practice the Robe of Stars Trigger and Meditation for one moon cycle. Keep a record of your experiences.

Focus with Motions: The Salutes

Like memorized passages and rhymes, salutes are triggers without words. They are a set of stylized motions performed by the working Witch to get things moving in the right direction. They can be as complicated or simple as you desire. Remember, if you open with a salute, you should close with a salute. Therein lies the difference between the salute and the pattern of hand motions you designed as simple triggers. Many individuals do the same salute in reverse to close. Others do a complicated salute to open and a very basic one to close. It is all in the mind of the Witch. The primary function of the salute is to serve as yet another catalyst for uniting with or honoring Divinity.

The Witch can perform salutes before a meditation begins, before entering sacred space, before a ritual, or simply when he or she walks past the altar and would like to touch Divinity. It does not always have to be a prerequisite to something more spectacular. It can just be. Salutes are like clothing—try different ones until you find or design something that is right for you. In a tradition, salutes are the same for everyone, or similar in nature to the degree the individual holds. This is to help focus the group mind; members in the circle who are spacing out might look at the person at the altar and say, "Oh, George is performing the salute. Now I know precisely where we are in the ritual and where my head ought to be right now." The salute helps everyone to focus on the task at hand. A few continental traditions salute with their hands at specific times during a ritual, such as after the drawing down of the God and Goddess, when someone says "So mote it be," or at other key intervals. Sometimes they all do the same salute. At others, the females perform one type of salute and the males another. Normally, the performance of these salutes is out of sight of guests, or not done at all. The main reason? They don't want the guest to feel stupid. It is not a deep, dark secret that only the initiated may know (although there are a few individuals who probably think so). It is a signal for the group mind to unite.

Salutes can be done with your hands or with props, such as a wand, cauldron, athame, or a candle. Although I prefer to use my hands, I sometimes work with a palm-sized, obsidian arrowhead given to me by a lovely Witch named Rowan. I may perform the salute with a stick of incense, the cauldron, etc. How you begin is also a matter of choice. One tradition salutes clockwise with incense at each quarter, then moves back to the altar to finish. I have seen stunning salutes with all the above. Base your salute on your preferences. Salutes can be gentle motions, or sharp, stylized ones. I've tried all of them, and I suggest you do, too. Choose the one that provides the most amount of focus for you.

The God/Goddess Simple Salute

Stand with your hands at your sides, feet together, head bowed, and eyes closed. Breathe deeply for as many counts as it takes you to calm, ground, and center yourself. Slowly raise your head and your arms. Cross your arms over your chest, right over left. This is the Salute of the God, called the God position.[2] (See illustration) At this time, you should be thinking of the Lord and what He means to you. Visualize the God, the power and strength He provides. Feel his forest home around you. This is your first indication to the Divine about the work you are going to perform. Some teachers tell you to wait a specified number of heartbeats (like thirteen, nine, seven, etc.) before continuing to the next portion of the salute. My only complaint with this is that the student will be focusing on counting rather than on Divinity. Counting is really for beginners, to help them slow down and get into the natural swing of a rite or ritual. If you find yourself rushing, then slow down and count. If you are taking your time, don't worry about it.

Next, move slowly into the Goddess position (See illustration) by spreading your arms out to your sides and up above your head, with palms up. Move your left foot out to the left. You'll find your feet naturally have about twenty-four inches between them. Tip your head back a bit. Envision the energy of the Goddess descending upon you. Let it flow around you and fill you with the hope of the Goddess. Her caring and strength encompass you. Envision the God and Goddess meeting and merging inside your body.

Begin to move your arms back into the God position (keep your feet apart). Envision capturing Divine energy between both arms, and pull it toward your body. By the time you resume the God position, you will feel this extra boost of energy entering your heart chakra. Relax and feel communion with Divinity.

---

2. Traditionally, the God position is wand in the right hand and the scourge in the left, held against the chest. This was called the Osiris position, named after Egyptian practices. The two shafts of the tools are grasped in clenched fists, wrists crossed and the shafts crossed again above them. More modern Wiccans are moving to the wand in the right hand and the sword or athame (knife) in the left hand. See the illustration provided for the Osiris position without the use of tools. Notice the body shape in the God position is phallic, while in the Goddess position it represents the cup or chalice.

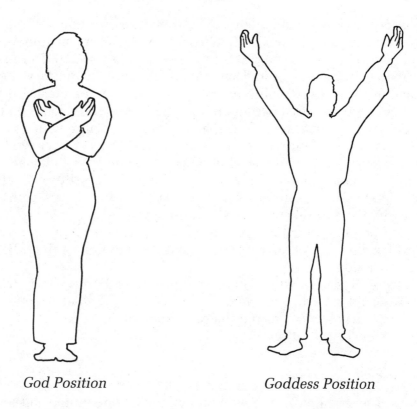

God Position   *Goddess Position*

When you are ready, return your arms to your sides and open your eyes. You are now ready to continue with the work you have planned. When you have finished your work, perform the same salute as your final act of closure.

The Sacred Symbol Salute

This one requires a choice on your part—what symbol summarizes your magickal and spiritual intent? Don't make a snap decision. Consider carefully what symbol you would like to integrate into your magickal and spiritual practices. There are various books on the market showing occult symbols from which to choose (see Appendix IV for a sample of these symbols). You may try all of them, or only a few. The choice is yours. What energies do you wish to manifest? You might try designing separate symbols for individual workings. You could even spend time choosing your symbol through the use of bind runes or other sigils, which I highly recommend. This makes your practices unique and totally individual. Every magickal application you perform on the physical reflects in the astral planes. One meaning of the Wiccan mystery "As above, so below" applies here. After all, that is the idea of doing a magickal or spiritual act—to request and use Divine or positive energies. If you create your own salute, it is a signal to positive astral entities that this is you and you're busy in the physical. Through meditation, you can even channel distinct positive energies to join you through your personal signature salute. This requires a complete meditation, in which you and astral entities agree on a relationship for spiritual work by using your signature salute like a telephone wire. The sacred salute is to be absolutely secret. Tell no one, ever.

To determine what sacred symbols you would like to use, write down on a piece of paper the specific energies you wish to manifest. Do you want direct connection with a particular archetype, or will the focus on the All do for you? Are you creating sacred space, or are you planning to do a complete ritual? Is your ritual for honor (one symbol); for work (another symbol)? What types of energies do you use (plants, gems, archetypes, totems)? There are unlimited combinations of signature and symbolic salutes. Is all this too much of a hassle? If your answer to this last question is yes, think carefully about why you feel this way before you scrap the idea.

If you are still confused about what to pick, do some research. Several other Llewellyn books carry occult symbols and their meanings. Perhaps one of these would suit you best.

Once you design your salute, try it out. How does it affect your application? How did it feel to you when you performed it? Rather than reversing this salute, you may wish to keep it the same and employ it again, near the end of your magickal application.

The Lunar/Solar Draw

There are several kinds of drawing down the moon/sun in Craft application. The Lunar/Solar Draw is the process of invoking the energy of the moon or sun for either little magicks, sacred space, meditation, or full ritual. It is for any phase of the moon (lunar) or any time of the day (solar), depending upon your intention. All Witches may use the Lunar/Solar Draw. Most popular, of course, is using this salute when the moon is full. However, should you wish to work with Crone energy, the new moon is best. If you wish to work with God energy, solar applications are best. The moon phases can match the working you are doing: waxing to build, waning to destroy (such as a bad habit, negativity, etc.).

The first type, and the one with which most Wiccans are familiar, is the process of invoking the Goddess (lunar energy) into the body of the High Priestess. This is done in a ritual circle cast to either work with or honor the Goddess energy. In some traditions, the energy is drawn in through the aid of the High Priest. Then, in turn, the High Priestess (as the Goddess) draws the power of the God (solar energy) into the High Priest. Why ladies first? The Goddess is seen as the birth mother of the God.

Other traditions begin by drawing into the God first (as He represents the power) and he, in turn, draws the energy into the Goddess (She who will wisely use the application of the power).

In other traditions, the Maiden (much like the second in command after the High Priestess) draws the Goddess energy into the High Priestess. The Maiden is seen here as the Divine Midwife.

These three practices are put into motion by either the Fivefold Kiss or the Eightfold Kiss, which are, in my mind, the most serious ritual acts performed in the Craft. Never, ever, laugh at someone performing either of these two ceremonial actions. Laughter here is both inappropriate and downright rude. When teaching my students these two salutes, I make them pair up and practice it until they are rolling with laughter on the floor. Why? This way they get the giggles out of their systems before an actual ritual.

The Fivefold and Eightfold Kiss are tradition-wide. This means the practice spans many traditions, including Gardnerian, Alexandrian, Caledonii, British Traditional, and Black Forest, to name a few. It is a common practice, especially during initiations and on the high holy days.

In the Fivefold Kiss, the Priest or Priestess kisses five points of the human body in the form of an upright star (inverted for second-degree initiations, but we are getting ahead of ourselves here). Fivefold means mouth, right hip (the kissee's right), mouth, left breast, right breast, left hip, and back to mouth. Notice this is the form of the invoking pentagram (see illustration). In the Eightfold Kiss, the Priest or Priestess kisses eight points of the human body: each foot, each knee, the genital area, each breast, and the mouth. Before you fire off a thousand letters to me: Yes, I know the Farrars call my Eightfold Kiss the Fivefold Kiss. This is just a difference in wording, nothing more.

The tools most often used for this salute are the athame or the wand. However, hands, flowers (especially roses), etc., are also effective. A staff or a broom might be a bit clumsy.

The Fivefold Kiss

This salute is not for ritual only. Let's say you are at work again with that idiot boss. Are you going to hike up your skirt and whip out the athame neatly buckled to your thigh, or open your briefcase or lunch box and brandish that glittering twelve-inch blade, complete with deer-antlered handle, under his nose? "Oh, excuse me, Mr. Pain-in-the-you-know-what, I find it necessary to settle something right now and I wish to perform my Lunar/Solar Draw. Would you excuse me?" That would surely impress him.

Stand and face your altar (or the moon/sun should you be lucky enough to be outside or near a window where you can see it).

Take several deep breaths. Relax.

Ground and center.

Hold the tool you wish to use in your strongest hand. Envision the sands of time stopping in mid-air—no clock moves, no bells chime.

Raise the tip of it to your lips. Kiss the tip of the tool, if you so choose. (I have never gotten over feeling stupid in front of groups of people when kissing an inanimate object. I reserve my kisses for people (and my dog, of course) as an expression of affection. I also like kisses to be reciprocated, and laying a big one on a stick or blade is not my idea of ultimate interaction.)

Extend your stronger arm out in front of you, keeping the tool at eye level. Elevate your arm so that you can see the moon/sun just above the tip of the tool. If you cannot actually see the moon, envision it.

Breathe deeply and envision the God/dess. In your mind, tell Her (or Him) why you need Her strength, power, magick, etc. Your reasons could be many. Perhaps you are in need of healing, protection, energy, a solution, etc.

Relax and feel Her energy moving toward the tip of the tool. Visualize it balancing on the end of the tool, then slowly work the visualization down through the tool, into your arm, and finally, into your heart chakra. Once in the heart chakra, let it expand in both directions throughout your body. Hold this position until the energy has reached both the tips of your toes and the top of your head. After you have performed this salute several times, you will feel the energy moving through you and your visualization need not be your only guide.

Breathe deeply.

Lower your arm.

At this point, you have a choice: Ground and center, immediately do the Reverse Lunar/Solar Draw, or wait until after the meditation/magickal application/ritual is completed, then perform the Reverse Lunar/Solar Draw.

The Reverse Lunar/Solar Draw

In your mind, say thank-you for the experience and energies given you. The tool should once again be in your strong hand.

Elevate your strong arm. Hold the tip of the tool out in front of you, just under the moon/sun.

Breathe deeply and center yourself. Reaffirm your oath of service.

Bring the tip of the tool slowly back to your lips. Breathe deeply. Lower your arm, then your head.

Imagine the sands of time trickling again, the tick of the clock, the soft chimes of the hour.

Ground and center.

The Lord and Lady Salute

Stand and face your altar (or the moon/sun, should you be lucky enough to be outside or near a window where you can see it).

Take several deep breaths. Relax.

Ground and center.

Hold the tool you wish to use in both hands, and stop time as before.

Raise the tip of the tool to your lips. Then move your arms outward, balancing the sun/moon on the tip of the tool with your arms out in front of you.

Breathe deeply and visualize the energy entering the tip of the tool, moving back through the hilt, splitting into God and Goddess energy (one fork for the right arm and one for the left), then joining in your heart chakra.

Lower your arms. Breathe deeply. Center yourself.

Perform the reverse salute now, or after the working. It is your choice.

Putting It All Together

How would all these nifty triggers, motions, and devotions go together? Here is a quick outline for you to consider:

1. Prepare (gather supplies, take a ritual bath, or ground and center).
2. Perform the Robe of Stars Meditation.
3. Perform a salute.
4. Perform an altar devotion.
5. Perform a quarter salute with incense.

❁ Your Work ✿

Project 1: Practice the God/Goddess Simple Salute with your daily devotionals for two full weeks. Record your experiences.

Project 2: Choose a symbol for the Sacred Symbol Salute. Try it with your daily devotionals, in meditation, then in a full ritual. Record your experiences.

Project 3: Practice both the Lunar and Solar Draw for one moon cycle. Work on variations that will feel natural to you. Record your experiences.

Project 4: Practice the Lord and Lady Salute for two weeks. Record your experiences.

Project 5: Put it all together. Begin with gathering your supplies, the ritual bath, and grounding and centering. Perform the Robe of Stars Meditation, then do your daily devotional. Continue with one of the salutes, the altar devotion, and finally, a quarter salute. Don't forget your rules of ritual. Record your experiences.

Focus: Choosing a Patron God or Goddess

Although it is quite acceptable to never move beyond the aspects of the Lord and the Lady, many working Witches choose to hone their skills and focus their religious energies in the direction of one or two particular archetypes. These Gods and Goddesses create symbiotic energies between the Witch and Divinity. Choosing a patron is neither a light nor a simple matter and takes time. Skipping from one Goddess or God form to another will not permit you to reap the benefits of a long association in terms of focus, spirituality work, or attainment of skills. Working with a patron is relationship-oriented in the sense of "working in tune with," rather than commanding or summoning. Should the solitary choose to work with a group (whether traditional or eclectic), his or her patron choice will enhance the workings of the group.

The patron encompasses the Witch's character, qualities, energies, known skills, heritage, and other attributes, and how they will mix with the known abilities of the God or Goddess. You may wish to make a list of several Gods and Goddesses, shortening the list over time, keeping in mind that the energies of the God and Goddess chosen must be compatible with each other as well as your desires and life-style. Refer to historical texts about your area, or texts pertaining to the mythos you are currently studying to assist you in your choice of energies. In many third-degree traditional rituals, there is a time when the elevated Witch is asked to choose his or her patron, thereby naming an astral temple after that choice. The Witch and the patron, connected in ritual, birth a new haven for brothers and sisters of the wise. As that Witch travels throughout life, the patron will be present at all magickal functions and life experiences, whether invited or not.

Many times the working Witch chooses specific patrons for special work. For example, during my third-degree initiation I chose the Morrigan and Herne to be the Patron Goddess and God of my astral and physical temple (hence the Temple of the Morrigan Triskele—the Black Forest Clan). Now, before you history buffs tell me that the Morrigan and Herne aren't specifically linked by legend and wonderful facts, let me explain that those choices work for me. I also have a patron deity for our hearthstone work inside the house and one for fountains and springs on our property. It is wise not to choose too many deity energies. Those chosen must carry energies in agreement with all those on the property and become activated through a ritual written by yourself.

Once the patron is chosen, it is time to get down to serious work. To begin, both a physical and astral shrine need to be established. Once you have completed this task, you are ready to do repeated meditation and energy work under the guidance of that patron. Your skills in visualization are something that cannot be bought, nor is there a short-cut to perfection. Many times I receive letters that begin this way:

> *Dear Silver, please help me. I have no money; all I can offer is my friendship. I am in major financial trouble, but I want to study the Craft. I want you to help me to do this. I don't want you to think I am begging for a handout, but...*

The first question in my mind is always this: What does money have to do with belief in a religion? Who taught these people that money and knowledge are one and the same? It is not that I scorn the letter-writer's friendship. However, it is obvious that the person feels money and religion walk hand in hand—you have to pay out one to get the other. That's another religion's ticket to the Divine. The greatest enlightenment of self comes from interacting with the Universe without money. It may come while you are holding a flower and finally feeling its energy. It may come while you are in a ritual circle and for the first time, you actually "see" the cast circle around you. It may come to you during a devotion, a meditation, or a hike in the woods. You cannot buy or sell spirituality. You can not steal it or borrow it. It is a free gift for all to share.

I can't, nor can anyone else, give you religious belief. Either you attain it on your own, or you go without. What you and Deity do together is up to you and your religious system. No amount of certificates, classes, workshops, tests, or friendships will create your religious beliefs. Of course, they will shape them, get you thinking, and fill your time in (hopefully) a progressive manner—but it simply doesn't take money to be One with the Universe, nor does it take a certificate or a diploma to be a religious person. When it becomes necessary to prove on paper that we are Wiccan, Christian, Buddhist,

Shinto, Muslim, Native American, or any other religion by means of expending money, we have missed the central theme of religion.

Learning magickal applications doesn't take money, either. It takes practice. The gifts from patron Gods and Goddess will assist you in your magickal work. You can't pay them for their services with currency. You can honor them, do positive works and deeds in their names to enhance the Universe, or seek to bring about harmonious balance in self, thereby affecting the Universe in a positive manner by being you. You cannot, however, use your Visa or MasterCard, nor is there a credit line on how much knowledge you can obtain in this lifetime. In the Craft, you can't buy your way into the Summerland with large donations or by erecting beautiful buildings.

Through working with the energies of Deity, ancestors, and planet spirits, the human calls in a triad of power. Thus, your patron deity should reflect this triad in the way you feel will be most beneficial to yourself and your work. You can either work through this patron to pull in the triad of power, or you can work with the patron deity to enhance the triad work. We will discuss this procedure in more detail when we get into quarter calls and circle castings.

Triad Focus

Let's travel back in time a bit before the amazing color wheel array of today. During my Pow-Wow research (and thanks to Thor and Audrey Sheil of the Trollwise Press in Staten Island, New York) I discovered the colors black, red, and white were common magickal colors with both my German ancestors and the continental Celts. Although there are many correspondences for these colors (such as the Norns), we are going to deal with them here as a representation of a triad.

Black: The fertile earth and rolling seas (water and land united, promoting growth)

Red: The blood of our ancestors (fire of creation, procreation, and heritage)

White: The energy of Divinity (the Divine breath of creation)

Clear your altar and try working with only these three colors. If you like, go to a florist and purchase a red rose, a black rose, and a white rose. Work with these or dry them, saving the petals in separate containers. Design an altar devotion that concentrates on dropping a petal or two of each color into a cauldron. Invoke the energies as listed above for a specific purpose, whether it be one of honor or one for future work.

Weave cords of these three colors together for a specific desire. In meditation, you can visualize each rose opening, spreading its energies around you. Use your imagination—that's what Witches do best!

The Shrouded Supper

One of the easiest ways to assimilate these three colors and their correspondences into your magickal work is through the Shrouded Supper. Do this event alone, or with several people. There are only four rules:

1. The event should take place in sacred space.

2. All food, utensils, plates, napkins, glasses, tablecloths, etc. must be red, white, or black.

3. No one is allowed to talk from the moment they walk through the door. They may speak after the ritual is over and they leave the room where the supper took place.

4. You must eat by the light of a candle or oil lamp.

As you are preparing and eating the food, focus on the colors and what they mean to you. By ingesting the food, you are providing a future trigger for the color. I know this sounds silly, but many profound experiences (including a rapturous state) can be achieved during the Shrouded Supper.

Although the Shrouded Supper works well at any time, you may like to try it at Samhain, where the ancestral forces are at their peak.

I hope this chapter led you to the following Wiccan mystery: There is no limit to spirituality. Now, it's your turn to zap up interesting ideas.

❁ Your Work ❧

Project 1: Choose a patron deity. Plan and execute a ceremony. Build a shrine to that deity.

Project 2: Triad Focus: work with the colors and attributes. Record your experiences.

Project 3: Perform the Shrouded Supper.

Project 4: Write a short paragraph to yourself explaining where you are at this point in time in terms of mental, spiritual, and physical abilities. What would you like to improve? What have you already improved upon? Set a list of ten goals for a six-month period.

Project 5: Keep going.

Conjuring the Mechanics of Quarters

'm ready to go. I have all my tools, my lighter, the water ... okay. Breathe deep ... good. Here goes the altar salute ... right on target—Yeah! Now, let's see, I wanna do the quarters next. I memorized this part; should be a snap. Got it out of a new book, don't you know. I turn to the North (right; I want to manifest something tonight) and I say:

> *Guardians-of-the-Watchtowers-of-the-North-Element-of-Earth-and-all-ye-in-the-in-the-realm-of-Dragon-I-Bubblefox-High-Priestess-of-the-Logging-Tradition-do-summon-stir-and-call-ye-forth-to-witness-this-rite-and-to-guard-this-sacred-space.*

Ha, I said that in less than twenty seconds and didn't screw up. I'm on a roll! What's next?

Whoa, Witchie! Park the broomstick, sheathe that athame, and sit a spell with me. What's wrong with this picture? First, never spout a quarter call all in one breath. You are not an auctioneer. Take your time and visualize precisely what you are trying to manifest. In this example, Bubbleface (oops, I mean Bubblefox) pulled something out of a book without thinking about it first. Let's dissect this particular quarter call and see what Bubblefox brought into the sacred space with her.

Guardians of the Watchtower of the North ... What's a Watchtower? Way back when, in tribal life and into the time of the castle, Watchtowers were built for the protection of the people and as cover for a look-out. Sometimes they were connected by elaborate wooden bridges or more sophisticated, stone walls running to the turrets at the four corners of a castle or fortress. Watchtowers were normally at the four corners of whatever needed guarding. When the Watchtowers are called, they are seen as the guards we talked about earlier—the fellows or ladies (as you please) with big muscles, flashing teeth, and nasty, pointy weapons. Thus, your sacred space really becomes a square, flanked by the warrior types of the Universe.

Element of Earth... Bubblefox now mentions an element. Is she looking for the element energy or an elemental? There is a big difference here. Is she seeing dirt and growing things in her mind, or is she concentrating on an earth elemental, such as a gnome? Or, is she seeing the elemental as many of us do—formless, but with life energy of its own that has the capability of manifesting earth gifts to help her?

And all ye in the realm of Dragon... Before one calls a dragon, I highly suggest working with it in meditation first. Personally, I adore dragons, but would you invite any passing dragon to visit you? Even more interesting, are you summoning, stirring, or calling on this big fella? He most likely came from a specific culture. If you are doing a Celtic ritual and pull a Chinese dragon by the tail, you may find yourself in a cultural energy flux. There is a difference.

I, Bubblefox, High Priestess of the Logging Tradition... We will hope that Bubblefox has done some sort of dedication ritual and properly introduced herself, or gone through an initiation ceremony before hollering at the Universe that she's doing some sort of ritual with the name of a tradition pinned to her torso. If she has done these things, then it is proper to let those she's summoning, stirring, and calling forth know precisely who on the mundane plane is making all this ruckus.

Do summon, stir, and call you forth... Here's the key: You summon elementals and element energies. You stir the ancestral dead (or anything that is sleeping and/or bigger than you). You call (nicely) the divine energies associated with that quarter (this includes anything on a higher evolutionary scale than yourself—there are lots of energies bigger than humans, with higher wattage).

How do these rules fit in with what Bubblefox is doing? Good question. I hope for her sake she is not summoning a dragon. They are a great deal older than we are and may not be interested in a pip-squeak person who calls herself Bubblefox. They expect humans to be well bred in their manners, which does not include frivolous demands on their time. A nice call of please-come-and-be-my-honored-guest-energy is appropriate for dragons.

How about the Watchtowers? Is she summoning, stirring, or calling them? That depends on what she is envisioning. If she's going to put a gnome in that tower, then she better be able to mentally tell him precisely what he is supposed to be doing, and therefore the word summoning comes to mind. If she is trying to connect with her own ancestral lineage (tradition or personal bloodline), then she would gently stir them. If she thinks she is addressing an angel, then calling fits the purpose. In traditional work, the quarters are also the home of a specific deity/totem animal. For example, if you were thinking of Artemis for the North, you would be using "calling" mode.

To witness this rite and to guard this sacred space... Who's supposed to be doing what? Are they all witnessing or guarding? How are they doing both? Can they be doing anything else? If they are guarding, they are facing away from you and are probably outside of the circle. If they are witnessing, then they would be inside the circle, facing you, and you asked them to watch, not help. Here's the clincher. If you are doing sex magick, for example, are you planning an exhibition for Divinity, the dead, and elementals? My, what a crowded room you will have! Not only that—which dead did you wake up? Or, should I say whom did you invite into your ritual or sacred space? Ghengis Khan? Florence Nightingale?

The point of this unusual example is threefold:

1. Always research any magickal formula before you use it.
2. Understand fully what you are saying and to whom you are saying it.
3. Visualize precisely what you mean and to whom (or what) your thoughts are being directed.

How you call your quarters sets the tone for your entire working, whether it be a simple spell, an act of devotion or meditation, or an important ritual. Don't overlook the importance of the quarter call. It sets the stage for a great (or a crappy) performance. The better (and more logical) the quarter call, the more successful the outcome of your work. The purpose of the preceding exercise was to help you focus on what is coming out of your mouth. In the movie *Dune,* there is a speech by the main character that begins something like this:

> *Some thoughts have the power to be equivalent to a thing. Through sound and motion, these thoughts can come into form.*

This character goes on to show how this can be done in their world with a metal box that emits a beam. In our world, the only tool you need is you.

Let's look now at the various energies we find in quarter calls, and whether they are used before a circle is cast or after.

❁ Your Work ✿

Project 1: Write down what you currently say to call the quarters. If you use more than one type of call, write them all down. You will use this information later.

Project 2: Think these calls through. Is there something missing? Is there something there that you never really thought about, but don't care for now? Circle these passages, then continue through this chapter.

Elements vs. Elementals

Depending upon what you believe, elements and elementals may not be the same thing. Some working Witches claim that those of the Craft do not use elementals at all—that this communication/procedure belongs primarily to ceremonial magicians. For the sake of argument, let's try to define some differences between elements and elementals. Then you can choose what you would like to work with, and what you would prefer to leave alone.

An element can be recognized by one (or more) of our five senses. An element is part of our mundane world, belonging to this plane. Therefore, the elements we normally work with in the Craft are Earth, Air, Fire, and Water. These four elements can describe the entire Table of Elements (remember science and the periodic chart?). I've always wanted to do a project where a spell is written for each element on the periodic chart. Anybody game? But, I digress (again).

An element does not think. If I pick up a handful of dirt and ask it how the wife and kids are, I'm not going to get an answer. When we pick up salt from the altar or dribble holy water to cleanse something, we do not envision that element as a thinking being. Elements belong to the plane where humans exist.

Elements are not considered dead because they don't have a thought process as we understand it. They do have energies to work with and are willing to share their world with ours. Elements can be invoked before or after a circle is cast. It is your choice.

An elemental, on the other hand:

Is normally invisible to the untrained eye

Has some sort of thinking process attributed to it

Is considered a spirit that represents an element

Does not normally belong to the human plane of existence

Is comprised totally of the element it represents

Elementals do not look the same to everyone. Some see them as vaporous forms, colored in the same way as the element they represent. Others envision them with human attributes, but not quite. Some people feel them as waves of energy. What makes elementals so hard to pin down is the variety of ways in which they are experienced by occult practitioners. The elementals I've been fortunate enough to see with my human eyes were in the form of lights and flames. I've seen balls of white light dancing before me as I walked the dog one fat full moon evening. I've watched blue tongues of flame zip merrily about the feet and arms of my Craft sisters. It is easier for me to see them at night.

When you see elementals, you may not realize it. You've got to be quick of eye and your brain must allow you to process the information. If you don't believe in elementals, you aren't going to see them.

There is also argument about the thinking process of the elemental. Most working Witches feel that elementals have more of an animal mentality—meaning they are not mean or good, nor can they plot a fantastic, page-turning novel. At least, not on their own. This does not mean they are powerless. Elementals are attributed to an element and direction, as the list indicates.

Gnomes: Earth, North. Givers of material gain and stability. The rulers of the forest. Seen as "Little People" or green light. Protectors of outdoor circles and groves.

Sylphs: Air, East. Givers of wishes, knowledge, and dreams. The rulers of the weather. Envisioned as "fairies" or white light. Delicate beings with beautiful wings. Protectors of magickal applications.

Salamanders: Fire, South. Givers of passion and creativity. The rulers of fields and fire or blue flames. Envisioned as dragons or lizards. Protectors of hearth, home, or business.

Undines: Water, West. Givers of love and friendship. The rulers of all water. Envisioned as merpeople, sirens, or pink lights. Protectors of the gates of death and karma.

The idea that the elementals belong to ceremonial magicians could have come from the tool that is used to employ and control them—the pentacle. I'm sure you know that the pentagram (usually with one point up) is the five-pointed star. It is called a pentacle when a circle is drawn around it. Each point of the pentagram stands for an element, and the uppermost point represents Divine Spirit. The circle signifies the melding of all elements through the work of humankind and indicates the Wiccan mystery of oneness. It has been rumored that King Solomon wore a pentacle on his left hand, and the pentacle/pentagram pre-dates Christian legends. Therefore, rather than belonging to a single religion, the pentacle can be considered Universal. For a complete definition of the pentagram, check Doreen Valiente's *An ABC of Witchcraft.*[1]

An upside-down pentacle represents chaos, and is rarely used by working Witches. However, as I have stated before, you will find it employed in a traditional, second-degree initiation ceremony. I have seen it used in one other instance, in a cauldron ceremony to prevent a fanatical group from marching in a large city where it was feared violence would ensue. The ceremony worked. The leader of the fanatics was jailed for another offense, and the remainder of his group was subsequently sued for previous actions. The march never materialized.

Oh, but we are not done yet. Next on this list are artificial elementals. Let's quote Donald Michael Kraig on this one.

An artificial elemental is something which you, by force of will and magickal techniques, create to do your will...a type of talismanic magick without the talisman.[2]

This type of elemental does not belong in quarter calls—it is formed for a specific magickal application, that includes using Watchtowers for quarter calls.

Now, would you summon, stir, or call elements and elementals? Remembering the information I gave you before, you decide. Elementals can be

1. *An ABC of Witchcraft* by Doreen Valiente, Phoenix Publishers, 1973. Page 264.

2. *Modern Magick* by Donald Michael Kraig, Llewellyn Publications, 1988. Page 409.

called/summoned/stirred before or after the circle is cast. (Notice I didn't give you the answer.) Again, there is debate here among magickal people. Some feel that only humans and Divine energy should be within the cast circle, therefore elementals are not welcome. Others feel that to use elemental energy, that energy must be permitted within the boundary of the circle. Finally, you must decide whether you are going to work with a cast circle when working with elementals. The predominance of opinion is: Never call an elemental unless a circle has first been cast. Conversely, it is quite acceptable to call an element into sacred space where no circle is cast. The choice is yours.

Elemental Calls

(Use together or alone.)

The East, the Sylphs, the Knowledge, the Wind
Positive forces, I call you in.

The South, the Drakes, the Hearth, the Fire
Aid this night in my desire.

The West, the Mers, the Love, the Water
I conjure my need into matter.

The North, the Gnomes, the Roots, the Grove
Bring your gifts, I make it so.

The Center, the Spirit, the Life, the Force
I call you now to open your doors.

Release

The North, the Gnomes, the Roots, the Grove
Fare thee well, I send thee home.

The West, the Undines, the Love, the Water
Fare thee well
Back you go to Gaia's cauldron.

The South, the Drakes, the Hearth, the Fire
Fare thee well and never tire.

The East, the Sylphs, the Knowledge, the Wind
Fare thee well, with peace I send.

The Center, the Spirit, the Life, the Force
I ask you now to shut the doors.

In perfect love and perfect trust
Hail and farewell.

❀ Your Work ❀

Project 1: Learn to work well with all of the elements. Scott Cunningham's books *Earth Power: Techniques of Natural Magick* and *Earth, Air, Fire & Water: More Techniques of Natural Magick* are excellent workbooks for both the beginner and the adept. Too many times more experienced Witches forget about the fun we had when this was new to us. It behooves us to go back through the element information from time to time. Like a good movie, you can always learn something new.

Project 2: In meditation, meet the gnomes, sylphs, salamanders, and undines. You may be surprised later, when your alert self takes the dog for a walk and runs into them.

Project 3: Develop a quarter call that deals primarily with the elements and use it in ritual. Record your experiences.

Project 4: Develop a quarter call that deals primarily with the elementals and use it in ritual. Record your experiences.

Watchtowers

We've mentioned Watchtowers before, but let's cover them again. If you use Watchtowers, you are working with a square, not a circle. There are four corners in this type of application, each attributed to a direction. Watchtowers can appear as those big guys (or gals) who look like they have spent a great deal of their time at the local gym. Considered warrior energy, they would be dressed according to the pantheon you are using. Watchtowers are summoned to guard; therefore, Watchtowers would be called after a circle is cast, giving them something (the circle and its contents) to guard. Viewed this way, there would be a square of energy outside your circle energy. You must make the choice whether you would be summoning, stirring, or calling these energies.

Again I remind you (lest a rabid reviewer begin to salivate with poisonous fangs over this book) that different Witches deal with magickal applications in a variety of forms. The subject of Watchtowers is a prime example. Some working Witches view the Watchtowers as a type of angel or angelic being. Others see the Watchtowers as a structure inhabited by a super/angelic being. In fact, you'll find Witches from a Catholic/Italian background who interpret the Watchtowers as *Grigori*. The *Grigori* are extremely tall male beings who supposedly took human female mates, fathering a race of giants.

There are evil Watchers and good Watchers. Those seen as positive in nature are familiar to just about any person, no matter their religious background. The familiar Watchers are Michael, Gabriel, Raphael, and Uriel.

Watchers and Watchtowers are connected to early stellar cults. The four stars (called the Watchers) were Aldebaran, Watcher of the East, attributed to the Vernal Equinox; Antares, Watcher of the West, attributed to the Autumn Equinox; Fomalhaut, Watcher of the North, responsible for the Winter Solstice; and Regulus, Watcher of the South, connected to the Summer Solstice. Astral towers were constructed to house the Watchers. When lunar and solar religions replaced the stellar cults, the Watchers were reduced to minor deities of wind (in the Greek pantheon) or principalities of air (like the Christian angels). The sigil showing that magick was either ending or beginning was the pentagram.

To some, Watchers are the same as both stars and angels, or referred to as beings of light. They have been called the Shining Ones (as we see in the Celtic legend of the Tuatha De Dannan) and were said to have fathered children with these shining (magickal) characteristics. Whether the Watchers came from the stars, or represented the stars themselves, is open to theological debate.[3] (I would like to thank MorningStar, a very close friend and tradition sister, who researched this stellar information.)

Another concept of the Watcher is an animal-like thoughtform designed and enhanced by the magician/Witch. Its mission is to gather data rather than to protect.[4] A final note here from the writings of MorningStar:

> *Witchlore also holds that it is the Watchers who assist in the spiritual growth of the Witch and who escort him or her to the next realm after physical death. Nothing is ever hidden from the Watchers, and some see them as the lords of karma. This is not to be construed as heaven/angels for the good or demons/hell for the bad, but rather the assurance that as ye sow, so shall ye reap. Karma is delivered promptly and objectively.*

Watchtower Call

> *Watchtower call*
> *Aldebaran light*
> *East I draw*
> *Come this night.*
>
> *Watchtower call*
> *Regulus might*
> *South I draw*
> *Protect this site.*
>
> *Watchtower call*
> *Witness Antares*
> *West I draw*
> *To work with star faries.*

3. The suffix "-el" on the names of many angels is the Sumerian equivalent of "shining." In Old Welsh, a shining being is *Ellu;* in Old Irish, *aillil;* in English, *elf;* in Anglo-Saxon, *aelf.*

4. *Psychic Self-Defense* by Dion Fortune, Weiser Publications, 1930/1993. Page 194.

Watchtower call
Fomalhaut aid
North I draw
With my blade.

Shining Ones
Of stellar sight
Assist me please
Throughout this rite.

Release

Hail and farewell
(Fomalhaut) (Antares) (Regulus) (Aldebaran) bright
Safe journey now
Into the night.

Peace and harmony reign supreme
Blessings upon you.

❁ Your Work ✿

Project 1: Either draw or find a picture of what the Watchtowers look like to you. In meditation, introduce yourself and learn to understand this energy. Record your experiences.

Project 2: Develop a quarter call that deals primarily with the Watchtowers and use it in ritual. Record your experiences.

Project 3: Try the Watchtower call given in this section. Record your experiences.

Faeries

There are reams of material available on faeries, so I'll be brief. The best place to research faery energy is not a book of magick, but tomes on myths, local legends, and archeology. For example, if you say: "Guardians of the Watchtowers of the North, element of earth, and all ye in the realms of faery...." after a circle is cast, this is what you are really saying:

I've cast a circle and called the Watchtowers from each compass direction to guard it. I'm asking the element of earth (not the elementals) to come in, and I'm calling everything (both good and bad) from the realm of faery. What I'm going to do with them depends on the remainder of my quarter call. Do I really want to ask them to witness and guard? There are all sorts of faeries—some considered good, others not so good. I've got to do my home-work when dealing with the enchanted world. Unlike an element or elemen-tal, the faery realm encompasses many levels of intelligence, ethics, and abilities. I must choose wisely.

Here is a table to get you started:

Direction	King	Color	Rule
East	Paralda	Red	Trees, flowers, winds, mountains
South	Djin	White	Fire, volcanoes, passions, fields
West	Nixa	Grey	Lakes, ponds, rivers, oceans
North	Ghob	Black	Earth, gems, minerals

Faery lore in the 1990s is a hotbed of debate among magicians. Every cul-ture and every country has its own opinions on what faeries are, where they came from, whether they are real or not, and how they should or should not be used. In the Craft, there are two distinct uses of faeries—by those who are primarily interested in the historical and archeological correctness of the information, and those who turn more toward the mythical and creative aspects of working with faeries. Since neither sect has blown up, I think it's safe to let intuition be your guide.

❀ Your Work ❧

Project 1: Develop a quarter call for the faery realm. Try it in rit-ual. Record your experiences.

The Airts

Airts (Gaelic) are associated both with compass points and with winds. For too long, American Witches have been using European correspondences when working with the winds/airts. In my Pow-Wow research, I discovered it is important that magickal people work with local weather patterns. This will require research on your part and you must answer the following questions:

Which wind brings heat and dry air?

Which wind brings cold and dry air?

Which wind brings warm breezes and rain?

Which wind brings chilly and wet conditions?

Match these winds to their cardinal points. While you are at it, consider unusual occurrences or landmarks in your locality. For example, is there a mountain in the West? Does it have a local name? How does it fit in with your magick? Have you worked with this mountain energy? Does the mountain protect you from storms? Are there any legends about this mountain? An unusual occurrence would be a type of wind or storm that is linked to a certain direction, or it could be an energy line, atmospheric conditions, etc.

The working Witch must be far-sighted. If you live in a tornado-prone area, then watch what you are calling during that season. The same would go for dry winds in a forest area or groundshaking magick on fault lines. Jumping up and down and chanting your guts out to wake up Mother Earth on a known fault is downright stupid.

I'm not trying to get you so superstitious that you lose your head and constantly worry about wild magick. I believe the Universe does have a safety net. However, you should still be responsible with your magick and carefully plan every action you perform, both mentally and physically. This includes doing the proper research for the area you live in, the tools and herbs you use, and the words coming out of your mouth.

One of the most difficult concepts I've dealt with in teaching is the power reservoir of the students' locality. I have a heck of a time getting students to understand that where they live and the energies that reside there are extremely important to the work they do. It takes several months to get this idea across. I haven't decided if this mental block comes from too much book-reading and not enough practical application, or from the technological age sucking something vital from their thinking process. To me, it's very scary. Regardless of the answer, it is useful to the working Witch to be fully aware of his or her surroundings at all times (magick or no magick).

Local legends can come in handy. For example, there is a legend is south-central Pennsylvania that goes something like this:

When Mary goes over the mountain wet on Ascension Day, there will be numerous rainstorms for the next forty days. However, with this rain comes hefty breezes, and the ground will be dry.

When Mary goes over the mountain dry on Ascension Day, there will be few rainstorms for the next forty days. However, the rain that does fall will nurture the earth.

Mary, here, of course, indicates Christ's mother. Because the legend gives her the power over earth and rain, she is also secretly associated with Goddess energy. I imply hidden because people in this area would have a cow if they knew they were talking about a Pagan controlling the weather. Whoever made up this saying was no magickal dumbo. If it rains on Ascension Day (again, we can thank MorningStar for this bit of trivia she picked up from a local farmer), then we can expect hefty breezes and dry ground. Therefore, if the Witch has planted herbs or special flowers, he or she will need to take extra precautions that all are protected/staked/and watered correctly. Never underestimate the power of local lore.

Getting back to the airts, then, we find a passage by Doreen Valiente that gives us the following information:

The Gaelic airts had a traditional association of colours attributed to them. The east took the crimson of dawn; the south the white light of high noon; the west the brownish-grey of twilight and the north the black of midnight.

She also gives us the following invocation (notice I don't say quarter call):

Black spirits and white
Red spirits and grey
Come ye and come ye,
Come ye that may!
Around and around,
Throughout and about,
The good come in
And the ill keep out![5]

With this invocation, you have called the four cardinal points (the four airts according to their color, with a bit of visualization) in one breath, rather than walking to each quarter. You are giving them a choice: "come ye that may." You've asked them to spiral on the outside of your circle, then invite them to come in. There is also a rider that says only the good spirits are allowed in and the bad ones aren't invited. The word "in" tells us that a circle has already been cast. Are we done yet? No.

Notice there is one thing you haven't included. You've not told them (the airts) which way to spiral in—deosil or widdershins—and does it matter? Well, you said "around and around," so that means circular movement, one way or the other. From your training, you know that deosil (pronounced jessel) is clockwise motion, and widdershins is counterclockwise. That means that you might be physically (or mentally) moving in a specific direction while voicing this invocation. If you were doing positive magick, you would be moving deosil while you speak (or perhaps you would be envisioning the airts coming in deosil). If you want to banish something, like sickness or a bad habit, you would move widdershins. How many times will they or you circle? That is for you to decide. An old legend says three times, which is why some people walk around the circle area three times. If you say the invocation three times, you've solved that problem. Didn't you do that already when you cast the circle itself?

Finally, at what direction do you begin? The invocation gives us a clue: black. Now, where is black? Black is the colour attributed to North, falling right into line with my training, which says everything comes from the North. However, not all Witches like to start things in the North. Many have a great affinity to the East—the rising sun and so on. Again, you have a choice to make. If you are an East person, you are going to have to reword the original incantation a bit and begin with what color? No peeking, please! Okay, the answer is red.

What's this? You see a problem? Very good, because that means you have been following closely and now earn one Witchie star. Let's look at the beginning of this invocation again:

1. *An ABC of Witchcraft* by Doreen Valiente, Phoenix Publishers, 1973. Page 2.

Black spirits and white,
Red spirits and grey...

Black spirits (North) and white (South)
Red spirits (East) and grey (West)

Ooops! What have we here is not a circle at all, but an equal-armed cross, a landing pad for the center of your circle, where the altar is. Ah-ha! Thus the call is an invocation and not a quarter call or circle casting, technically. Top, bottom, right, left is also the gesture of Thor's Hammer and we move into another pantheon entirely. The equal-armed cross can refer to the four quarters of the earth as well as the four elements. Are you confused yet?

I beg Doreen Valiente's pardon for slavering over her invocation—personally, I love it and use it a great deal in my work. My point to you is this: As there are any number of Witches, there are any number of ways to work magick. Somewhere, someday, someone will take your creations and tear them apart, piece by piece, to tell you what they like, what they think is inferior, or what doesn't follow form. You must experiment until you find what works best for you. And, yes, indeed, it certainly is a lot of work. I've lost some very promising students because they had no idea as to how much work magick can be, how much research it takes, or how much experimentation is needed. They think that I am going to tell them the one fail-safe method for any number of things that include a blink and a zap, and that's the end of it. Nope. I'm a tough taskmaster (we Virgos are good at that). A closed mind is the enemy, whether it is yours or someone else's.

Doreen Valiente's invocation is a good one. In the spring of 1994, I tried several experiments with this very invocation, without a long and drawn-out ritual or the obligatory quarter calls. I wanted to see what would happen. If it could stand on its own with the visualization I conjured ahead of time, linking the words to both thoughts and feelings, then I could share this with you, the reader. (You see, I never write instructions or mention anything as okay for you to do that I have not tried myself.)

When you have studied for a while, you will be able to conjure a mental circle and mix a spell or invocation at the same time. However, let me be quite clear that you must first do the basic stuff (like in *To Ride a Silver Broomstick* or any of the other wonderful beginning books on the market today) before you can jump into the mental thing.

Back to my experiments. The first was planned. My daughter was having trouble with that mouthy neighbor kid again. (Yes, the one you read about in *HexCraft: Pennsylvania Dutch Country Magick*.) Her little mouth was rattling on, calling my daughter a Satan worshiper and other such nonsense and causing great difficulty with my daughter's friends. I had had enough.

I bought a small plastic container and filled it with the following:
Rose petals
White sugar
Brown sugar

Vervain (to make it go)
Dragons' blood (for more power)
A slip of paper with my daughter's name on it

I called my daughter into the room and together we sealed the container. I shook it to mix the contents, drew a pentagram in the air over it, and placed her hands on top of the container. I passed a dried, undecorated gourd over the container nine times in the beat of my Pow-Wow magick. I placed my hands over hers, recited the Airt Invocation, then went into an ad-lib:

Oh lovely Lady of the moon
Grant now this day a little boon
Around my daughter there shall be
Peace, good will, and harmony.
In perfect love and perfect trust
I conjure this spell the way I must.
For the free will of all and with harm to none
Now this spell is truly done.

Of course, I always add:
May all astrological correspondences be correct for this working
(from Laurie Cabot, and)

May this spell not reverse or place upon us any curse
(from Sybil Leek)

As with everything, especially when dealing with volatile human emotions, the next day showed only a little progress between my daughter and her acquaintances. You will notice that I did not target the other little girls. I have two reasons for that. First, my daughter must learn to step into harmony rather than plunging into rage. Second, a cardinal rule of the Craft is never magick a child. If you are the guardian of the child, as with my daughter, it's okay to do positive things for him or her. However, we never magick children for whom we are not responsible.

The word child here can mean one of two things (yes, I'm getting technical, but this is a modern world). For example, let's say you live in a very bad part of the city. You've done your protection spells, but you are still worried about the safety of your child. Of course, you have several choices, including moving. Sometimes, though, circumstances may not permit flight. If you know for a fact that a thirteen-year-old or a nine-year-old is packing a weapon (such as a gun or knife), you can work to render both that individual and the weapon harmless. This child has taken on an adult responsibility—one of honoring (or not honoring) life. Therefore, you are not dealing with your everyday cookies-and-milk energy. You can (and should) also tell the appropriate authorities. I have always gone with the old adage "Render unto Caesar what is Caesar's" and I don't give a fig that it's a Christian saying—if it fits, wear it. Another rule of the Craft is defend. Traditional Witches have different rules of practice on how they would handle such a situation. An evil or wicked person must not be coddled. Errors in harmony should be dealt with quickly. How you do that is an important part of your training and your moral fiber.

The final result of this magickal operation? It took about a week and a call to the school counselor, but the animosity moved from a fever pitch to grumbling to silence. One of the little girls got caught hitting my daughter while she was standing in line and the other was severely reprimanded.

Is this the end of the story? No. A moon cycle passed—all was quiet on the daughter front. The next cycle commenced and hell broke lose. This time that nasty little girl ganged up on my daughter and my kid was physically hurt. Step one? Well, I aspected the Morrigan and went brooming into the school. With the counselors, I straightened out the difficulty with the girls, but dragged home a very unhappy and tearful little daughter.

Back to both the magickal and mundane drawing boards. Doreen's invocation worked perfectly the first time. The magick held for thirty days, but karma is as karma does, and sometimes, no matter what you do magickally, it is not going to solve the problem forever unless you take strong action on both the mundane and the astral planes. After much contemplation, I discovered my daughter was suffering from low self-esteem and that the fear bug had bitten her with malice. She was pulling conflict toward herself. She is smaller than all the other children in her class and was allowing their size and their big mouths to intimidate her. This time I worked magick to raise her self-esteem and sent her to karate school. No more problems.

The second experiment I have to share came up unexpectedly. One June evening, a nasty storm began to blow. Before the rain descended upon us, I ran outside to rescue the flats of flowers my father had not yet planted in our yard. With them stowed away, I turned to face the oncoming storm. I've experienced many of these spring tantrums before. The light from the patio cut through the darkness to outline the perfect flower beds and garden my father had worked so hard to plant in the last two days. I knew the storm stood a good chance of destroying everything he had done. His work would have been for naught and he truly loves the land we live on. Each plant nestled in the ground, put there with great care. I couldn't stand by and allow them to be damaged, or worse.

I am sure my neighbors now think I am possessed, for I was wearing one of those long, lightly-knit dresses with plenty of skirt (pink, no less). I rarely, if ever, make an overt show of magick, especially in public. But "cut and be damned," as a friend of mine used to say, so I stood with my back to the street, facing the yard and the jaws of the oncoming storm. Putting my hands out in front of me, I closed my eyes and became one with the storm. I could feel the wind whipping around me, my hair stinging the air like the Morrigan herself, and my pink skirt billowing out behind me. At that point, I recited Doreen's invocation, concentrating on my visualization of the four airts, how I wanted them to move, and where I wanted them to go. Rather than ad-libbing words this time, I mentally showed my concern for all the living creatures and plants in our yard, letting my love for the earth lent to my family permeate my entire being.

In my mind, I visualized the storm blowing over our yard, not touching a single blade of grass or stem of flower. I did not command. I asked nicely in perfect love and perfect trust.

During the visualization, the wind died to a standstill three times, then picked up with renewed force. I lowered my hands slowly, grounded, and centered. At the moment I clicked once again with the mundane world, the back screen door slammed.

"What 'cha doin?"

Ah, kids. They'll do it to you every time. A working Witch learns to be patient. As my child walked out to meet me on the patio, there was no magnificent change in the weather. I put my arm around her and walked into the house. One does not add negative thought to any magickal working. We talked about popsicles, then I went back to my writing.

The result? The rain came in gentle waves. No thrashing winds. No screaming, howling gales rending our flower beds or garden. No shingles, trash cans, or patio furniture spewing forth across the lawns—just soft, gentle, life-giving rain.

Two days later, a tornado sped toward my town. When it reached the town limits, it picked up its tail, skipped over the town, and set back down in the next one. Guess I did something right.

❀ Your Work ✿

Project 1: Get to know the weather patterns of your area. Buy a local map and pinpoint where you are. Keep a record of all types of weather patterns and how they associate with your area in everyday life, during the full and new moons, or when you work magick.

Project 2: Work with the indigenous energies of your area.

Project 3: Try Doreen Valiente's invocation. Record your experiences.

Angels

Before the argument begins, let's shut it down. Regardless of what you may have been taught, angel energy has been mentioned in legends and historical records long before the advent of Christianity. Angels do not specifically belong to the Christians, though their scholars have done a tremendous amount of research and myth-building to accommodate them. In fact, if you desire to do some serious study, you will find that angelic beings appear in many cultures, races, and religions across the globe.

We had a discussion one circle night on the subject of angels. Remember that our tradition holds many people who have risen beyond "this is this" and "that is that." It is possible for a Jewish woman to practice both the Craft and Judaism. It is possible for a Catholic gentleman to practice the Craft and Catholicism. It is possible when you let go of the idea that one group is right and the other is wrong. It is possible when you transcend the idea that Divinity belongs to only one group of individuals. It is possible when you understand that Divinity manifests in a variety of ways within the human mind, and without it. The human, thank goodness, is not the center of the known Universe.

So, what was our discussion about? Well, I thought you'd never ask. There is a difference in how angels and angelic energy are perceived and used in the standard religions of today. In Judaism, they fit within the Tree of Life. An angel is responsible for each sphere and other angels who work within that sphere. In Catholicism, angels fall into a detailed hierarchy called the Nine Choirs. In Protestant sects, angels are rarely identified. In fact, in the King James version of the Bible, only three are mentioned by name: Michael, Gabriel, and Raphael. I guess this is because you aren't supposed to ask them for help. This brings up another point one of our Baptist-in-her-past ladies mentioned: "We were told that you couldn't talk to them. It was like they were prevalent at the time of the story, but are dead to us now." So true.

Many Witches get skittish when discussing angels. Angels, after all, may have been a large part of the religious structure they left behind, and they therefore do not wish to incorporate them in their Craft studies. I don't have a problem with that. It is their choice. Other Witches feel that angelic energy is strictly new-age stuff. Since many new-agers have heart failure around Witches but really like angels, I can see how this train of thought could occur. However, that doesn't mean you can't believe in angels or angelic energy if you are a Witch. Again, we are discussing a matter of choice, not a matter of hard doctrine.

If you are going to use angelic beings in quarter calls, you will have to do some research. For example, in the Nine Choirs breakdown, Seraphim (not the Archangels) are the head honchos. However, Seraphim may not be the energy you want; after all, they are dragons, have six wings, four heads, are flaming— and, oh yes, their wings are covered with eyes. As a Seraphim is the closest to Divine energy, they resonate pure thought and pure love. Since anything pure is beyond human comprehension, I don't think it is such a hot idea to call a Seraphim. But (yes, I realize you are not ever supposed to start a sentence with this word; however, this is important) you should also be aware that certain angelic beings hold various ranks, and therefore it is okay to work with them. Michael, for example, is considered a Seraphim and an Archangel. Go figure.

You can do a lot of interesting work with angelic energy, Witch or no. Guardian angels come from the lowest level of the Nine Choirs and are closest to humans. So close, in fact, that they have many humanoid attributes and are most susceptible to human failings. The rulers of this choir or sect of angels are familiar to you: Michael, Gabriel (often seen as the only female among the group), Raphael, and Auriel (sometimes seen printed as Uriel).

Angel	Quarter	Responsibility	Color	Depiction
Michael	South	Protection	Blue	Big dude with a nasty sword
Gabriel	West	Regeneration	White	Triple Goddess with lily
Raphael	East	Healing	Green	Big guy with six wings
Auriel	North	Manifestation	Red	Associated with the ever-turning sword

I've not given you much description, simply because I want you to do your research. This should include both scholarly work and meditation practices. If you are thinking, "Gee, Silver must've been Catholic before she was Wiccan and that's why she's giving me all this angel stuff in this manner"— wrong. Of the research I've done on angels, the Nine Choirs method of cataloguing appears to be the easiest. I am well aware that there are Judaic angels, Islamic angels, Zoastar angels, etc. If any of these structures appeal to you, by all means investigate them.

> *A 1978 Gallup poll showed that fifty-four percent of Americans believed in angels.... in 1988, the Gallup survey found that seventy-four percent of American teens believed [in angels].*[6]

I would like to know what that poll states now, as I don't know a single person, Witch or no, who doesn't believe in some type of angel.

It is generally agreed that angels and angelic energies are beings unto themselves. As humans are not horses nor horses humans, neither are angels capable of being human or vice versa. Angels are considered higher on the evolutionary scale than humans. They are not the same as the archetypal energies with which Wiccans work. It is also agreed that most angels like to help humans. Angels don't always look human, either. Cherubim have four faces and four wings (not the cutsie babies you might imagine); Thrones are huge spinning wheels with lots of eyes; Dominions speak fire; Virtues are too brilliant to look at; Powers are dualistic—some good and some bad. The good ones look like people with wings and the bad ones like leopards. The Principalities are assumed to look a bit like humans, as well as the Archangels and Angels. However, when you are working with angels, you are in a different ball park, and you must research the rules of the game thoroughly before suiting up.

During our circle work, especially when the need is great or when I'm not feeling up to par, I will pull angelic energy into the spell. When I do, MorningStar has a habit of looking over at me with a secretive smile. She says, "You were pulling in those angels again, weren't you?"

There are scads of stories about single angelic helpers or even legions going into battle during World War I to assist the Allies.[7] New-agers have latched on to angelic beings with fury. Why? Because they don't have to move far from structured dogma to include angels. It is okay to believe in other

6. *Know Your Angels* by John Ronner, Mamre Press, 1993. Page 38.

7. Ibid.

planes if angels are the inhabitants. Therefore, the possibility of other worlds and other spirits removes the fear of the end without sending them to hell for believing in something their religious doctrine dislikes. While this type of belief is not a surprise to Wiccans, the working Witch should always remember his or her own awe when encountering various planes and beings before condemning other individuals for their belief in angels. To each his or her own is an important Wiccan mystery.

❀ Your Work ❧

Project 1: Choose an angelic system and study it.

Project 2: If you would like, work in ritual with angelic beings. Record your experiences. Even if you do not choose to work with them, keep them in mind for your non-magickal friends who are in trouble. Your studies may well assist someone in his or her time of need.

Totems

Humans have always marveled on the skills and cunning of animals. It is natural for us to seek companionship and sometimes a particular quality from the animal kingdom. In the Craft, you will find animals (totems) associated with quarters, although it is not necessary. Many working Witches have personal totem animals with which they work that do not coincide with specific directions or are not involved in their personal quarter calls. Totem energy is also found in the art of shapeshifting.

Most traditional Witches have a specific totem animal or animals attributed to each of the four quarters. Sometimes these energies are activated with the quarter call, and other times they are not. This choice depends both upon the tradition and the type of work to be done. Totem animals are viewed as mystical powers rather than a singular animal. However, singular animal totems do come into play in more personal work, such as in vision questing. Traditional totems usually come from the indigenous animals of the area where the tradition was born. For example, Celtic totems include horses, bulls, stags, ravens, wolves, bears, and boars. (There are other amimals; this is a simple list.) These animals were all found around the area where the Celtic peoples lived.

Before creating or drawing in totem energies for quarters, you will have to do some research for yourself. Your choices should be based on:

Your affinity for the animal.

Its mundane and spiritual characteristics.

Its availability in your locale.

Long before you call this energy, you need to introduce yourself to the totem while in sacred space and have a chat, or at least learn how to mix your energies with those of the totem. If mixing scares you, don't sweat it; work around your fear. Here, I will admit, the traditionalists have it over the solitaries as these animals are pre-chosen for the working Witch. However, that doesn't mean the traditionalist Witch cannot work with other totems independently. Regardless, he or she must still learn to work with the pre-chosen totems, just like the solitary has to educate him or herself about the chosen totems. There is no way of getting around it.

Refined totem work can be extremely advantageous to the working Witch. As I am sure you have guessed, the wolf is one of my totem animals, although it is not part of my traditional totem array. When I want to send a strong message to someone, the wolf carries that information for me.

Here is a prime example of how it can be used (Don't you just love these stories?). As you know by now, I have both an open study/healing group and a closed group. During one open evening, Diane began to tell the others around the table about an astounding vision she'd had the week before. "I was lying in my bed," she said, "I opened my eyes, and there was this big silver wolf standing over my chest. It scared the hell out of me, with its mouth open and fangs dripping! What do you think it meant?"

Diane was fairly new to our group. Some of the oldsters cast a sidelong glance at me, but didn't, thank goodness, say anything. Later, when most of the others had left, I turned to one of our regulars and grinned. Diane was chatting to another woman on the other side of the table. "So," I said, "what do you think of that wolf thing?" Some of the women started to snicker.

Diane looked over at me and smiled half-heartedly. "What's so funny?"

"How'd ya like the wolf?" I said again.

Her smile got bigger, but her eyes were questioning. "What do you mean? I don't have a clue."

One of the women close to Diane jabbed her with a finger and said, "Silver. Wolf. Message. Get it?"

Diane has the most beautiful dark eyes. They were roving at this point.

"Oh. Noooooooooo," she said, finally fixing me with a hard stare.

Yes, indeed. The week before, Diane was approached by one of the more unstable floaters who visit my house from time to time. Most of the people in the group know who they are and don't think much about it. My house serves as a safe place for many types of people. Those who come here regularly keep an eye on those who breeze in and out. Along these lines, we found that one of the occasional visitors had a habit of trying to whip up business deals in which others work their cans off and those with the idea rest on their laurels. (History does precede everyone.) Diane had been approached by this person and I was trying to warn her to watch her step, hence the materialization of the wolf as she was considering plans with the unstable individual.

"Oh, duh!" was all Diane said after the explanation. I tease her now about sending silver wolves—has she seen any lately?

There is debate on the origin of power animals. Some magickal people believe that the formation of an astral power animal is much like an artificial elemental, meaning it is entirely built by your thoughtforms, or your energy work. Others, like myself, believe that it takes both the collective consciousness of the animal kingdom from whence you draw, and the energy/will of the magickal person. The choice of what to believe is yours.

Working with power animals is not difficult, if you have been a good working Witch and have practiced your meditation sequences faithfully. In meditation, call forth your chosen animal. Make friends with it. That's all you do for the first month. Each evening, spend a few moments getting to know the astral animal. Supplement your impressions with research at your local library on its characteristics, natural environment, food requirements, etc.

During the second month, pathwork with your chosen animal in meditation. Go for walks with it, envision various scenes and what the animal's response would most likely be, etc. Keep a record of your experiences. Begin talking with the animal. Yes, communicating in your natural language is okay. Hold conversations, tell jokes, spin stories together. Your power animal is now becomming your best friend.

In the third month, you will go into meditation, call on your power animal, and ask it to perform certain small tasks. For example, I would ask the animal: "What color hat is my friend Lisa wearing today?" Of course, the questions should be those that have answers that can be checked out later, but you don't know the answer at the time the question was formulated. Send the animal out, come out of your meditation, and go about your business. Sometime later, go back into meditation and call upon your power animal to give you the answer to your question.

This is a small example of the use of a power animal. For more information on power animals and shapeshifting, please refer to *To Ride a Silver Broomstick*[8] for detailed instructions.

❁ Your Work ✿

Project 1: If you haven't chosen a totem animal already, do your research and find one.

Project 2: Work with your totem animal both in meditation and ritual.

Project 3: Learn to send your totem animal out as a watcher.

Project 4: Learn to send your totem animal out as a protector.

Don't forget to record your experiences with these projects.

---

8. *To Ride a Silver Broomstick* by Silver RavenWolf, Llewellyn Publications, 1993.

Archetypes

In your Wicca 101 studies, you should have throughly covered the various forms of Deity. In Wicca, we call many of our deities "archetypes." If you have not covered this information before, you are going to have (yes, it's true) more research on your hands; you will need to refer to some introductory books for this information. Check the suggested reading list in the back of this book for a detailed listing.

If you have already chosen your pantheon, or work with several pantheons, all the better. Here again, traditional Witches have a specific set of deity energies they work with regularly. Various members of the pantheon take their places at the quarters in ritual. There is no reason why a solitary Witch cannot do the same thing, though it will take planning on your part. Remember the old rule, and don't mix systems or pantheons.

Instructions to these deities during a quarter call should be specific. They are to guard, bring energies, protect, etc. If you are planning to do a separate invocation during a rite to a deity, it should be different from those at the quarters, and belong to the same pantheon and system of the quarter deities.

❁ Your Work ☙

Learn to work with different archetypes, one at a time.

Mighty Ones/Ancient Ones

These are beings like the Watchtowers, with one exception—they are humans who have transmuted through many incarnations and hold ancient knowledge that can be beneficial to us along our path. Ancient Ones have no delineated names, other than belonging to an element or cardinal direction. Ancient Ones should not be confused with archetypes, who might have once been human. These beings can also been seen like the Grandmothers and Grandfathers of our chosen lineage. This is especially true in traditional work, but there is no reason why a solitary cannot meditate and research his or her own lineage or chosen pantheon blood line. Many working Witches light a candle to their ancestors with every working they do, asking for assistance from either energy or blood lineage. By the act of bringing the flame into being, you are:

Mystically lighting your path across time

Dispelling ignorance and fear of the unknown

Linking your energies with the energies of the Ancients, which remains open until you psychically close the door, or physically close the door by extinguishing the candle

Keep in mind that a few Witches see these Mighty Ones with the same characteristics of guardian angels, which is perfectly acceptable. As I was trying to write this chapter and explain these concepts, one of my friends said, "Why are you attempting to fix what isn't broken?" I thought about that for awhile and came up with the following answer.

I'm not trying to repair something that is damaged. I'm trying to define and mold it to what will work best for me. Not everyone is comfortable with traditional verbiage, even traditionals. Sometimes, when we try to change things, we don't think them through clearly enough, or we get too poetic for our own good. We need to keep the reasoning behind our actions clear. We need to understand what we are saying and why we are making a particular motion or gesture. The only way we can do that is to tear apart what we know already works, and figure out why it does. In that way, we can find the true meaning and stop pooing around with the junk that creeps in over time.

✿ Your Work ✿

Project 1: In meditation over several days, meet the Ancient Ones.

Project 2: Invite them into ritual and work with them.

Quarter Review

Let's go over the different energies that can be called from, into, or around a quarter:
1. Elements (Earth, Air, Water, Fire)
2. Elementals (Spirits of Earth, Air, Water, Fire, Akasha)
   a. Devas
   b. Sylphs
   c. Undines
   d. Salamanders
   e. Gnomes
3. Watchtowers
   a. Stellar
   b. Angelic
   c. Otherworld beings of strength
4. Airts
   a. Black (North, midnight)
   b. White (South, noon)
   c. Red (East, dawn)
   d. Grey (West, twilight)

5. Angels
   a. The Nine Choirs (Catholic)
   b. The Tree of Life (Judaic)
   c. Zorostar
   d. Islamic
6. Totems
7. Archetypes
   a. Minor deities
   b. Legendary figures
8. Mighty Ones/Ancients
   a. Blood lineage
   b. Psychic/initiation lineage/current group mind
   c. Guardian beings
9. Winds (covered in the sacred space chapter)
10. Dragons

These are all practical Wiccan mysteries/ceremonial Wiccan mysteries that can be drawn upon at any time (remember, time as we understand it does not exist). You can begin working with one set of mysteries, then evolve into another, and another. Eventually, as did the Ancient Ones, you will wish to mix and match the various energies to your liking. All it takes is (groan, growl, pant) a little research and a lot of experimentation.

We've talked about these quarter calls in and out of the ritual circle. To this point, I've talked about them as a set, a group of four. Usually they are linked to compass points, no matter whom or what you summon, stir, or call. Also until now, I've talked about the ritual circle but have not conjured it for you. That is in the next chapter. I had a good reason for this. Before you begin casting your little fingers about, you should be thinking about what you will be doing and planning carefully. What you are going to put into your ritual circle should be decided in advance, not slung in as an afterthought. Your quarter calls are as important as the casting of the circle itself—never forget that.

When you become more experienced at working with the above list, you may not wish to call, summon, or stir the entire set of energies. For example, when Diane works for regeneration and psychism, she opens only the West quarter after casting her circle. Those energies she calls include:

Element: West (Water)
Totem animal: Horse (Epona)
Archetype: the Calliech (wisdom)
Ancient Ones: of her blood (Irish) and traditional (Black Forest) lineage

Rather than using her full altar (which remains in the North, as our tradition dictates), she uses a large, portable flat stone. Therefore, within her ritual circle stand both the permanent and portable altar. If her work is serious enough, she may first call the entire set of Watchtowers to guard the circle, but will not make motions at each quarter. Rather, she will invoke their aid (as in the call of the airts), then continue her work from there.

The Wiccan mystery here is this: One learns to call, summon, or stir only what one needs for a given task.

When MorningStar works a circle, she calls a specific quarter for a planned task and acknowledges the others. You do not need to wake up every energy being in the Universe to tell them you are performing a given magickal or ritual task. You don't need to be Ma Barker, pounding a wooden spoon on a big kettle at the top of your mountain to let everyone know it's dinner time. The only instances when bells and whistles in the Craft (notice I did not say in ceremonial work) are to be rung are:

A dedication of a Witch

A Wiccaning (a birth)

An initiation or eldering of a Witch

A passing of a Witch (a death)

A Sabbat or high holy day

When the Witch is in life-or-death shit

In this text, we will cover some of the instances above. As there are many excellent books on the market discussing Sabbats, dedications, and initiations, I'll not be covering those. I will, however, share some of my own religious and magickal rituals, as well as a few get-me-out-of-trouble-please-thank-you-very-much-in-advance practical rituals that have worked for me, or others with whom I practice the Craft.

Whether you are a solitary or traditional Witch, take some time to write out a few quarter calls for yourself. Start with an easy, generic one, and then work into a few that are more complicated and require both research and meditation exercises. You will be amazed with what you create.

Things to Keep in Mind

One of my students recently remarked, "I always wondered what the heck I was supposed to be doing when I'm working with the quarters. I would get up there and feel a wave of confusion as I spoke. This feeling of uncertainty would follow me throughout the whole rite, whether I was doing it by myself or with others. In fact, when I was doing my own stuff, I would invariably forget something. By the time I was done, I felt I had failed in the whole process."

Here are some helpful hints:

Say the quarter call, circle casting, or invocation slowly. If it will help, shut your eyes so you can focus better. I've never read anywhere nor have been taught by anyone that you must have your eyeballs focused on the room or area in front of you. Mundanely, there is nothing there, anyway. You are calling otherworld energies, or at least things you can't usually see with the human eye. If it helps you to concentrate, then by all means, shut your eyes. I do.

When working with quarters, remember that you are dealing with a portal or passageway to other worlds of some kind. Envision it as a door, an opening, a curtain parting, even a tube connecting that world with your circle world—it doesn't matter, as long as you understand the concept of *opening*. To help you, design a gesture or visualization of this act. I remember reading that Dion Fortune visualized a personal sigil of power on a curtain before she proceeded with astral work.

Visualize what is to be coming through or guarding any quarter while casting your circle, invoking deity, or aspecting deity. Again, do your homework. You need to see very clearly in your mind who or what you are pulling toward you.

Feel, with your sixth sense (or other senses), what is happening around you. Do you feel hot, cold, calm, edgy? If you have done your homework, you know what feeling to expect. You may tingle, want to giggle (too bad for you if you are working with others who have no sense of humor), or feel the need to move. If you have a negative occurrence, stop, shut it down, and come back another day.

If you are participating in a group and you have been given the job of a quarter, you are responsible for that quarter from the time you open it until the time you close it. This also includes a circle casting, invocation, or aspecting. You are to be monitoring the energy—don't just stand there gazing blandly at the group. Do your job. Quarter energies are funny, depending on what you are summoning, stirring, or calling. Most energies don't like slackers and a few are irritated by a lazy Witch.

If you are working alone, you've got your hands full. Don't call all the various quarter energies or invoke a ton of deities if you can't handle them (times four, no less, if you are discussing quarters). Choose wisely and you won't feel tired after your rite. Inundate yourself and you'll probably want to sleep for a week, or feel vaguely out of sorts for the next few days. Rome wasn't built in a day; neither is an adept working Witch created in one rite or ritual.

All quarters/energies must be dismissed/closed precisely in the manner in which they were called. Poetic license is wonderful—don't take it here. The mark of an adept working Witch is a proper closure and take-down of the circle energies. A lazy Witch will be a hazy Witch the following day and have all sorts of strange things floating around his or her ritual space after all is supposedly completed. You also risk insulting the energies you have so graciously brought into your circle, then kicked out with a mere dismissal.

If you have:

Summoned: Dismiss and thank

Stirred: Farewell in peace and safety and thank

Called: Hail and farewell and thank

There is nothing worse than an ill-bred working Witch. A thank-you, whether it be in a quarter call or when you leave the house of the High Priestess/Priest, is definitely in order.

Also keep in mind the order of what you have done when you began your ritual. For example, if I cast my circle first, then called my quarters, then invoked Deity, I should reverse the order of closure. I would thank Deity, dismiss my quarters, then draw up my circle.

All workings with both Divine energies and those of other planes should be done in perfect love and perfect trust or, as in sacred space—perfect love and perfect peace. Never conjure quarters, cast a circle, or work a spell without complete harmony in your heart. Even if you are angry, you must reserve that special place in yourself that can rise above fear and hatred. As your spirit evolves, so does your magick. This also requires a balance in your life. If your world is in tatters, don't do magick for others. Ask for mundane and spiritual help for yourself.

All workings should have a goal. Haphazard work is not good in any type of religion or science. One needs clarity of thought at all times.

Our purest intentions are those in which we succeed the best. Here is where the Universe steps in. Okay, so you forgot to call a quarter, missed a beat on a chant, chose the wrong planetary hour. These things can be transcended by purity of thought and goal. This doesn't mean you are supposed to be sloppy on purpose—then your intention would no longer be pure. It does mean that higher powers always look out for us, their children, and will fill in the gaps when we try our best. Seek to turn evil into good, rather than good into evil.

A working Witch does not mind summoning, stirring, or calling power, but is not driven by the quest of power for itself. Rarely do Witches use the ultimate power at their disposal. If one fears the medium or seeks to control limitless power, the Craft is not their home.

A working Witch carries no delusions, either of self, intentions, or others. Know the pond and your place in it.

A working Witch does not seek to control unlimited minions, either human or astral. We are not into the groupie scene. Each person must journey on his or her own path of spirituality alone, with his or her free will intact.

Now that I've beaten this subject to death, are you up to digging into circle conjuring? I certainly hope so, because that's where we're headed, yes? All aboard!

Symbol of the Vesta Witches

Casting Circles

Ten thousand years we've struck the fire,
Creation's music freely sung
With Magick joined we've praised the stars
Since first the world begun.
Our spirit lives in timeless dance,
The Tarot and the Rune,
And nights united in the power
Of Drawing Down the Moon.[1]

According to practically every mystical text, the most desirable magick circle is nine feet in diameter. Traditionally, magick circles in the out-of-doors were ritually marked by bits of clay, stones, trees, or a circle in the dirt drawn by the athame or finger. Inside, general consensus says salt, herbs, or a mixture of both were used to form a mundane boundary, and could be swept away easily. More modern Witches use carpets with a circle either woven into it, or painted on it. Some have even painted directly on the floor, then covered the circle with a big rug when not performing ritual. (Wouldn't the vacuum cleaner salesman be surprised!)

A nine-foot circle is great, provided you have the space, but really isn't practical (or necessary) for the solitary practitioner. If you are practicing around people who do not approve of your work, your permanent circle is as

1. By David O. Norris, 1994.

far away as Mars. When not participating in group work, that huge circle can be more of a pain than a boon, and I can personally vouch that I have a high success rate (as do my students) without the nine-foot circle. Many of us work in less than three feet, some of us even work in unique, visualized circles.

In this chapter, we will cover all sorts of circles, from psychological ones to those that are fairly uncommon. By uncommon, I mean that I personally have not seen these types of circles outlined in any other text currently on the market, nor have I seen them in the numerous Books of Shadows I've been fortunate enough to glue my peepers on. Among other interesting things, this chapter will show you how to conjure a circle in the palm of your hand and throw a circle into form.

> *Properly prepared he must always be...According to the rules of the art; Otherwise, he will never succeed in the works he undertakes. The circle must always be properly cast and purified and he must be purified beforehand by ritual bathing, if possible. All weapons used in the magickal arts must be properly consecrated and all doors securely latched so that he never feels in danger that someone may come when he is working.*[2]

Properly Prepared

Traditional teachings require the seeker to be properly prepared before he or she enters the magickal circle. I owe a great debt of gratitude to Bried Fox-Song, a British Traditional Clan Mother in New York. Without her, I never could have made deosil or widdershins out of my traditional lessons. These days, no matter what the question or the hour I call her with it, Bried is always there. It is Bried who first explained to me what a proper person is supposed to do and how he or she is to perform. The list of proper person qualities looks like the Girl Scout Laws. (I kid you not.) Among those qualities expected in the Witch before he or she enters the magickal circle are:

Reliability
Trustworthiness
Responsibility
Loyalty
Cheerfulness
Humanitarianism
Honesty
Fairness
Consideration
Respect for authority
Resourcefulness

---

2. *The Alex Sanders Lectures,* Magickal Childe Publishing, Inc., 1984. Page 68.

Can keep a secret
Devotion to Divinity

A friend of mine used to play an interesting trick on her students. She would not let them eat at the feast unless they could recite the qualities listed above, in one breath, in less than thirty seconds. They learned them quickly.

Conjuring the Circle of Balance

Whether you entered the craft six months or fifteen years ago, the idea of conjuring balance in your life should never change. Before you entertain the thought of helping AnaBelle with her torrid, soap-opera life, you should have:

A high sense of self-esteem (not to be confused with megalomania).

Put your life in order, including both mundane and spiritual goals. You should have accomplished most of the first goals you set, and prioritized or re-evaluated those you have not met.

Come to terms with how you view Divinity and in what manner you associate with it.

Learned to balance your spiritual life with your mundane life. After all, that's what you are here for. If you were to float around in spiritual jetsam all the time, it would not be necessary for you to be on the earth plane. You might as well buck up, my little camper, and get with the earth program.

Come to grips with the fact that there are "fringe-Pagans" who practice sometimes and manage to muddy the water for the rest of us. Let's face it. Some people like to play politics and enjoy the megalomaniac trip. Learn to tell the serious seekers from the space cadets in any religious arena.

Conjuring balance is not a simple matter until you realize that balance already exists—you simply have to tap into it. Rather than allowing yourself to get sucked into every emotional maelstrom that comes along, school yourself to take three deep breaths and stand back. Become an observer, not a participant in the hellish hurricanes of others.

The Circle of Fear

There is always debate among magicians on precisely what one casts a circle for. I've found four camps (so to speak):

1. Those who feel the circle is cast to keep astral nasties away and protect the practitioner.

2. Those who feel the circle is cast to contain power until the magician chooses to release it.

3. Those who believe both 1 and 2 apply equally, as well as viewing it as a psychological trigger for the work at hand.

4. Those who don't cast a circle at all (these people are rare and normally do not believe in a power more potent or higher than themselves—not what I would call Wiccan theology).

Depending on what type of work you are doing, I go with number three. However, before we begin practicing circles I feel it is imperative to tell you there is nothing to be afraid of. I have had innumerable students tell me (at length) their various fears about circle conjuration. Nothing is going to happen to you, unless of course, you are stupid enough to conjure something evil on purpose. Then, you deserve to fry.

The first year *To Ride a Silver Broomstick* came out, a comedy cable television show in Massachusetts held up the book on Halloween and tried to conjure Beezelbub. I was incensed. Personally, I hope all the minions of the underworld descended upon them. In my mind, they asked for it. Therefore, another Wiccan mystery presents itself to you: Learn to be responsible for what comes out of your mouth, whether in the world of the mundane or of magick.

I have lost students because they were petrified to conjure a circle. The one problem with teaching groups is that many participants tend to rely on the group magick, rather than working on their own. This happened in my group. Many people were studying for months before I figured out they were skipping their personal practice sessions and working circle magick only with their peers. This is a no-no. To be an accomplished working Witch, you must be able to conjure any type of circle at any time. Although traditional Witches can tap into the group mind with special words of power, it isn't going to do all the work for them. It will lend energy and assist in stability. In the long run, those students who were not working solo found themselves floundering behind.

The Circle of Inadequacy

If you are teaching students, beware of the "I'm so inadequate" syndrome. It often comes up in conjunction with the practice of circle or quarter conjurations. This is a major flag that the person isn't doing his or her homework and may be working with a bad case of fear or inadequacy. Catch it before it gets too far, or the person will insist that you are responsible for not teaching properly, when in reality, it is a lack of dedication on the student's part. More frightening, the student may feed on his or her own self-esteem, and you will discover the person blubbering in your kitchen, cursing in your dining room, or belaying with great fervor that someone close is being attacked by astral nasties this very minute! You think I jest?

In our tradition, we encourage Witches to work as much on their own as possible. Group work is great and has its place, but removing solo practice from the working Witch cripples him or her severely. (Yes, I am quite aware I am repeating myself here, but I wish to drive this point into your brain—

quoth this Raven, ever more!) Often, those who only work in groups find themselves in fifty feet of poop out in Kansas while they are on vacation and their group is back in Maine. One of our first-degree requirements is that the Witch can handle both quarter energy and conjuring circles alone, and if we can, insist they perform for a group rite as well. They are also required to write a solo full moon ritual and a new moon ritual, and perform it, with the appropriate notes of results. We have several other requirements as well that involve hands-on work. It is the only way they are going to learn—by doing.

The Magick Circle

The magick circle is a fundamental requirement of all kinds of occult ceremonial work, and one of the most ancient. The magicians of Babylon and Assyria used magick circles in their rites. Descriptions of their workings have come down to us, together with the name they gave to the magick circle, usurtu.[3]

Like quarter calls, there are as many circle conjurations as there are working Witches. The best circle conjurations carry a twist that belongs entirely to the working Witch. In this chapter we will cover several types of conjurations, from simple to complicated. Don't forget that many working Witches conjure the circle first and then call the quarters, as appropriate to the working.

The Simple, Personal Circle

If you have been meditating every day like a good Witch, you have already done the simple circle. It is the mental enclosure of your body with some sort of energy field, whether you have visualized mirrors, a blue bubble, an invisible shield, or whatever. This is the simple circle and can most certainly be used in emergencies and light spell casting (often called minor magicks) that include the following:

Petition magick
Mind programming
Candle magick
Cord magick
Gem magick
Element magick

Some of the more complicated magicks (such as Tarot and runic) also use a simple circle. In these two cases the difficulty lies in knowing the two systems mentioned, rather than the performance of the spell.

---

3. *Witchcraft for Tomorrow* by Doreen Valiente, Phoenix Publishing, 1989. Page 66.

One of my best friends became a tradition sister through the casting of a simple circle, with a complicated twist.

"I think my husband is a psychic vampire," she said. I said nothing. I've known this to happen. The lady, let's call her Suzanne, was distraught. She was honest and trying to deal with a situation that most people would not believe, and she wasn't so sure she believed it herself. This is good. I liked her immediately. Always question logically things like psychic vampirism, psychic attacks, etc. People do get carried away with these ideas. Look at Pennsylvania during the height of the Hexmeister scare back in the forties, or these stupid Witch wars we hear of today.

Back to the story. "I don't know what to do," she said. "Am I crazy?"

When someone comes to you with concerns about these topics, listen very carefully. Keep your mouth shut until the person is through, only interjecting enough to allow the full story to come out. Sometimes you will find the individual is mentally unbalanced or simply a victim of his or her own overactive imagination. These situations have different responses. In this case, I felt Suzanne's fears were legitimate and she was willing to do something about it, rather than take up my time by lamenting in a pity-me-whine-but-I'm-too-weak-to-fix-it.

We were not talking about a case of an overzealous magician. No, this person was one of those extraordinary charismatic he-man types. No more, no less. What to do? A simple circle with a very complicated twist.

Conjuring a Hologram of Paradox: An Advanced Personal Circle

The following conjuration takes approximately six weeks for the beginner to learn, a week or less for the advanced working Witch. It involves repeated meditations, so gear up to the standard format of quiet time, sacred space, etc.

The Dragon's Loop

The Dragon's Loop is a shielding exercise that leads to an excellent form of psychic self-defense, though it can also be used to protect objects within and outside the home. In essence, you will be creating an infinite loop of protection that can not be destroyed. Here's how it works.

Choose something that you want to protect, either yourself, a loved one, an animal, or a thing. If your choice is a person or animal, choose a piece of jewelry or a pocket item for a person, and a collar or tag for an animal. If it is a small animal, use its cage.

Personal items can be jewelry, crystals and gems, a handkerchief, lodestone, or some other favorite bauble. For a room, choose a statue, a plate or cup, a small picture, or mirror.

Step One: Get to know the item by using all your senses—smell, touch, taste, hearing, etc. You must know every contour of the item with your eyes closed, so it is best to use the bird's eye view, ant's eye view, and person's eye view exercise given in *To Ride a Silver Broomstick*. Do this exercise for one week. By the time you are finished, you should be able to close your eyes and immediately conjure the complete image of the item immediately. If you cannot, take another week until you can.

Step Two: Now it is time to meditate with the object in your hand. I chose a dragon ring given to me by Lord Serphant of North Carolina. If you are ill, nervous, worried, or hold any negative feelings at all after you have grounded and centered, end the session and begin again the next day. Negative energies will deplete or weaken the shield you are constructing and you will have wasted both time and energy.

With your eyes closed, expand the image of your object until it is approximately fifty percent larger than the actual object. Open your eyes and place that expanded image over the object—as if you are looking through a transparency (or holographic image) and can see the three-dimensional object. Practice this image-over-image visualization for one week.

Step Three: The third week brings you into more complicated visualization. This time, go into your meditation. First, see the object. Second, see the hologram around the object as well. Now visualize the person you want to protect, such as yourself. Watch yourself put the object in your pocket, around your neck, on your finger—whatever. Expand the hologram image of the object around yourself (or the subject). Practice this for one week.

Step Four: You are now nearing the end of this exercise. Enter your meditative state, and go through step three. When that is accomplished, begin building a web of light from the object to the hologram and back to yourself. These strands of light will look like those energy globes you buy at a novelty shop. You know, the ones where you touch the outside of the ball and little lightning bolts flash out of the center and feed toward the outside of the globe. Practice this for one week.

Step Five: Repeat step four above, then empower with Divine energy. You can use whatever Divine universal form you want, it doesn't matter as long as it is a force you trust completely. Visualize a pure white light cascading onto the shield (like the outside of a dragon's egg) and hardening the dragon shell. At this point, you must be absolutely confident that nothing, not any single thing, can pass through this shell. The shell can be quite beautiful if you like, or very plain; it is up to you. Practice this for one week.

Step Six: Not all of us are confident all the time. Here is where the dragon energy comes in. During this week's meditation, conjure yourself a friendly dragon who will be willing to assist you when the chips are down—sort of an extra reserve of energy. Watch as the dragon fire hardens the egg with an extra coating of protective energy. When you need it, a mist will break free to obscure the shell and make it invisible to astral eyes.

To maintain the connection between self, object, and hologram, practice steps five and six about once a month, to keep yourself fresh. Suzanne accomplished this visualization in one week. She reported back that she was no longer fatigued, nervous, or carrying around that drained feeling. I've taught many individuals this technique. It only works if you take the time and practice it.

The Standard Circle

If this text happens to be the first book you have ever read on the Craft and you intend to start practicing, please, please, *please* learn the standard circle conjuration first and practice it diligently. Do not jump into the advanced techniques. You will be doing yourself a disservice, believe me. You've got to know a standard conjuration/ritual inside and out, upside down, with your eyes shut and in your sleep—that's where the real work comes in.

The standard circle sticks to four quarters that match (same system, pantheon, etc.), and usually the circle conjuration is somewhat in the same line. Most of these conjurations are short and to the point.

> *I conjure ye, O circle of power, so that you can be for me a boundary between the worlds of men and the realms of the mighty spirits. A meeting place of peace and trust, love and joy, containing the power I will raise herein...*[4]

Whenever you utter a circle conjuration, you should take your time and listen to yourself. If you rush to get through it, you are doing yourself an injustice and allowing room for failure. A circle conjuration should be done with reverence. You, this one little person on the planet, are about to do what few can—walk between the worlds.[5] This is no easy task. The act of circle conjuration should put you in awe, no matter how many times you do it or where you do it. If you are in front of people, half-close your eyes as you walk if you don't like being on parade.

The standard circle conjuration is often done on the move, with athame, staff, or wand in hand. Many Witches walk thrice around the circle. Some walk only once, and we will get into conjurations like that later. Remember that you

---

4. *A Book of Pagan Rituals,* Herman Slater, Weiser Press.

5. Walking between the worlds is a suspension in time and space best described by Starhawk's famous circle opening and salute:
The Circle is cast.
We are between the worlds,
Beyond the bounds of time,
Where night and day,
Birth and death,
Joy and sorrow,
Meet as one.
(*The Spiral Dance* by Starhawk, Harper and Row, 1979. Page 57.)

are conjuring a bubble, not a circle drawn on the ground. The bubble encases you and whatever else you want. It is your visualization and your circle. This bubble is also "above and below"—an important visualization to remember, because you are supposed to be visualizing while you walk and talk. What type of visualization do you use? Here are some I've heard of or done myself:

A blue, gold, or silver bubble

A mist that slowly conjures and forms into a bubble (my favorite)

Blue fire that springs up, then forms into a bubble

Pulsating energy formed into a bubble

Dragon's scales formed into a bubble

Fairy wings draped and formed into a bubble

A woven circular tapestry that molds into a bubble

A circular spider web that knits into a bubble

A green hedge that grows into a bubble

I'm sure there are dozens more, but you get the drift.

A Craft elder visiting my home once told me this story. I liked it so much, I want to share it with you.

The elder moved to a new home. He notified the authorities about his religion and indicated that he would be hosting rituals on his property. If they liked, they could attend one to see what actually happened. One afternoon, the local sheriff did indeed drop by for a chat. The conversation must have gone well, because the afternoon shadows gently blended to dusk and the sheriff was still ensconced on the front porch of the elder's home, rocker tipping gently to the beat of the melting ice in the lemonade pitcher.

As the sun slipped below the horizon, the elder smiled at the sheriff and indicated it was time for a ritual to begin. The afterglow of dusk, the time of in-between, was at hand. Would he like to join in? The sheriff said no, but he would wait on the porch and watch them. The elder nodded and he and those participating walked down to the grove.

Let me make it clear here that from the elder's front porch, the full grove could be seen. Nothing was hidden from the sheriff. The ritual proceeded on schedule and went well. Afterward, the elder walked back to the porch.

"Well, what did you think?" asked the elder.

The sheriff scratched his head. "You know," he said slowly. "I could see everything clearly up until the time you walked around in a circle and said some words about erecting something and then—I'll be darned—everything down there got fuzzy. I couldn't see a thing clearly, but I had a peaceful feeling inside, anyhow."

That, evidently, is what a cast circle looks like to some mundane people on the outside. Even with all the comings and goings at my house, most of my neighbors think I'm having a Tupperware party (can you believe it?).

I don't often see circles myself, but I can feel them. For me to actually see them with my regular eyes, they've got to be well-cast and strong. Witches can put distinctive twists on their circles to make them their signature and work well for them. Lady Maven casts a circle that looks like a ring of blood-red that explodes at the apex, then drips down around the bubble. (She's great with the athame, by the way. We always give the dedicants to her. Quite exciting.) Lord Merlin has a sorcery twist on his, and the circle gets so thick sometimes that my eyes actually water until he cuts a door and lets me in. I don't like to wait outside too long, let me tell you. Lady Bats has a fuzzy, whipped cream sort of circle that looks like it came out of an aerosol can. Put your hand out to touch it and it springs back like the Stay-Puft Marshmallow Man. Lord Shadow's circle appears much like his magickal name—a shadowy essence that feels weightless, but carries a hint of steel. As scary as these circles may sound, let me assure you that they are not cast with evil or wicked thoughts; quite the contrary. These are very strong, warrior-type people, who cast their circles to both raise energy and protect, nothing more.

Why all this fuss about circle casting, anyway, if it is to be followed by a dynamite invocation, excellent ritual format, or fun working? Like anything you build, the foundation must be firm so nothing can rock the proceedings. The circle conjuration needs to be correctly worded, visualized properly, and erected securely. If you do not take your time and concentrate, you will probably have many of those psychic disturbances that happen to others during ritual, visit you.

Regardless of what a few Witches will tell you, psychic disturbances rarely happen in or directly outside a well-cast circle, and if they do, they are more like Divine manifestations, rather than things going bump in the night and scaring the poop out of you. Unless you are breaking a hex, working weather magick, or doing some type of major exorcism, you should not have things flying around the room or screeching wildly in the grove. Remember, acts of harmony should not create chaos on any plane of existence.

Yes, I know manifestations are fun and they make you think you are actually doing something, but often they mean the psychic seas are rough and you need to work on some fine-tuning that includes both inner and outer balance in your technique. I do want to warn you, though, circles get hot—literally. This is not an uncommon or undesired occurrence. While we are at it, I'd like to dispel another myth: the act of circle conjuration itself is not a lot of work. If you are expending huge amounts of personal energy, you are doing it wrong. The working Witch is a Crafter; he or she crafts a circle out of the natural energy around him or her. If you are straining, you aren't doing it right. Wiccan mystery number—well, whatever the heck number we are on.

How Many Circles?

Before we go further, I would like to touch on the subject of how many times a working Witch walks around his or her circle when casting it. I have never seen more than three, and I have seen (and have done) less than one.

Let's break down the standard, three-time pass, and how a working Witch may visualize the intent while speaking the words of conjuration.

The first pass is for the Goddess
The second pass is for the God
The third pass is for the All

The first pass is for the Elements
The second pass is for the Ancestors/Faeries/Spirits/Angels
The third pass is for Divinity

The first to cleanse
The second to consecrate (bless)
The third to empower

Some working Witches make three passes, but not while speaking the words of conjuration. For example, they may do the altar devotion and salute before they walk the circle, then ritually cleanse the area in a circular fashion with salt and water on the first pass, and fire and air on the second pass. Back at the altar, they ground and center, then make only one more pass while speaking the words of conjuration.

I don't know where the three-pass idea comes from. Yes, I realize I'm showing my ignorance here. I've seen some old Books of Shadows with the three-pass poem, and since the number three has been considered magickal since people decided they could count, who really knows?

Other working Witches (me included these days) do a great deal of the conjuration process in their minds. This is fun, challenging, and exciting, but takes practice. We'll get to that, hold on to your broom—I won't disappoint you.

One of my favorite circle conjurations (given below) was written by Doreen Valiente[6] and fits well with the invocation designed by the same author in an earlier chapter:

Black spirits and white
Red spirits and grey
Hearken to the rune I say.
Four points of the circle, weave the spell,
East, South, West, North, your tale to tell.
East is for red for the break of day,
South is white for the noontide hour,
In the West is twilight grey,
And North is black for the place of power.
Three times round the circle's cast.
Great ones, spirits from the past,
Witness it and guard it fast.

There are working Witches who pass three times, tracing their footsteps, and others who pass first in a large circle, second in a smaller one, and the third pass is close around the altar. The latter is mostly for solitary work. Again, the choice is yours.

---

6. *Witchcraft for Tomorrow* by Doreen Valiente, Phoenix Publishing, 1989. Page 157.

If you plan to write your circle conjuration, take into consideration the following:

It should be designed in prose that is acceptable to you

It should be the length it takes you to make the chosen number of passes

It should be specific to trigger an appropriate visualization from yourself

You should explain precisely what the circle is going to do

You may invoke the quarters, if you wish

You may invoke the ancestors, if you wish

You may invoke Divinity, if you wish

Wording Circle Castings to Work for You

As with the quarter calls, let's break down a conjuration and figure out exactly what we are doing, and why. Here is a variation of the first conjuration I gave you:

I conjure thee, O great circle of power... You are specifically stating what you are going to conjure: O great circle of power. In this instance, you are creating neutral energy.

So that you will be for me a boundary between the world of men and the realms of the mighty spirits... Now you are cutting the boundary between the world of the mundane and the world of spirit, creating a safe space to collect the energy.

A meeting place of perfect love, trust, peace, and joy, containing the power I will raise herein... The function of this circle is to hold power until you are ready to release it.

I call upon the protectors of the East, South, West, and North, to aid me in the construction of this circle... You've enlisted the guardians of the four quarters to assist you in building your circle and lending their energies, mixing them with yours. You can envision these protectors any way you like.

In the name of the Horned Lord and Radiant Lady... You are calling on Divinity and using their names, leading more power to your circle.

Thus do I conjure thee, O great circle of power! This is an affirmation of what you have done.

This circle is sealed. Meaning nothing is getting in here, unless I want it to.

Now, what if we aren't planning to do a ritual or magickal working, but feel the need to cast a circle of protection? How would we do that, using somewhat the same formula?

I conjure thee, O circle of protection... Prime function stated.

So that you will be for me a boundary between all negativity and all that is dear to me... Here the line of purpose is drawn and you are including yourself and your loved ones.

A safe place of perfect love, trust, peace, and joy, containing those I wish to protect herein... The function of this circle is to protect all those who are within it, either physically or in your heart/mind.

I call upon the Guardians of the East, South, West, and North to aid me in the construction of this circle... Again, you are calling upon the building and constructing energies of the quarters.

In the name of the Morrigan and Cernunnos... Here two strong Celtic divinities known for their protective qualities are chosen.

Thus do I conjure thee, O great circle of protection... I have affirmed my intent.

This circle is sealed! You've hermetically sealed and locked the area, magickally speaking.

Okay, let's get fancy. How about a circle conjuration for healing?

I conjure thee, O great circle of healing, so that you will be for me a boundary between good health and dis-ease, a healing place of perfect love, trust, peace, and joy containing the positive, healing energies I will raise herein. I call upon the angelic beings of the East, South, West, and North to aid me in the construction and healing purpose of this circle, and to help me dispel dis-ease from _____ (a specific person's name). In the name of the Golden Lord and the Silver Lady thus do I conjure thee, O great circle of healing. This circle is sealed!

Of course, you could choose two deities (preferably a male and female to hold the balance) of your favorite pantheon. By using Golden Lord and Silver Lady, we have also touched on the healing properties of the sun and moon.

See what you can do if you use your imagination? Every time you experiment, you pull yourself toward a higher sense of spirituality and knowledge. Don't let anyone try to convince you that your theory of magick, ritual, or energy work may be wrong before you have tried it—and remember not to take one failure as all-inclusive. Try again.

Why specialize a circle casting? Like anything else, the more precise, the better the result. By specialization, you are directing the energies toward a single intent. Of course, you wouldn't use a healing circle for a Sabbat celebration. However, if your friend is very sick and you want to do everything you possibly can for him or her, a healing circle brings you closer to a speedier conclusion. Tight, focused circles are the hallmarks of a working Witch. Much can be accomplished without group energy.

Casting Mind Circles

In the simple circle, you conjured a bubble around your body. The mind circle is a little more complicated and takes practice and time. You are going to sit in a quiet place where you know you will be undisturbed for as long as you need. Close your eyes and move into your favorite meditation sequence. From there, begin your altar devotions, preparation of sacred space, circle conjuration, and quarter calls in your mind. Don't get frustrated if this takes you a while to do and many tries until you can get it right. You will find that the more you do it, the faster the visualization goes. I learned to do this technique by practicing every night before I fell asleep.

Why bother? Not all circumstances are conducive to a full ritual that includes quarter calls, altar devotions, and a circle casting. There will be times when speed is of the essence. There will also be occasions when you don't have access to your equipment. Finally, the more you can do in your mind, the higher your self-esteem. As you progress, you gain confidence. It is a a relief and an exhilarating feeling to know that regardless of the circumstances, if you can keep your head, you can do practically anything. Some people would regard this as a psychological puff of power, but I do not. To me, it is a wondrous thing, this religion of the Craft, and I am constantly in awe that I, one human in many, can touch such a wide array in this magnificent Universe.

❁ Your Work ❧

Write a circle casting for a specific purpose, match the quarter calls you will need, and perform it. Keep a record of your results, including date, time, planetary hour, astrological sign, and moon sign. How did you do?

Casting Advanced Circles

By now, you know how it feels to do the altar devotion, the circle casting, and the conjuring of quarters. The energies are familiar to you and should bring a feeling of peace and tranquillity—a harmonious atmosphere. The following exercises/circles should be practiced first in a non-productive vein. You will be working only on conjuring without the express purpose of a rite, ritual, or casting a spell; however, you will need to follow through and take down even a practice circle. Get the technique down before you use it in your work.

Casting a Circle in Your Hand

To cast: Burn some incense and create sacred space. This can be done mentally or physically, though while learning this technique, I suggest practicing physically. You might use the words (first said by Scott Cunningham):

> *I call Air for speed*
> *Fire to cleanse*
> *Water to bless*
> *Earth to manifest*
> *Spirit to seal*

Place a flat, portable altar stone in the middle of the floor with a bowl of water and a single, lighted candle. Sit in front of the stone.

Perform an altar devotion with your hands, then stand.

Hold your hands over the altar, cupping them in front of you.

Visualize a ball of energy in your hand. The intent must be clear that it is formed to grow into a circle.

This next part is tricky because your visualization and focus must be very good. Drop the ball of energy and imagine that it explodes out in all directions to form a perfect circle that encompasses you and the altar. You can make the circle as large or small as you like. This type of circle depends upon your visualization. It can grow slowly or very fast, and be colored or not. Never forget that your final intent is a bubble, as when you walked and cut in the standard circle casting discussed earlier. When you are satisfied, say:

> *As above*
> *So below*
> *This circle is sealed*

One of the best ways to check yourself is with a partner who can either see energy with his or her mundane or third eye, or a person who can feel the quality of energy.

To take down: Contract the energy the same way you expanded it. Open your receptive hand and pull the little bubble back into it. Either give it to the Universe for healing or absorb it into your hand, envisioning that it is transformed into healing energy before it enters your body.

Casting the Hand of Glory Circle

The legendary Hand of Glory was part of a gruesome story that originated during the Middle Ages. Credit for this horrific spell is given to Albertus Magnus. The working called for the severed hand of one who had been hanged or strangled. The hand was dried and dipped in virgin wax. The light of the taper was said to "paralyze completely the faculties, both mental and physical, of everyone who comes within its influence." The working had a dual function: To protect the practitioner and to control evil.

Of course, no one uses the hand of a corpse today; however, a modern Hand of Glory spell is used by some magickal practitioners to control negative situations that involve rapists, stalkers, abusers, etc. (See Chapter 8 for the modern version of the spell.)

Although the myth of the Hand of Glory was a rather negative one, here we turn it toward positive energies. The Hand of Glory circle is a lot of fun.

To cast: In this circle, the energy is directed by your index finger. You point your finger at the center of the floor and imagine a glowing dot. This dot will expand, rushing across the floor in all directions at once. The right side will lift toward the heavens, then descend the left side. As the right ascends, the left side will descend beneath the floor or ground (depending where you are)—together they form a perfect orb.

To take down: Reverse the visualization and balance the ball of energy on your receptive index finger. Either give it to the Universe for healing and protection, or absorb it into your body, visualizing its transmutation into positive energy.

Casting the Exploding Circle

This is one of the most exciting circles I have ever seen conjured and it is done by one of my students, Lord Merlin, now an elder of the Black Forest Clan.

To cast: Stand at the altar and perform the altar devotion. Ground and center until you have reached total harmony within yourself.

Not moving (still facing the altar) and with your eyes shut, begin weaving a net of purifying energy clockwise around the room.

When you are finished, envision the net catching all the positive energy you will need to form the circle.

Pull all the energy into your left hand and concentrate on angelic beings collecting power to enhance your work. Breathe in the power. Pull the net into your left hand.

> *Elemental spirits*
> *Lords of old*
> *This altar fresh*
> *I now behold.*
>
> *Love and peace*
> *cling to me*
> *in truth and serenity.*

I charge you to assist here
Our light
Our love
shall be our store.
This place is in perfect harmony
As I will, so mote it be![7]

In one movement, turn to your right, lift your left arm, and throw the energy on the ground (visualizing a circle emerging in one quick swoop), stamping your left foot at the same moment your energy throw hits the ground. The energy explodes into a perfect circle—as above, so below. It sounds bizarre, but it is a marvelous experience for everyone in the room. To cut his door, he visualizes a camera lens opening, then closing after all have been anointed.

To take down: Mentally turn the circle back into a net. Pull it in like the cartoon Spiderman. (Remember, his web retracts into his glove.) You will retract the circle either into a tool or into your body, transmuting the energy into positive essence before doing so.

Casting the Circle of Mist

This is one of my favorite late-night circles, when I am alone and in the mood for a little mystery. I use one prop, an old oil and vinegar bottle.

To cast: Do your altar devotion, and ground and center.

Place a large, flat stone in the middle of the room. Place the bottle exactly in the center. Put all the tools for the working you have planned in the center of the stone, around the bottle. Place one illuminator candle beside the stone.

Sit in front of the stone and hold the open bottle in both hands. Imagine it collecting the needed energy from the Universe to create a secure, harmonious circle. When you feel the bottle is full, cap it.

Place the bottle back on the stone and stand up.

Uncap the bottle and speak the following words of conjuration while guiding the mists from the bottle. Envision the mists cutting the circle in a clockwise direction.

Mists of North, East, South, and West
Rise with haste per my bequest.
Thrice circle round, in and out
From the bottle, out the spout.

Surround me now in harmony
Fire and sky, land and sea.

---

7. The conjuration used by Lord Merlin comes from a book entitled *The Magick Power of Witchcraft* by A. Manning.

Ancient Ones of lineage old
Bring spirit strong, and circle hold.

As above, so below
This circle is sealed.

To take down: When you are done with your working, set the bottle in the middle of the floor, say the following, and envision the mists returning to the bottle in a widdershins direction. Cork the bottle after the closing is said.

Mists of West, South, East, and North
Return with ease as I called you forth.
Once circle round, up and out
Back into the bottle, down through the spout.

Leave me now in harmony
Fire and sky, land and sea.
Ancient Ones of lineage old
Farewell to thee, back to the fold.

If you will notice, this conjuration and deactivation conjures the circle, the elements, and the Ancients. There is no need for a quarter call. An invocation can be done immediately after the conjuration, and the work of the evening begun.

This conjuration is particularly effective outside if you store dry ice in the bottle ahead of time. It makes quite a show and gets everyone in the mood. For a solitary ritual, you can also use a perfume bottle, especially the clay ones designed to absorb fragrances.

Casting a Circle for Pow-Wow or Folk Magick

Folk magick is the birth cauldron of the New Generation of Witchcraft. No matter how you write it, say it, argue it, or revere it—those little kitchen Witch practices are indeed a basic building block of both the old Craft and the new. A fellow in England had a hissy-fit because of my presentation of the Craft as "new generation." I look at it this way: our ancestors were wise and much of what they knew is lost. Those practicing today fill in the holes with modern tools and ideas. Our sciences have found additional planets, propagated new forms of vegetation, and given us goodies we can use to work magick. I realize, as my father repeatedly tells me, that there is nothing new under the sun. However, place a Witch from the 1600s in today's magickal community, and I bet he or she would have heart failure. The energy we are using may be the same, but we have changed and our practices have changed, whether we wish to admit it or not. This leads into another Wiccan mystery: The Craft ever-grows, ever-changes. That is what keeps it alive, fresh, and strong.

Pow-Wow is the American form of Witchcraft, and is practiced today as a form of folk magick, best known for healing. Folk magick does not require a full

112

circle or ritual, but should be practiced in a magick circle. Often the circle casting is tied directly into the invocation/spell work. How many of us have found great spells in old cookbooks and diaries, but there is no explanation to go with them? Here is a circle casting to close the gap for those folk magick gems that take only a minute to perform.

To cast:

Witches' lair and wolverine night
Ancient Ones bring second sight
Blood and bones of those before
Help me with this little chore.

Thread and pins and natural things
At my bidding, magick bring.
East and South, West and North
Circle round, bring power forth.

Land and sky, fire and sea
Open now for Divinity
Spirit rise and seal this place
I work now in sacred space.

To take down:

Open now this sacred space
Send all energies back to place.
Fare thee well and safe return
Let not my magick ere be turned.

Casting a Circle for Goddess Worship

Dianic Craft is popular in the United States today. I started on my path through the writings of Marion Weinstein—her work was an inspiration to me. Here is a conjuration in her honor.

By the strength of Witch's honor
I conjure the magick circle
Feminine steel, a powerful boon
I am safe within the Goddess' womb.
A sacred place, a world apart

Where enchantment births and magick starts.
With Air and Fire, Water and Earth
I circle round, the Mother's girth.

The Legions of life await my word.
This circle is sealed.

Casting a Circle for God Worship

What if we want to work with the God? The male mysteries are touched upon less than Goddess-oriented or balanced worship in modern Craft. Yes, I know there are pockets of God worship; however, many Witches run for cover when the God tries to stand alone. Too close to Christianity, I guess. But that does not mean you cannot honor the God in your private workings.

Black and White, Light and Dark
In-between the balance starts.
Strong and powerful, safe place about
God's strong energy I circle out.

With Earth and Air, this circle grows
I activate; His spirit glows
With Fire and Water, the circle blend
I conjure all His energies in.

The Ancestral Circle of Sands

This one appears in the preface of this book. Place a bowl of sand in the center of the proposed circle. Stand over the bowl, feet apart. Take a handful of sand and intone the following conjuration, allowing the sand to slip from your fingers, back into the bowl.

To cast: Raise your hand over your head and move it in a clockwise circle above your head.

Slowly spiral your hand down until it is directly in front of you. As you do so, envision the circle turning above your head, then descending around you to the place where your hand is. The circle will continue to turn clockwise around your body, but will not touch the ground yet. Take a few moments to envision it as purifying energy.

Slow the movement of the circle down until it stops. Turn your hand so that when you open it, the sand will drop directly into the bowl. Say:

I conjure thee, O great circle of power
I transmute thy pure energy into a cauldron of enchantment.

Slowly open your palm and allow the sand to slip into the bowl while saying:

As the sands of time dissolve into the oneness of the Universe
I call forth the Ancient Ones to protect me and impart their wisdom.
Ancestors of Old, keepers of my lineage
I stir thee now.
Arise and join the energy bridge that awaits you!

When all the sand has fallen into the bowl, clap your hands loudly and say:

As above, so below
This circle is sealed.

Envision the remainder of the circle dropping like a curtain, enveloping all who are present in a perfect bubble of protection.

To take down: Envision the circle returning to the bowl of sand, while you move your hand in a widdershins circle above the bowl. Take your athame and stab it directly in the center of the bowl (don't break the tip, mind you), envisioning all the positive, transmuted energy entering the blade. Say:

This circle is open
But never broken.

Taking Down Circles

Although I believe there are 101 ways to do almost anything in the Craft, I get a little testy when it comes to taking down a circle. Too many times I've watched inexperienced Witches botch the job, only because they don't know any better. Drawing up a circle is just as important as casting it. By the same token, if you have put a great deal of effort into erecting a circle, why in pentacle's name would you take any less time dismantling it? What, you snap your fingers and poof, it isn't there anymore? Why did you bother to erect it at all if it is that simple?

Want to hear me screech like the real Witch I am? Tell me you are going to "dismiss" the circle. One does not dismiss a circle. This wording reminds me of a Victorian lady, waving her lace hankie. "Shoo! Go away, little circle. I am dismissing you! Off to where you belong." Where, may I ask, are you dismissing it to? I don't want to play anymore, so go back to your own energy sandbox?

If you take the responsibility to build a circle of power, you must also take the responsibility of taking it down. What goes up, comes down, with precisely the same amount of care it took to put it there in the first place.

To put it bluntly, you can dismantle, pull up, draw in, take down, draw up, or pull in a circle. You don't "dismiss" it.

When Not to Cast a Circle

There are few times when you shouldn't cast a circle; naturally, they are the same times when you shouldn't practice magick.

When you are very ill. Have a friend work for you.

When the moon is void of course. The odds are very much against you.

When you are angry. There is no focus in harmony if you are mad.

When someone is with you who does not approve of what you are doing.

These ideas in circle casting are a simple jumping-off point. Take the information you have learned in this chapter and design some of circle castings for yourself. Experiment with them, have fun, and begin to count your successes. If you put thought and effort into it, you won't be disappointed.

❀ Your Work ❧

Project 1: Choose one Sabbat, one Esbat, and one minor working. Do any historical or working research necessary.

Project 2: Compose a ritual outline for all three for a solitary practitioner, including accurate colors, correspondences, deities, etc. Incorporate a new salute, a new quarter call, and a new circle casting.

Project 3: Choosing one of the three outlines, write the ritual or working from start to finish.

Project 4: Perform this ritual or working.

Quick Outline of General Ritual Procedures

Esbats

> Altar devotions
> Salute
> Cast circle
> Call quarters
> Anoint
> Unite energies (if more than one person is present)
> Invocation/Drawing Down the Moon
> The work to be performed
> Cakes and ale
> Salute
> Dismiss quarters
> Release circle
> Feast

Sabbats

> Altar devotions
> Salute

Cast circle
Call quarters
Anoint
Unite energies
Invocation/Drawing Down the Moon
Ritual enactment of festival
Circle dance or raising of power
Cakes and ale
Salute
Dismiss quarters
Release circle
Feast

Detailed General Ritual Format Outline for the Wiccan Seeker

I. Opening Choices (choose one or more from A, B, C, D, or E)
   A. Altar devotions only
   B. Altar devotions and mini-circle
      1. Sprinkle salt/herb circle
         a. Draw a magickal alphabet in salt or chalk
         b. Sprinkle a special herb or mix with the salt (choose one or more)
            (1) Angelica and rosemary (protection)
            (2) Vervain and dragons' blood (as a magickal catalyst)
            (3) Yarrow and lavender (healing)
            (4) Chamomile and patchouli (psychism)
            (5) Roses and apple seeds (love)
            (6) Cinquefoil and mint (monetary or possession gain)
      2. Sprinkle holy water on salt
      3. Salute
      4. Cast circle (choose one or more method)
         a. Wand
         b. Athame
         c. Staff
         d. Stone
         e. Incense
         f. Hand
         g. Mind
      5. Call quarters (choose one or more)
         a. Elements
         b. Elementals
         c. Watchtowers
         d. Airts
         e. Angels

       f. Fairies
       g. Totems
       h. Ancients
       i. Archetypes
       j. Winds
       k. Dragons
   6. Open quarters (choose one)
       a. All
       b. Open one, acknowledge others

C. Altar devotions and full circle (see above for details on choices)
   1. Sweep area with broom with words of purification
   2. Carry incense in deosil pattern with words of purification
   3. Carry candle in deosil pattern with words of purification
   4. Sprinkle water in deosil pattern with words of purification
   5. Sprinkle salt in deosil pattern with words of purification
   6. Salute
   7. Cast circle (choose one or more method)
       a. Wand
       b. Athame
       c. Staff
       d. Stone
       e. Incense
       f. Hand
       g. Mind
   8. Call quarters (choose one or more)
       a. Elements
       b. Elementals
       c. Watchtowers
       d. Airts
       e. Angels
       f. Fairies
       g. Totems
       h. Ancients
       i. Archetypes
       j. Winds
       k. Dragons
   9. Open quarters
       a. All
       b. Open one, acknowledge others

D. Mental
   1. Ground and center
   2. Altar devotion and salute
   3. Draw energy down and in
   4. Use mini-circle/full circle or mental circle

E. Qabalistic cross
  1. Ground and center
  2. Altar devotion and salute
  3. Draw energy down and in
  4. Use mini-circle/full circle or mental circle
II. Workings (choose from A, B, C, or D)
  A. Sabbats
    1. Anointing (choose one or more)
       a. Holy water
       b. Herb water
       c. Oil
       d. Wine or juice
    2. Opening remarks/unification of energy (choose one or more)
       a. Humming
       b. Chanting
       c. Reciting a poem
       d. Singing
    3. Drawing down moon/sun (choose one or more method)
       a. Wand
       b. Athame
       c. Staff
       d. Stone
       e. Incense
       f. Hand
       g. Mind
       h. With another person
    4. Invoking Deity as needed (choose one method)
       a. High Priestess only
       b. High Priest only
       c. High Priest and High Priestess
       d. Group aspecting
    5. Honor Deity or season (choose one or more method)
       a. Skit
       b. Poetry
       c. Speech
       d. Single-person dramatization
       e. Group participation (choose one or more)
          (1) Meditation
          (2) Pathworking
          (3) Other project
    6. Raise Power (choose one or more method)
       a. Song
       b. Dance
       c. Chant
       d. Drumming

     e. Mental
   7. Cakes and ale
B. Esbats
   1. Anointing
     a. Holy water
     b. Herb water
     c. Oil
     d. Wine
   2. Unification of energies (choose one or more method)
     a. Humming
     b. Chanting
     c. Reciting a poem
     d. Singing
   3. Drawing down the moon/sun
   4. Invoking Deity as needed (choose one or more)
     a. High Priest
     b. High Priestess
     c. High Priest and High Priestess
     d. Group aspecting
   5. Name the working (choose one or more)
     a. Healing
     b. Talismans
     c. Tools
     d. Psychic work
     e. Other
   6. Perform the working (choose one or more)
     a. Minor magicks
     b. Major magicks
   7. Raise power (choose one or more method)
     a. Song
     b. Dance
     c. Chant
     d. Drumming
     e. Mental
   8. Cakes and ale
C. Consecrating tools/talismans
   1. Unification of energy
   2. Purify item
   3. Invoke Deity or other energies needed
   4. Ask aid in the work to be done
   5. Instill proper energies into the item
   6. Thank those energies for assisting
D. Open circles with guests
   1. Purify and banish room before arrivals
   2. Anoint people as they enter

3. Prepare smudge bowl[8]
   a. Draw pentacle of holy water on inside bottom of earthen bowl
   b. Draw pentacle of oil on outside of bottom
   c. Cover one to two inches with small stones
   d. Cover one to two inches with sand
   e. Add appropriate herbs/incenses/candle
4. Ground and center
5. Unification of energy
6. Invoke Universal/positive energies
7. Draw a banishing pentagram in the air with the bowl
8. Pass to next person
9. Place in center of the circle
10. Begin your work

III. Closings (must always match the openings as far as types, quarter calls, tools, and energies)
   A. For Open Circles and Workshops (choose one or more)
      1. Closing poetry
      2. Closing spell
      3. Closing focused prayer
      4. Benediction
   B. For Rituals
      1. Salute
      2. Thank Deity
      3. Dismiss quarters
      4. Pull up circle widdershins (choose one)
         a. Into tools
         b. Into a positive thoughtform
         c. Into hands and body
      5. Benediction
      6. Ground and center

---

8. Some Wiccans/Witches smudge rather than anoint. In smudging, a bowl is needed to burn sage (or another preferred herb). The bowl is cooled, and the ashes are used for body purification. Others simply allow the sage to burn on a piece of charcoal, much like incense, and carry it around a room to purify the area. In either case, the bowl is fireproof clay or ceramic and normally fits in the palm of one's hand. The bowl can be plain or decorated to match a pantheon, tradition, or personal practice.

Conjuring Power and the Aspects of Divinity

Everyone wants to conjure power. Intimidation on the job, mind-games in relationships, wearing masks of fear when others get too close—all these head trips are the result of someone wanting power and someone losing it. Being a powerful magickal person won't get you shit in the end if you do not work in balance and harmony. The secret to power is not attempting to take it from someone else or strategically overcoming an opponent. The mystery lies in moving through life without disturbing or disrupting the harmony of other humans or the Universe in general. To be powerful, you must learn to remove negativity from yourself and your environment, and become one with the Divine energies of the Universe. Only at that point will your magick be above the others. And then, you won't care.

Although the work in any ritual or rite is most important, it cannot be done effectively without some sort of acknowledgment to Divinity, even if that acknowledgment is silent, as in most folk magick. It is assumed that you have worked numerous circles and drawn down both the moon and sun in standard ritual format before you begin this chapter. Here, we are going to explore conjuring on a deeper level, learning to raise power and accomplishing harmony in all facets of your life.

In modern Witchcraft, there are ten ways to raise/enhance power:

Meditation
Aspecting (a form of possession) and invocations
Trance and astral projection
Potions, including herbals, incense, and wines
Dancing and/or drumming and rattles
Blood control, as in biofeedback (not in trying to strangle someone)
Working with stellar/earth/sun/astrological energies
Chants and sacred breath
Spells
Sex

Notice I left out the scourge. I did that on purpose. You can not tell me that beating on yourself or someone else is an action of harmony. It's demeaning, and it doesn't belong in the Craft of today. With all the other wonderful ways to raise power, I can not believe anyone would choose this. You are most welcome for that soapbox dissertation, now on to better stuff.

Traditional Witchcraft speaks of the eight paths to power, most of which are listed above (minus the scourge). Due to my years of study of Pow-Wow chants, I have learned that chants and sacred breath do not necessarily fall in the same category as spells, where you mix this and that to satisfy a need. Therefore, I've separated chants from spells. Of course, you can use chants and spells together—they work great in unison.

These ten ways of raising power can be combined, if you'd like. For example, you can drum, chant, and aspect together, or perhaps mix an herbal tea, use a rattle, and cast a spell. It is your choice and you should pick the combinations that work best for you. Of course, the only way you are going to find that out is if you take the time to experiment.

The Wiccan mystery here is this: Learn to aspect power by melding with it. This will add speed to what you wish to accomplish.

The Power Wheel Game

This is a game of challenge that you can play by yourself or with your magickal friends. You will need:
One large piece of poster board
A compass
Colored markers (Ten different colors and black)
One game spinner
A one-minute timer (you can get hourglass ones or use a stopwatch)

On the poster board, draw a big circle using the compass, and divide the circle into ten slices. Color each slice a different color. Label each slice with one of the ten paths. Attach the spinner to the middle of the circle.

To play: Spin. You must make up a rhyme about that path of power and say it three times in one minute. You cannot repeat another person's rhyme or use another individual's idea. For example, if the person beside you made up a rhyme about a blue egg meditation, you cannot use the same theme. There are lots of laughs with this game and fierce competition. If you get the rhyme in one minute, you receive ten points. If you fail, you lose ten points. When you are tired of playing, add up the points and see who is the winner!

❀ Your Work ✿

Project 1: List the ten paths of power and describe each one until you understand fully what they entail.

Project 2: Play the Power Wheel Game.

Project 3: List the ten paths of power and design a working to go with each path. Perform as many of these workings as you can. Keep accurate records.

Drawing from Mother Earth

I cannot take credit for the original idea of this conjuring. MorningStar came up with it for an assignment on circle casting and quarter calls in our advanced classes. She wrote:

We as pagans, spend a great deal of time drawing down energy, celestial energies of the moon, the sun, the stars, or perhaps all three. I believe that we need to address the imbalance that we thereby create and begin to draw up energy from the Earth. Consider that the earth is infinitely and eternally bathed in the energies of the heavens: the planets, the stars, the sun, and the moon are constantly sending subatomic energies via light and motion that interact with the atmosphere and particulate makeup of our planet (Earth). This energy is absorbed/dispersed/used by the planet, which is a living entity unto itself. This energy is also converted for use by the living creatures that inhabit this planet. Solar, lunar, stellar, and planetary energies that wind up in storage in the Earth are probably stored in the Earth's core. The rest of the energy resides in objects that humans term inanimate (read: inferior), rocks and minerals. Pagans and magicians are well aware of the power that resides in crystals. They are also aware of the ley line energy that traverses the Earth, plotting of which allows them to pinpoint the locations of power places. There are sacred objects/tools which are repositories of energy, mostly from being charged by a magickal practitioner, but these energies are minuscule in relation to the amount of energy available in the Universe.

Rather than passively grounding, as we all do, MorningStar proposes we begin to actively receive earth energies and draw them, as we already are familiar with drawing celestial energies. Some of you will say, "Well, I already knew that!" Before you scoff too loudly, try this magnificent, personal circle-casting and invocation.

The Circle of Stars

Much like in the original Pow-Wow folk magick stance, stand with your feet apart, with your receptive hand at your side. Move your hand out about one foot from your body.

Open your palm, and hold your palm toward the ground. Put your dominant hand down at your side, and move it out in front of you about eight to twelve inches. Turn your palm up.

Imagine you are slipping the palm of your dominant hand into a handle on a big lid. Close your fingers around that handle. (Now you will have a fist.) Close your eyes and imagine you are touching Earth Mother and pulling her toward you. Very slowly begin to pull up on that handle.

Take your time and keep pulling. You will feel the energy moving up through your feet and into your solar plexus (where it may explode a bit—keep pulling).

Keep pulling until the energy reaches your crown chakra at the top of your head. (Believe me, you'll know it when it gets there). Your arm should be folded by your head by this time. Allow the energy to pulse until you think you can't hold it anymore.

Quickly straighten your arm out in front of you, open your hand, and hear a "Kaboom!" in your head.

Wasn't that fun? Now let's do it again and take it a step further. This time, rather than "Kaboom," envision a golden beam emanating from your hand. Make it a beam of love for the planet. Envision it leaving your hand and creating a waterfall of golden healing life for the planet. How did that feel? Different?

Let's try another tactic. Think of a person you want to send loving, healing energy to. Put the person's picture on a wall in front of you, at eye level. Stand back about four feet. Raise the power again. This time, shoot your hand out toward the picture and drop your palm down to direct the beam of loving energy toward the picture. Record the time you did this. Contact your friend and ask how he or she felt.

Call a different friend on the phone. Tell your friend that you are going to conduct an experiment. Ask him or her to sit by the phone for the next five minutes. Hang up. Raise the energy, think of your friend, and send a message of "call me" with the beam of energy. Did your friend call you back? How quickly? How did your friend feel during the time you were raising power? Record your experiment and explain to your friend that every time he or she gets that feeling, you will be trying to make contact.

Let's go back to the "Kaboom." Creating sounds in your head helps generate power. For example, you can start stalled cars by raising energy and thinking of the sound the car should be making if it is running. Once you practice, it works all the time. Try raising power again, but this time when you "Kaboom" it, envision a circular web of golden sticky stars around, above, and below you. You have created a magick circle whose job is to collect positive energy until you let it go—and you've done it in less than a minute.

If you don't like the all-in-one shot, try this. Raise the power, then quickly drop your hand, with your palm slanted out. Direct the beam of golden light and walk the standard circle. How did that feel? Try it again, but this time use the following chant:

> *The cauldron of the Mother*
> *Her mysteries wise and deep*
> *Rise now as I call thee*
> *This sacred space to keep.*
>
> *The Mother supports me*
> *The Consort defends me*
> *The Guardians surround me*
> *With a web of golden stars*
>
> *Above and below*
> *Around and about*
> *I charge this circle*
> *In and out*
>
> *And legions await my word.*
> *So be it.*

To take down this circle, stand in the middle and raise your arms over your head. As you bring them slowly down to your sides, say:

> *The web of life is an endless circle*
> *never to die*
> *only to change form.*
> *What was begun*
> *now is finished.*
> *Welcome home*
> *these energies borne.*
> *The circle is open*
> *never broken*
> *It is so.*

Stop your arms at your waist until you finish the chant, then drop them quickly (in one motion) to put the energy back into Earth Mother.

Perhaps you do not wish to cast a circle. Try the following prayer while drawing up earth energy:

> *Mother of all enchantments*
> *Queen of the Devas*
> *Provider for all Nature*
> *Thou who casts thy green ray*
> *upon the children of Earth.*
> *Smile upon thy Witch and Priestess/Priest*
> *Who seeks thee here above*
> *And lend thy sacred energies to this task of love.*

Try pulling up energy from Mother Earth for simple matters:
Relieving stress
Re-generation during the mid-afternoon
Before an important business meeting or contract signing
Before a job interview
Before a divination sitting
When you are feeling blue
When you are in deep poop and time is not on your side

Trying pulling up earth energy while:
Chanting
Drumming or using a rattle
Dancing
Doing an invocation
Working cord magick
Mixing incense or potions
Having sex (where both of you know you are doing this)
Working weather magick
Holding a healing session

Drawing Father Energy in Group Ritual

I've got another story for you. Not only does it show you a nice ritual, it has a lesson in it.

On June 16, 1994, MorningStar and Bats performed a group ritual for Summer Solstice for our open women's group. MorningStar worked very hard on her ritual. She and Bats practiced long and hard for this special occasion. So hard, in fact, that they scared Bats' cat to a useless ball of fur every time they practiced invoking the God energy—but that is another story.

Even though we are traditional, working Witches, we hold eclectic open rituals. We do this to afford those who normally cannot attend a chance to worship with a group, and to keep our students on their toes by assigning them rituals to write and perform. We are not incredibly picky about who can come, other than my standard rules: no drugs, no children under ten without their parents, no alcohol. It usually works out very well.

On this particular evening, we had three guests and seventeen of our traditional Witches. The evening began in a very upbeat way. All were encouraged to bring instruments, so we had quite a collection of drums, rattles, cymbals, bells, etc.

MorningStar began her ritual by doing a lunar salute and an altar devotion. She moved into her experimental circle casting, which she has permitted me to print here:

In this place that is not a place
In this time that is not a time
By my will I create
The "Is To Be"
The Mother supports my feet
And Her consort is by my side.
Above me, below me, and all around me
Are the guardians
Forming a web of golden stars
That contain the power raised herein
Until I release it.
The legions await my word.
So mote it be!

The circle went up. It was steady, with a light vibration. With this circle casting she did not move about thrice, as is the custom. Instead, she stood in the center and erected her web of golden stars with her mind and her hands, as in the drawing Earth Mother example given previously. We wanted to see if it worked with so many people in the room. It did.

MorningStar proceeded to call the quarters. She mixed our traditional quarter call (that includes Celtic deities and totem animals) and added a request for a particular set of angels to appear. Although unusual, it worked. For some reason, several of us can see the angelic forces come when they are called. We have found that no matter what pantheon you are using, angelic forces meld with the other energies you choose for a specific working without any problems or chaotic after-effects. Several of us have been experimenting with angelic beings for quite some time with the express purpose of sharing our experiences with both our group and you. To that end, I found nothing strange in her quarter call. She summoned what she was supposed to, stirred what needed to be nudged a little, and called what had to be called for the ritual she designed.

The ritual proceeded. Deity was invoked through a mixed group of male aspects to enhance the power of the summer season. Although unusual, among the Celtic names, the Angel Michael managed to sneak in. I tell all my students not to mix systems; however, for every rule, there is a reason to break it. MorningStar's logic was to mix male energies from the Celtic pantheon with one angelic being, to match the quarter calls previously given. It worked. The energy raised was astounding.

> *Great one of heaven*
> *Power of the sun*
> *We invoke thee in thine ancient names*
> *Michael, Balin, Arthur, Lugh, Tarvos, Cernunnos, Pan*
> *Come again as of old into this thine land*
> *Lift up thy shining spear of light*
> *To protect us*
> *Put to flight the powers of darkness*
> *Give us fair woodlands and green fields*
> *Blossoming orchards and ripening corn.*
> *Bring us to stand upon thy hill of vision*
> *And show us the path*
> *To the lovely realms of the Gods.*
> *So mote it be!*

MorningStar then passed out tea candles for everyone. Outside, my father filled a small pool with water. It was dark. The moon shown gloriously in the heavens. The yard was hushed and waiting. Silently, we filed out of the house and encircled the pool. Each woman lit her candle from the needfire cauldron, and placed it in the pool to float, uttering the name of a forefather or ancestor whom she wished to honor or ask for assistance.

"Summer Solstice is a time second only to Samhain," said MorningStar, "for accessibility to the other worlds. Since it is a God festival for us, it seemed appropriate to stir the energy of benevolent forefathers, either Craft, Pagan, or in our personal lineage, to honor the male energy of the God. I borrowed from and slightly modified the Japanese custom of sending out little boats with lanterns in them as they observe their Day of the Dead. We wore black and white, which served to delineate the preponderance of light versus darkness, yet the light is waning as the Holly King takes over until Yule." (In our tradition, we celebrate two divine births during the year—that of the Holly King and that of the Oak King.)

We filed back into the house. MorningStar passed out candles twined with male holly sprigs. The following prayer was repeated after her, one line at a time:

> *I will serve the Great Goddess*
> *And give reverence to the Great God*
> *I am a Pagan*
> *A stone in the ancient circle*
> *Standing firmly*
> *Balanced on the earth*
> *Yet open to the winds of heaven*
> *And enduring through time*

May the old gods witness my words
Blessed be.

MorningStar thanked deity, released the quarters, and took up the circle. Again, she used an experimental procedure, where she did not move in the widdershins fashion. She did not move at all, but pulled it in with her hands.

It was lovely, moving in like a sweet golden mist. I was impressed. So, I thought, was everyone else. I, in my infinite stupidity, forgot we had guests. I have a nasty habit of doing that. Silly me, I really believe in perfect love and perfect trust—especially in ritual.

The group mind is an interesting entity. One can always tell if something is not quite right. Perhaps a gut feeling, a tingling in the arms, a niggling something at the back of your mind—everyone has their own warning bells. We must all learn to listen to our particular bell. That night I was fulfilling my function as elder (and homeowner, which always puts me on my toes), and my inner bell was clanging louder than a marching band in full swing.

In the silence of the final bits of the ritual, I looked over at Bats. Her upper lip was sticking out. I nodded at her. She knew what she had to do. As the circle deflated, I swept over to MorningStar (in elder-type fashion, which is so much fun) and told her very loudly what a wonderful ritual it was. I hugged her and soon many of the "regulars" moved toward MorningStar, telling her what a great job she and Bats had done. No one looked for Bats as she is known for melting into the shadows after a show. The group began to break toward the kitchen, beelining to the coffee, or out to the food tables on the porch.

Bats, in her wonderful, mystical style, melded into the woodwork, circling the various small groups. I headed for the porch. Everyone was having a good time with lots of laughter and chatter. Slowly, they began filtering home.

"What did you come up with?" I asked Bats as she fluttered to my side.

"It's the one holding court in the dining room."

My eyebrows darted up. "Oh, no."

"Mmmm, yes. This new one claims to be some sort of psychic."

Bats meandered back into the dining room, with me trailing behind. There was our guest, seated in the middle of the floor, doing her thing, which normally is fine. We love new people and new skills, but the air was bad and my band was marching again. I looked over at Maven, who now carried a stern-old-lady look set firmly on her brow. Shit. I walked out to the porch, leaving Bats to keep an eye on our unusual princess.

I noted throughout the evening that our guest hardly spoke four words to me, though she knew she was visiting my home. She didn't even say good-bye or thank you for allowing her to come. You know, the usual nice things you say to people, even if you hated the party. Bats, ever-vigilant, watched through the evening as the princess performed her feats of divination for many of our regulars. The only thing she said to any of us before she left was, "So, where is it next week?" The girl had no clue—no clue at all.

When most were gone, MaraKay, Maven, MorningStar, Cinnamon and I sat bleary-eyed, discussing the evening. We do this a lot. Bats settled in the corner, as is her normal habit. The rest of us bantered ideas, observations, and good chatter about.

"So Bats, what did you think of our guest?" I asked.

Bats lips drew into a pencil point.

Maven was stoic.

MaraKay looked down from her vantage point of a chair, peering over her glasses at the rest of us on the floor. MaraKay hates to sit on the floor; besides, she has an excellent effect when she does the glasses thing.

Cinnamon busied herself by stirring a hole in the bottom of her coffee cup. I considered asking her if she was banishing or conjuring, but held my tongue.

"I despised her," whispered Bats.

The others mumbled in agreement.

I said nothing. None of them are usually judgmental.

"She told MorningStar—to her face, mind you—that she made several mistakes in her ritual, and that she shouldn't have called any angels."

MorningStar's face went pale, her eyes downcast. I was outraged.

We never saw our guest again, and in truth I never did know her name. Of course, she probably didn't show for her encore because I did a manifest spell, which I will explain later. Our guest broke a cardinal rule of the Craft: she was impolite. A working Witch or Pagan (or whatever you choose to call yourself) never behaves badly in public, and never purposefully hurts the feelings of those who have worked hard to bring happiness and peace to others. This too, is a Wiccan mystery.

If you visit a magickal person, whether or not it is in a group atmosphere, always do your best to be polite. Bring a small gift—a token of your appreciation for being invited. This goes back to your training as a child. You should already be well aware of good manners. If you are not, take heed to what Mother Silver says: "Show the integrity of your lineage at all times. In that way honor and respect will walk with you always and precede you." We're not called the Children of the Shining Ones for nothing, you know.

Drawing Up Energy for Healing[1]

This is a simple task. It can stop a nosebleed in seconds, aid in healing wounds in half the normal time, reduce swelling for bee stings, etc.

Hold the area to be healed with your receptive hand.

Hold your power hand in the normal stance, and pull up the energy from the earth (do not use your energy; if it kicks in, fine; if it doesn't, don't worry about it).

---

1. In two of my previous books *(To Ride a Silver Broomstick* and *HexCraft)* I concentrate on various aspects of healing. Although the process is simple once you are familiar with it, I suggest the student check these two books (or any of the other fine magickal and self-help books on the market) to get a complete background on magickal healing.

Touch Divinity with your mind.

When your right hand reaches your shoulder, open it and visualize the energy you raised pulsing from your power arm to your receptive arm and into the person you are healing.

When you are finished, ground and center.

Drawing up Plants to Help Them Grow

Even though you planted your little friends at the correct phase of the moon during the right astrological time, there seems to be a problem. Some are coming up fine, but others are showing signs of being obstinate. Try this:

Look at the plant and consider mentally what its Deva looks like. Is it large, small, bright, soft?

Put the plants in front of you (on a sacred, flat stone if you can). Shut your eyes and think of the Deva.

See the Deva and move into it (keeping your conscious separate, but allowing the Deva to touch you and you to touch the Deva). Mentally request assistance for the health of the plants before you.

Move out of the Deva. If it stays, fine; if it goes away, that's okay, too.

Recite the Mother Earth prayer as you put your hand over the plants, and begin to pull up the energy of the Earth through the seedlings/seeds.

Release the energy as a gentle rain over the plants. Thank the Deva and thank the Goddess of the Earth.

I tried this for my moonflowers. My father had a great idea. We would plant moonflowers and morning glories, alternating them, beside the patio. We would hang taut strings to allow them to climb. That way we would have a beautiful fragrance both during the daytime and during the evening. The morning glories went to town. The moonflowers sat there, doing nothing. By mid-June, we were frustrated. Time for working Witchie-poo to do her thing! I erected an altar beside the neat little plant paddies. Yes, I said paddies. My father is a garden nut. (By the way, should you have the secret for getting rid of slugs, please let us know. We've tried everything from beer to orange peels. Nothing, I mean nothing, works!)

My dad mixed special growing things for the moonflowers and morning glories and put them in cute little containers right beside the bed they were to go in as soon as they got strong enough. I used the technique previously given, which greatly enhanced the growth of the moonflowers. How fast? The next morning, half the seeds had broken through the soil. Yowser! I also timed the procedure. Every evening, from new moon to full, I worked with the plants. I told them how much I loved them and that it was time to wake up and enjoy the harmony in our yard. I stroked them, tapped on the side of their little containers, and banished any negative energy around them with incense as close to midnight as I could. I figured moonflowers would have a thing for the Witching Hour, just like we do. To enhance the process, I used my New Moon Rattle. The result was spectacular. Further into the growing season, I would shake the New Moon Rattle to trigger the energy and say hello to the plants.

If you have a garden, try the following experiment:

Mentally, split the garden into thirds. Every morning draw down the energy of the heavens on one third. Draw up the energy of Earth Mother on one third. Leave the other third alone. On paper, so you don't forget, check their growing process. What happened to your garden?

My garden went crazy. I had broccoli plants the size of banana trees (so I'm exaggerating a little bit). I harvested beans out the bazoo and my tomato plants got so big they advanced upon my strawflowers with vengeance. My father wants to know why the peppers are as big as softballs. Well, only the Devas know for sure.

Conjuring the Power of Wind and Rain

Weather magick is not hard if you take the following into account:

Seek harmony first.

Understand that elements have their own process of life, which is not the same as yours.

Learn to become One without fear.

After you learn the technique, never play with the weather simply because you are bored.

I first learned to work with the sun by associating it with Kernunnos. Every day during the summer season, I walked outside and around my property, thanking the God for blessing us with His sunshine and the Goddess for sending Her gentle rains. I would close my eyes and become one with the warmth upon my face, touch the red behind my eyelids, and mentally move into the energy of the sun. Once I was familiar with the energy of the sun, I moved into a more complicated arena—storms.

Storms are another matter, and I briefly touched on that issue earlier. The technique is simple. The only thing required on your part is trust.

Step into a storm. You don't have to physically step into a storm, but when you are learning, physical contact does make it exciting and helps to set the energy of the storm in your mind. A word to the wise here: Don't be a fool. If a tornado is coming your way, don't stand in its path. If it is thundering and lightning outside, don't become a human lightning rod. Use your common sense, please. You can easily stand at your window and look outside while the storm is active.

Become one with that energy. Focus on the physical aspects of the storm. Close your eyes and reach out with your mind. Touch the storm gently, allowing it to understand you are there.

Focus on harmony and peace. Ground and center, as in any magickal practice. Allow the calm inside you to move outside your body and around you. Allow the calm to touch the storm.

Move into the energy of the storm with your calm mind. You must not be afraid. If you fear, it won't work. If you seek personal power, forget it—you may even sizzle on the spot.

Talk to the energy of the storm and introduce yourself. You don't have to talk aloud, you can speak in your mind.

State your need and why you need the storm to abate, lessen, move on, etc. Your intentions must be pure. If you move the storm away from your home, it will go to someone else's backyard. Is that what you really want? Consider carefully your intentions and instructions.

Move out of the storm. Focus again on yourself by grounding and centering.

Focus on peace and tranquillity. Walk away, where you cannot see the storm.

Trust that your request will be carried out.

After you have worked this way a few times, you will be able to touch storm energy for various purposes from mundane to magickal. For example, one Sunday afternoon I ran out for groceries. I could see there was a storm hanging in the heavens, but the cupboards were bare and I had to go; besides, although we'd had a lot of rain that spring, the ground was dry as a bone. Remember the Mary going over the mountain on Ascension Day thing? I knew all the plants and trees needed the water. It wasn't my place to begrudge the world some rain.

It took me an hour to do my shopping. As I was standing at the check-out, sheets of rain slashed into the parking lot. People everywhere ran for cover.

"Could you put everything in plastic?" I asked the bag boy.

"Don't want it to get wet, huh? Well, you could pull up to the front here and one of our boys will get wet for you, and put your groceries into your car."

I nodded politely. Since when did any grocery employee stand out in pouring rain to load groceries into your car? I don't know how it is where you live, but when it rains in Pennsylvania, grocery employees scatter like leaves in a fall wind. You're stuck loading your own darn groceries.

The girl continued scanning my food and the fellow rammed things into the plastic bags. I looked out the big plate-glass windows at the ominous clouds and mentally called to the God and His symbol of the sun, asking for a brief respite until I could get to my car and load my groceries.

In a minute or two, I turned to the bagger and said, "Look at that, the clouds have broken in the middle of the parking lot and the sun is shining."

He shrugged his shoulders and went on stuffing.

I paid my bill and walked outside. I thanked the God for His sunshine (right over my car), and asked the rain to be gentle as I made my way to my vehicle. The rain now fell in light, misty droplets. I loaded my groceries, returned the cart, and thanked the rain for her kindness and asked her to make sure the plants and trees in the area got enough water.

As I drove out of the parking lot, the clouds closed over the sun. At home, I removed all the groceries from the car and brought them into the house, then turned and looked out the screen door. "Thank you again," I said, "for allowing me to drive home without danger from the torrential rains."

With that, the storm took up where it had left off about twenty minutes before. I closed the front door and attended to my family. My husband wandered in from the living room to help me put away the groceries.

"Did you get wet?"

I grinned as I pulled a honeydew out of one of the bags. "No, not really."

To pull high and low pressure areas toward/away from you, get a map and watch the weather on television. Pinpoint where you are. Watch where the weather is that you wish to access/deflect. On the map, draw a path from where the weather is to where you want it to go. If you wish to stall a weather front, draw a spiral over it. To deflate disastrous weather, draw a red X over it or make a balloon around the bad weather, and put a big pin in the balloon. Of course, a word to the wise here. Don't mess with the weather for fun because you will get your little paws smacked sooner or later. Always ask permission before you go fooling with the order of things.

Invoking/Aspecting Divinity

Working Witches differ on this topic. Some feel that asking for the presence of Divinity in the circle is enough. Others feel that the only form of Divine possession that should be practiced is through the process of drawing down the moon or drawing down the sun in generic form by saying "The Goddess" or "The God." When one draws down the moon/sun, it can be done alone or with a partner. Here is a drawing down the moon ritual designed for those who like the Celtic Craft and wish to incorporate the powers of the Morrigan. Before you scream, let me assure you:

It works.

I've done it many times.

I'm still breathing.

My life is good.

Drawing In the Morrigan

(by MaraKay Rogers and Silver RavenWolf)

Begin with standard options (Altar devotion, salute, circle casting, and quarter calls).

Stand in the North (the home of the Morrigan). Say the following while you anoint yourself with oil:

> *Blessed be my feet, that have brought me to the gates of Lir.*
> *Blessed be my knees, that kneel at the sacred altar of the Morrigan.*
> *Blessed be my womb (phallus) which brings (hath brought) life into the world.*
> *Blessed be my heart, may it beat in wisdom and strength.*
> *Blessed be my arms, that shall wield the power of the Morrigan.*
> *Blessed be my lips that shall utter the Sacred Names and speak only the truth.*

Close your eyes, raise your arms with palms out, and say:

> *Hail, great Goddess Morrigan, Queen of the Sildhe,*
> *ruler of Uindimagos.*
> *I of the realm of Fal salute thee in adoration.*
> *The Guardians of the Four Cities lay down their treasures before thee*
> *But all I can offer is my love and trust in you.*

Draw an invoking pentagram in the air. Again, close your eyes, raise your arms with palms out, and say:

> *I call upon thee, O great Morrigan, threefold Goddess of power.*
> *From the depths of Lir, from the world of man, from the reaches of Uindimagos,*
> *Do I call on thee*
> *To descend upon my body*
> *Thy servant and priestess/priest*
> *And lend your energies to me this day*
> *As I walk in the human world*
> *Ever seeking balance.*

Isn't that great, you say. So, what do I do with it? First of all, in this particular case, you would be aspecting Divinity. Before you begin, you must focus in your mind what you wish to work for, be it more stability in life, wisdom, protection of home and family, physical prowess (she is a battle Goddess, after all), winning a courtroom or boardroom battle, dealing with a criminal, etc. These are all good topics for the Morrigan. Of course, you could use any archetype, the Morrigan is simply an example. The main difference here is that when you close your circle, you are not going to release the energies of the Morrigan.

Instead, you will hold the energies with you until you have finished the task for which you called her. This is called aspecting and works very well, as long as you remember to work in harmony with the Universe.

Aspecting should always be done in a magick circle, and you should always be specific on both your intent and the archtypal energy you choose to use. When aspecting for a focused working, keep in mind the use of planetary hours, astrological movements, and moon phases. All these can enhance the practices of a working Witch and give you a safety net to overcome the various things that can cause a working to fail. For example, if you are tired or stressed, but it is the right lunar phase; it may be the wrong lunar phase, but the right planetary hour and day, etc. Angelic beings are incredible sources of power for healing rituals or invocations, and can override the wrong day, wrong hour, or wrong lunar phase.

Aspecting energies of particular archetypes can last from a few days to over a month, depending upon the circumstances. Here is one I wrote for the retrieval of wisdom. Try it and see what you think.

The Retrieval of Wisdom

Best phase: New moon.
Best day: Monday for wisdom, psychism, and a close relationship with the moon (if you need wisdom for a specific working, check your correspondence tables).
Best hour: Moon.
Best sign: Pisces.
Supplies: One large, flat stone; one iron cauldron; one black candle; ¼ charcoal briquette pre-soaked in lighter fluid (If you are outside, you can use three or four); a small bowl of water; illuminator candles, if needed; a small handful of dried patchouli.

Setup

Place the stone in the West. Put the cauldron in the center of the stone.

Put the black candle on the Southern edge of the stone. Put the bowl of water on the Western corner of the stone.

Ritual

Begin with standard options (Altar devotion, salute, circle casting, quarter calls to guard only).

Go to the West and light the candle.

Light the briquette(s) and sit before the cauldron, meditating until the briquette(s) becomes a glowing ember.

Take several deep breaths; ground and center.

At the end of each stanza, flick a drop of water from the bowl into the cauldron, then sprinkle a tiny bit of patchouli through the steam.

Invocation

> *Perfect is the Cauldron of the Calliech*
> *It glitters and glows in the dark*
> *In the Sanctuary of the West*
> *In the land of Tir-na-nog.*
>
> *Wisdom is what I seek of the Calliech*
> *Power to do what is right*
> *My mind is freed in Her presence*
> *My heart is open to Her sight.*
>
> *Clarity I hunt in Her Sacred Grove*
> *Attendance from Her guardians I seek*
> *From the land of the living I journey*
> *To protect and to bless the weak.*
>
> *The Wolf, she now howls in my favor*
> *The Raven, she circles in flight*
> *The Bear, she brings me her power*
> *The Stag, he brings me his might.*
>
> *In the company of the Calliech I stand*
> *In the circle of the ancestral stones*
> *I call forth the essence of the Ancients*
> *To fill this Witch's bones.*
>
> *Magick now dances around me*
> *Upon the rim of Her cauldron bright*
> *I pull in the wisdom that's needed*
> *And let mystery move in the night.*
>
> *The Eyes of the Spirit are upon me*
> *For I have been given the sight*
> *It is with reverence I bow now before Her*
> *In thanks for this gift of light.*

Relax and meditate. When you are through, ground and center. Thank the Calliech, dismiss the quarters, pull up the circle, and clean up the area. If you can, allow the briquettes to continue to burn.

One note of caution: Charcoal briquettes are dangerous to your health if burned indoors, which is why I suggested using only a small piece, should you be inside. This ritual is better done outside or with something else as your source flame.

Conjuring Power with Drums and Rattles (and Things Your Mother Tried to Take Away from you When You were a Kid)

The beat—it's all in the beat. There is a Celtic holiday on March 1 called Whuppitie-Scorrie, when adults and children alike take whistles, musical instruments, rattles, and drums and prance about the property to raise the sap in the trees and wake up Earth Mother. If you don't own any instruments, don't despair. The first year our family celebrated this holiday we used wooden spoons and pots and pans. It was great. My neighbors thought we were insane—me in the lead on a cold, frosty day, trailing four children madly banging pots and pans both inside and outside the house. In the summer, our kids take up the assorted instruments we've collected around here and "make music for the Devas." Although only one of my children is musically inclined, the Devas on our property don't mind much. Everything grows nicely.

Don't despair if music is not in your soul. My mother constantly played out the "let Papa sleep" scenario when I was a kid. My father worked night shift for many years, hence my mother's hatred for any noise above a whisper. Also, I can't read musical notes—to me they look like black bubbles with dangly strings playing kick the squiggly "S" thing on the side of the page. That doesn't stop me. I've got lots of toys that don't require musical knowledge—bells, chimes, rattles, drums, cymbals, and whistles from all over the world that even an inept like myself can handle. My favorite is a round, clay whistle (the size of the palm of my hand) from Peru called an ocarina (oh-kah-ree-nah). It makes sweet, flute-like sounds and is supposedly one of the oldest musical instruments known. This pre-Columbian instrument was used throughout the Andes to imitate the songs of birds or call herds down from the mountains. (So said the tag when I bought it.) I can make it imitate the sound of doves, which is an old trick to bring good weather. I also use it to call the various Devas on my property. Through meditation I designed a soft call for each one.

All musical instruments, including rattles and drums, can act as triggers, much like you were taught earlier with the hand motions. To achieve a specific state of mind, delve into using different patterns of sound. If you can't make a lot of racket (and I understand this completely—you won't find me stomping on the floor and banging a drum at midnight when my children are sleeping—I play out the "let children sleep" scenario quite well), don't worry about it. There are many small instruments out there you can purchase inexpensively that won't wake both the living and the dead. A small set of pan-pipes, for instance, can make a strong musical note or a simple whisper, like a breeze meandering through a summer night. My ocarina can be played softly as well. Small rattles are quiet, too.

Another fun adventure is to make rattles all by your lonesome. As I am not musically inclined and don't know much about the subject (and you thought I could do everything—fooled you!) I tend to look toward more practical and easily-made objects. During the harvest season, pick up five nice-sized gourds. (I do it every year. Someone can always use a rattle.) Dry the gourds over the winter. Hang them in a loft, or in one of those metal baskets for storing vegetables. Don't worry if they get weird in color or look like they are molding; keep turning them and they will dry. In the spring, begin shaking them to loosen the seeds inside. Eventually, they will break loose and you have the makings of a great, natural rattle. If you want to get ingenious, choose the power month of August to decorate them. Design and paint one on the full moon, the new moon, and the dark of the moon. Use them for moon rituals that deal specifically with those phases. Use the fourth rattle as a sun rattle, and the fifth, if you like, as a rain rattle. Heck, you could even make lunar and solar eclipse rattles! There is no end to the possible creativity. Make a Deva rattle by wrapping it in silver bells to wake everyone up, including the neighbors, of course, on Whuppitie-Scorrie!

Conjuring Moon Power

Working Witches are familiar with the standard phases of the moon:
> **Full:** good for almost all types of magick and power raising
> **New:** especially good for new beginnings
> **Dark:** for lifting or throwing curses, banishing unwanted energies
> **Waxing:** growth
> **Waning:** disseminating

These are the five standard phases of the moon that occur in thirteen cycles throughout the year.

A delightful way to draw down the moon, no matter her phase, is by using a small hand mirror. This can be done either alone or with a partner, and is best done outside. You can also give everyone a small hand mirror in a group ritual. Here, though, the elder of the group is responsible for overseeing the process. She, or he, quietly walks clockwise in the circle, maintaining the energy flow, checking for blocks, and aligning mirrors where needed.

When: Full moon.

Where: Outside, if possible.

Supplies: One large flat stone in the center of your circle; one drinking chalice or cauldron and cup with fruit juice or another beverage; one hand mirror; one silver candle (place in the South—do not light); one small cauldron or bowl containing water (place in the West).

Setup

Go outside in full view of the moon. Put your chalice or cauldron and cup on the stone. Keep your mirror in your hand.

Ritual

Ground and center. Salute with the mirror and perform an altar devotion with the mirror.

Put the mirror in the palm of one hand and angle it so it reflects the light of the moon, slanted down, as you walk the circle thrice, repeating the casting. Keep your free hand positioned palm down to the ground.

> *I stir forth my ancient ancestors of the moon*

walk once around,

> *I call forth the Mighty Ones of the hidden realms*

walk once around,

> *I summon forth the primordial protectors of the quarters.*

walk once around and stop silently at each quarter

> *Bless and surround this sacred space with both*
> *power and protection.*

Seal the circle by holding the mirror to your lips and placing it face down on the ground in the center of the circle, on top of your stone.

> *This circle is sealed.*

Begin at the North:

> *I acknowledge and bless the Element of Earth.*

Draw your personal sigil with your finger on the ground.

> *I acknowledge and bless the Element of Air.*

Draw your personal sigil with your finger in the air.

> *I acknowledge and bless the Element of Fire.*

Light the candle and draw your personal sigil in the air with the silver candle.

> *I acknowledge and bless the Element of Water.*

Draw your personal sigil with your finger in the cauldron.

Invocation

> *In this night and in this hour*
> *I call upon the moon's great power.*

Great Goddess of the Moon
Queen of every realm
Lady of infinite destiny
Protectress and Mother of Witches.

I call upon your wisdom
To pierce through the night
Cast upon me your Priestess/Priest
Thy loving gaze.

The enchantment has begun
From the heavens
Power will come.

Raise your mirror and angle it so that the rays of the moon are reflected from its surface and onto your body. When my daughter, Falynn, and I do this in our garden, our backs are to the moon, so that we can capture the reflection before us. Begin with your genital chakra and work up, slowly, to the crown of your head. Bring the mirror back down and pull the energy of the moon into either your third eye or your abdomen chakra.

When you are finished, turn the mirror so that the light is now reflected in the cauldron or cup in the center of your circle. Let the rays of the moon cleanse, consecrate, and empower the drink. Put the mirror down and drink the liquid, imagining that it contains great wisdom and power.

Spend some time meditating or raising power for a specific purpose. Ground and center. When you are through, thank the Goddess, acknowledge the quarters once again, and bid them farewell. Take up the circle in the manner you like best. Clear your area. Leave a gift for the Devas.

For a group ritual, try the following:
As early as you can in the growing season, plant moonflowers. When they begin to bloom, plan a ritual on the full moon. Follow the ritual above, except add a large mirror in the center of the circle. Place the moonflowers around it along with some stones. You can use the stones to help tilt the mirror to reflect the moonlight during the ritual.

Conjuring Sun Power

Summer is my favorite time of the year and I love to do sun rituals. In the Craft, the sun can be viewed as either male or female, so it appeals to everyone. Due to the high humidity in our area, I prefer to do my sun rituals at dawn or dusk. Every year I plant sunflowers and gather them in August, under the sign of Leo, as my tradition calls for. Before my harvest begins, I perform a ritual much like the one following.

Ritual

Ground and center. Salute with the mirror and perform an altar devotion with the mirror.

Put the mirror in the palm of one hand and angle it so it reflects the light of the sun, slanted down, as you walk the circle thrice, repeating the casting. Keep your free hand positioned palm down to the ground.

> *I stir forth my ancient ancestors of the sun*
> *Bright Gods and Goddesses, one by one*

walk once around,

> *I call forth the Mighty Ones of the hidden realms*
> *Sunrise (or sunset) energy at the helm.*

walk once around,

> *I summon forth the primordial protectors of the quarters*
> *Sun energy at the borders.*

walk once around and stop silently at each quarter.

> *Bless and surround this sacred space with protection.*
> *Power of the sun be my reflection.*

Seal the circle by holding the mirror to your lips and placing it face down on the ground in the center of the circle, on top of your stone.

> *This circle is sealed.*

Begin at the East (place of the sun):

> *I, son/daughter of the Shining Ones*
> *Acknowledge and bless the Element of Air.*
> *The rising sun, wisdom won.*

Draw your personal sigil with your finger in the air.

> *I, son/daughter of the Shining Ones*
> *Acknowledge and bless the Element of Fire.*
> *The midday flare, the dragon's lair.*

Light the candle and draw your personal sigil in the air with a gold candle.

> *I, son/daughter of the Shining Ones*
> *Acknowledge and bless the Element of Water.*
> *The sinking orb, where transformation is stored.*

Draw your personal sigil with your finger in the cauldron.

> *I, son/daughter of the Shining Ones*
> *Acknowledge and bless the Element of Earth.*
> *The midnight hour of ancient power.*

Draw your personal sigil with your finger on the ground.

Invocation

> *On this day and in this hour*
> *I call upon the sun's great power.*
>
> *Great Goddess/God of the sun*
> *Queen/King of every realm*
> *Lady/Lord of infinite destiny/protection*
> *Guardian and Mother/Father of Witches.*
>
> *I call upon your wisdom*
> *To pierce through the day*
> *Cast upon me your Priestess/Priest*
> *Thy loving gaze.*
>
> *The enchantment has begun*
> *From the sun*
> *Power will come.*

Raise your mirror and angle it so that the rays of the sun are reflected from its surface onto your body. Begin with your genital chakra and work up, quickly, to the crown of your head. (We don't want anybody burned). Put the mirror down. Face the sun. Mentally pull the energy of the sun into either your third eye or your abdomen chakra.

When you are finished, turn the mirror so that the light is now reflected in the cauldron or cup in the center of your circle. Let the rays of the sun cleanse, consecrate, and empower the drink. Put the mirror down and drink the liquid, imagining that it contains great wisdom and power.

Spend some time meditating or raising power for a specific purpose. Ground and center. When you are through, thank the Goddess/God, acknowledge the quarters once again, and bid them farewell. Take up the circle in the manner you like best. Clear your area. Leave a gift for the Devas.

There are numerous Gods and Goddesses of the sun. In the Celtic traditions, a nice trio is Brigit, Lugh, and Bel. For Dianic practitioners, try Sulis, Aditi, Solnitse, Hestia, or Lucina. Sulis is a Celtic Sun Goddess; Aditi is of Hindu derivation, meaning the Mother of the Lights of Heaven; Solnitse is a Russian Sun Goddess; of course we know that Hestia is a Greek Goddess attributed to hearth-fires and fire drakes; Lucina is a Roman Goddess sometimes called the Mother of Light.

The Eskimos consider the sun a female aspect and the moon Her male counterpart. Grian in Irish and Scottish Gaelic is feminine. Other Goddesses associated with the sun are Amaterasu (Japanese), Brunissen (Celtic), Hsi-Ho (Chinese), Igaehindvo (Cherokee), Knowee (Australian Aboriginal), Nahar

(Syrian), Sapas (Phoenician), Sekhmet (Egyptian), Sul (British), Surya (Hindu), and Suwa (Arabian).[2]

An Irish name for the sun is Tethin (to the Scots, Teth; modern version Teine or Tine), meaning burning or fire, and is feminine. Dineen's 1923 Irish Dictionary gives the noun Mor (or Mora) to indicate the sun. She Who Shines on the Elves relates to Sunna. There are a few Wiccan traditions that celebrate the dual Goddess on Midsummer—Grian and Aine. Grian represents the birth of the sun, and Aine the death and withdrawal of the skirts of the sun's rays into the realm of fairy.

If you are into Egyptian stuff and the cycle of the sun, you may wish to choose Ra for sunrise, Ahathor for noon, Tum for sunset, and Khephra for midnight. Ra is a falcon-headed God, whose head gear includes a solar disk with a serpent, sign of Osiris. Ahathor (better known as Hathor) is definitely feminine. She wears a headdress of horns and a solar disk, and has the head of a cow (not extremely romantic, I know). Hathor, by the way, was that good old golden calf that Moses was so bent out of shape about. Guess that female competition was too much for him, eh? With Tum, we are back to male again (which is fine—I'm a supporter of balance in all things); he is bearded. In Khephra, we are dealing with a sacred beetle (not Beatle, for you sixties fans) facing a sun disk. In envisioning this symbol, look to the scarab.

If you are a Southwest American fan, check into Anasazi, the Ancient Ones, for seasonal cycles of the sun in the Hopi and Zuni Indian traditions.

Conjuring Star Power

Many individuals, working Witches or no, believe our ancestors reside among the stars. Some think they will be back to collect us some day. Others feel they have never been far away and have been keeping track of our progress. We know the stars are always there, so the time of day you choose to conjure star power is entirely up to you. For maximum effect, a starry night, whether winter or summer, is ideal.

Ritual

Ground and center. Salute with the mirror and perform an altar devotion with the mirror.

Put the mirror in the palm of one hand and angle it so it reflects the starlight, slanted down, as you walk the circle thrice, repeating the casting. Keep your free hand positioned palm down to the ground.

I stir forth my ancient ancestors of the stars

walk once around,

---

2. *The Witches' Goddess* by Janet and Stuart Farrar, Phoenix Publishing, 1987. Page 40.

I call forth the Mighty ones of the starry realms

walk once around,

I summon forth the primordial protectors of the quarters.

walk once around and stop silently at each quarter.

*Bless and surround this sacred space with both power
and protection.*

Seal the circle by holding the mirror to your lips and placing it face down on the ground in the center of the circle, on top of your stone.

This circle is sealed.

Begin at the North:

*I, a child of the stars
Acknowledge and bless the Element of Earth.
Bring Earth energy to create and meld.
North star, send me your blessings.*

Draw your personal sigil with your finger on the ground.

*I, a child of the stars
Acknowledge and bless the Element of Air.
Bring Air energy to create and meld.*

Draw your personal sigil with your finger in the air.

*I, a child of the stars
Acknowledge and bless the Element of Fire.
Bring Fire energy to create and meld.*

Lite the candle and draw your personal sigil in the air with a white candle.

*I, a child of the stars
Acknowledge and bless the Element of Water.
Bring Water energy to create and meld.*

Draw your personal sigil with your finger in the cauldron.

Invocation

*On this night and in this hour
I call upon the stars' great power.*

*You who are the mystery of the cosmos
Who gives life to the Universe
Great Goddess of the stars
Queen of the heavenly realms*

*Let there be beauty and strength
Power and compassion*

Honor and humility
Mirth and reverence
Within me
As I drink from the cauldron
Of your starry night.

Thou hast been with me from the beginning
And you are that which will be attained
At the end of my desire.

I call upon your wisdom
To pierce through the night
Cast upon me, your Priestess/Priest
Thy loving gaze.

The enchantment has begun
From the stars
Power will come.

Raise your mirror and angle it so that the stars reflect from its surface and onto your body. Begin with your genital chakra and work up, slowly, to the crown of your head. Place the reflection either at your third eye or your abdomen chakra.

When you are finished, turn the mirror so that the stars are now reflected in the cauldron or cup in the center of your circle. Let the stars cleanse, consecrate, and empower the drink. Put the mirror down and drink the liquid, imagining that it contains great wisdom and power.

Spend some time meditating or raising power for a specific purpose. Ground and center. When you are through, thank the Star Goddess, acknowledge the quarters once again, and bid them farewell. Take up the circle in the manner you like best. Clear your area. Leave a gift for the Devas.

Notice the star chant contains a variation of the Words of the Star Goddess, which are as follows:

> *I who am the beauty of the green earth, and the white moon among the stars, and the mysteries of the waters, and the desire of the heart of man. I call unto thy soul to arise and come unto me. For I am the soul of nature, who gives life to the Universe. From me all things proceed, and unto me all things must return; and before my face, beloved of Gods and of men, let thine innermost divine self be enfolded in the rapture of the infinite. Let my worship be within the heart that rejoiceth; for behold, all acts of love and pleasure are my rituals. And therefore, let there be beauty and strength, power and compassion, honor and humility, mirth and reverence within you. And thou who thinkest to seek for me, know thy seeking and yearning shall avail thee not unless thou knowest the mystery; that if that*

which thou seekest thou findest not within thee, thou wilt never find it without thee. For behold, I have been with thee from the beginning; and I am that which is attained at the end of desire.[3]

Conjuring Power with Trance Work

Trances are states of deep meditation. They are not Madame Rosie uttering gibberish at a seance, feigning to speak to the dead among the tingling of bells and the heightened fear of her clients. States of trance have been practiced by spiritual and magickal people all over the world, in almost every religion, since the concept of Divinity was incorporated in the human condition.

The trance work I am familiar with contains eight levels. Notice my words here—I am familiar with. Different mystical schools have various opinions on the levels of awareness that can be achieved. As with all mystery training, what works best for you is important.

The eight levels are:

1. **The Gate of Healing:** Imagine a large, circular shower area decorated with thousands of mosaic tiles of every color imaginable. When your spirit/mental self steps into this shower, all negativity of this plane and any damage done to you (either mentally or spiritually) will be washed away and repaired. The working Witch should stand within this astral shower every day to enhance abilities and maintain good health.

2. **The Gate of Dreams and Creation:** Includes dream workings of all types, both during regular sleep time, induced sleep, and meditative experiences. Here, ideas, passions of creation (music, dance, artwork, writing, etc.), can be accessed to their heights and depths.

3. **The Gate of Knowledge:** Deals primarily with communication, including telepathy, astral projection, conversations with both the living and the dead, and those waiting to be born. This also includes guides, guardians, teachers, and masters.

4. **The Gate of Memories:** Here we find your personal history, all the lifetimes you have lived, the lessons you did and did not incorporate, the abilities and skills that you have and have not taken advantage of. Remember that you can aspect skills and pure qualities of yourself in various lifetimes to assist you in this one.

5. **The Gate of History:** Holds the hall of akashic records, the thousands of temple records stored over the centuries, the history of any lineage, people, clan, or group of souls.

6. **The Gate of Purpose:** Reveals the mechanics of almost anything, from actions of people to countries and assists the seeker in the positive arrangement of his or her own life. It also may be accessed to help others, should

---

3. Version by StarHawk, whose fine spiritual work has aided each and every one of us.

your intentions be pure. On a more distinguished level, it reveals the purpose of the Universe and your place within it. The gate of what is yet to be.

7. **The Gate of Unity:** The home of perfect love and perfect trust—the silver thread that binds the Universe together. The realm of perfection in all things, both past and present, living and inanimate, as well as things yet to come.

8. **The Gate of Divinity:** Few are able to go here, the place of the union of all selves with the Divine.

❀ Your Work ☙

Project 1: For the first week, carefully study each of the gates indicated. Check your research material, search for correspondences and rituals that may assist you. I suggest that although you plan for several of the gates, do the work in linear fashion until you create a pattern for yourself. For example, in wishing to work with the Gate of Dreams, you could make a dream pillow of herbs that both magickally and medicinally reduce stress and bring peaceful sleep. Timing, such as a Sunday or during a full moon, would be ideal for such a special journey.

Project 2: On successive weeks (beginning with the Gate of Dreams), start with your meditation sequence. You will move naturally into a trance state. You will know you are there—colors are more vivid, and sometimes so beautiful they are breathtaking. Sometimes they are colors that, in the mundane world, you have never seen. You may hear melodious sounds not thought of, or meet creatures not familiar to you. Keep a record of these experiences. From the Gate of Dreams, explore the second gate. Walk around; take in the sights. Above all, learn to be patient. Slowly, begin to explore the various avenues now open to you. Keep very good records. Your work on recall is as important as the journey itself.

There are also eight levels to the Underworld. Unlike the eight gates previously mentioned, which can be accessed without sacrifice, the eight gates of the Underworld, the realm of the Dark Goddess, can only be entered through the willingness of the seeker to give some part of self they hold most dear. This, in the Craft, is the purpose of the second-degree ceremony (using the three-degree system as an example). Here, the Goddess (the seeker) journeys to the Underworld, giving up things held most dear in self, to be reborn in the eyes of the Great Mother. Illusion is stripped away, and the seeker is reunited with the world of the living at the end of the ceremony. Is the descent only a story? No.

Can a solitary Witch do the descent alone? Yes, I've seen it done, quite by accident, with no ill results. In fact, I've seen traditional Witches who have earned their first degree create the descent unconsciously through situations orchestrated by their higher selves. There are times when first-degree Witches are held too long by their teachers, for whatever reason, and the Goddess takes it upon Herself to lead the seeker down the spiral of the descent. No human can stop the designs of the Mother. Either She will lead the Witch to another teacher or assist the seeker in his or her descent alone.

The descent to the Underworld information is not given to you in hopes you will rush about and prepare a ceremony for yourself. It is provided to enlighten you about another of the Wiccan mysteries available to the traditional Witch that is not seen or used by the eclectic or solitary Witch who has not had professional training. In mystery groups of old, drugs or snake venom were used to heighten or induce states of trance. Today, we teach the student that this is not necessary, because the human mind is quite capable of attaining such altered states through practice, rather than using a drug for a jump-start.

Before you go further, check the legends and mythos of your pantheon to examine how the various aspects of the Goddess and God fit into the eight Gates of Light and the eight Gates of the Underworld. Are any of the deities gatekeepers? Do any of the archetypes fit a particular level? Work first with those archetypes with whom you are familiar, then research to find others who will help you access the other worlds. Record your findings. If they do not assist you in the future, they may assist another who comes to you with a question.

There are two ways to work the Gates of Light. The first is by passing through gate one to get to two, then through two to get to three, etc. always beginning and returning to gate one. Other individuals prefer to see the gates in a circle, where all can be accessed from the same starting point. Do not be surprised if, during meditation or trance state, a gate is barred to you. There could be many reasons, from the state of your health, the point of learning you have attained, to your destiny. Do not judge yourself too harshly should you not be admitted to the gate you choose.

The eight gates of the Underworld are dealt with in a linear fashion, from one to two, and downward until you reach the Dark Goddess. From Her, you go back up, from eight back to one. I do not know anyone who has worked with these gates in a non-linear fashion, nor have I met anyone who has entertained the thought. The descent can entail a massive personality change and should not be done on a whim. In our group working, the seeker actively performs the dance of the eight veils (remember that one? Now you know where it came from) and meets the Lord of the Underworld. If we are working with a male initiate, he performs the march of the eight banners, and encounters the Dark Goddess upon her throne. Both ceremonies are equally moving.

151

When working with the Gates of Light, many people prefer to call a guide or angel as a companion. However, when working through the Gates of the Underworld, the seeker must go alone—no guide is provided or permitted.

If you are currently running some type of group, pathworking exercises can be designed by one sister or brother, and narrated by the individual in the group with the most pleasing voice, or one skilled in hypnotherapy. If you are working alone, you may wish to begin your journeys with peaceful music, and you can use various songs to act as triggers for the various gates.

The information you gather in trance state hold great power for the pure practitioner. Use it for selfish or cruel purposes, and the gates will be closed to you; the gifts you have received will be taken. Many working Witches report higher levels of psychism as they work through the Gates of Light or travel to the Gates of the Underworld. If you fear working alone, choose a good friend who is not condescending to assist you. If one is not available, ask the Mother. Surely She will provide one. You must only have patience and believe.

A note of help: When you move through the gates for past/future life information, it is far better to move with the intention of wisdom gained, rather than expect an instant replay of a lifetime for your viewing entertainment. Look for information that will enhance your current studies and further your spiritual path, rather than worrying about lost loves or romantic fantasies. This gate will serve you better if you work with a sound goal in mind.

Divinity and You

Because I run a group, I've heard a few interesting sagas. I've seen bad choices (including some of my own), bad judgments (ditto here), magickal and mundane failures, and romances that have gone down the tubes or up in rockets, hearts, and roses. I've watched insecurities surface and abilities soar.

"I like Wicca," says Lady Bats, "because it is something I can live everyday. It is simple and harmonious. Sure, I don't have everything I want, but I'm happy."

The most disturbing thing I've found in group work is a little monster called self-imposed politics. Its root is insecurity. The insecurity is germinated from the seeds of lack of faith and lack of practice. Scott Cunningham was right when he said you must live Wicca every day in order to reap its many benefits. It is not a sometime thing, to be dabbled with when the chips are down or you are bored. When members of my group run into extreme difficulties, ninety-nine times out of a hundred, I find out they have not been practicing their religion on a daily basis. They have not been doing their altar devotions. They have not been working on self-improvement rituals. They have not been banishing negative influences or energies from themselves every day. They have not been working magick on a regular basis in order to improve their skills. In plain words, they have not been doing all the solitary things that are required to become an adept. You must learn to work alone in all phases of the Craft to reach your life goals.

If you really want power, you must be dedicated to your work. I can teach you every ritual, spell, or trick I know and you won't get the appropriate treat if you don't apply yourself all the time. Sure, working Witches take breaks, vacations, or simply chill out for thirty days. However, these breaks are ritually begun and ritually finished. You cannot attain balance if you do not understand the nature of balance. Not working or fulfilling personal religious needs creates an imbalance in our lives. If you do not include Divinity in your everyday life, power ebbs away from you rather than pooling with you. You can not conjure harmonious power if you do not respect and honor Divinity every day. Me, myself, and I have got to learn to wing it together before we flock with others.

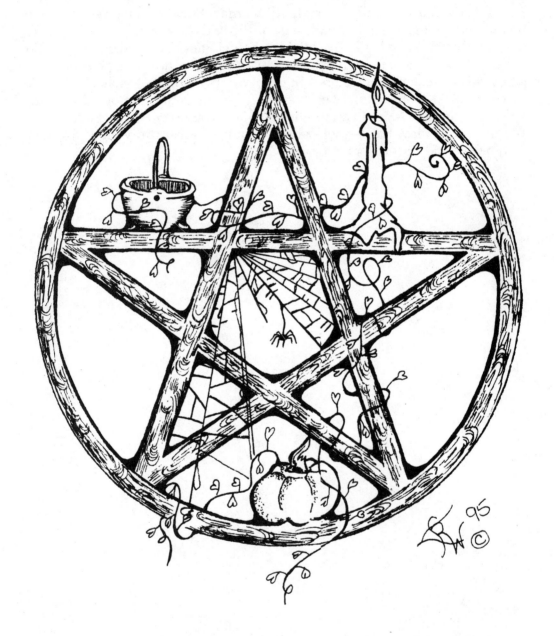

Conjuring Minor and Major Magicks

Not even gravity can keep a good Witch down. After all, who knows better how to work between the worlds where the gravity of any situation can be transmuted? Major and minor magicks help us combat boredom and negative thoughtforms. They also assist in bringing abundance and joy into our lives. Magick, including spell casting, is not difficult. Generally, it follows an easy formula with distinct steps that can be used for a variety of purposes. You do not need money, fancy tools, or exotic plants to work minor magicks. Major magicks sometimes require a small investment, depending upon your interests and where you wish to take your studies. For both minor and major magicks, you must have faith in yourself, a positive attitude, and connection with Divinity.

This chapter has very few spells in it. Sorry to disappoint you; that comes in the next chapter. Right now, we are concerned with the mechanics of spell casting, what it is, how it is done, etc. The actual spells are icing on the cake—no, sugar in the cauldron!

What Does it Take to be a Real Working Witch?

It takes courage, guts, and determination to be a Witch. How do you know an adept has cast a spell or done a major working? You don't; that's the point. An adept is so good, he or she can even cloak another magickal person's divination attempt. Real working Witches are bold. They go beyond the whining stage of "Why me, Oh Lord, why me?" They get their hands dirty. They move right in and do what has to be done, whether it is a mundane action, casting a spell, or performing a ritual. They don't quibble over politics, worry about who is Queen of the Sabbat this week, or brag about how much community service they have done, how many students they've taught, or how many people showed up at their house on circle night. They don't worry about having a retinue, and they don't use people to get what they want. They simply *do,* for themselves and others, in the best way they know how. They aren't always right and may make mistakes here and there, but that is all part of the human condition and the lessons that have been presented to them to learn.

Real Witches don't abuse their power, or seek to remove or denigrate others. They don't abuse children, spouses, or students. People who practice such abuses are fakes, frauds, and con artists. A real Witch doesn't make fun of another individual's handicaps or level of achievement, whether they be magickal or not. Every religion has them—these spineless jellyfish play-acting as wolves. As a community, we should be watching out for each other and taking out the trash. If no one is making a move on a particular situation and you see it for what it is, take it to the Goddess. She is always watching, and Her justice isn't blind.

Lady Bats says, "It is a blatant fool who plays big-Witchie-magickal-person. They gonna go down. Yes, they is. And the Goddess ain't mighty friendly when they gets to the bottom. No sir, that She ain't."

Spells? Prayers?

Although many working Witches explain spells as prayers to those who have no clue about the Craft, that is not exactly correct. Don't worry, I'm guilty of it myself because the hoped-for end result of a spell is the same as a prayer. Spells, unlike most prayers, as we've covered before, are focused acts. Mind, spirit, and body are attuned to a single desire. Groveling and mentally beating yourself is not required.

By now, you should not be muttering about whether spells work or not. Nor should you be in the throes of ethical vacillations. That's for 101 people, not you. If you have any doubts about spell casting, go back to the beginner books and work through those sections again. As an added kick, here is what Z. Budapest has to say about spell casting:

> Casting a spell, in self-defense or in self-interest is not selfish, but positive, life-affirming. You have been given powers, the very same powers that society devalues … What if it comes back tenfold? Well, don't be a fool. Never use your magick to attack the innocent. Then you have nothing to fear …. Don't be frivolous or cowardly. If your course is righteous, and your tools ready, go to it.[1]

1. *The Holy Book of Women's Mysteries* by Zsuzanna Budapest, Wingbow Press, 1980. Page 17.

In teaching students, I focus on the Witches' Pyramid. The foundation consists of the following:

To Know
To Will
To Dare
To Be Silent

These four principles, when focused, are the springboard of all Craft magick. Let's do something different. Rather than my rambling about the four principles of spell casting, how about I put it in outline form:

Spell Outline

I. The Witches' Pyramid
   A. To Know
      1. Know yourself
      2. Know what you want to accomplish
         a. Write down the specifics in long-hand
         b. Factor down to phonetics
         c. Factor down to initials
         d. Create a sigil with those initials
      3. Know how to work in moderation
   B. To Will
      1. Belief in yourself
      2. Belief in Divinity
      3. Belief in your skill level
      4. Belief in the abundance of the Universe
      5. The will to practice again and again
      6. Meditation skills
         a. Practice for visualization
         b. Practice for relaxation
         c. Practice for reaching Alpha
         d. Practice for speed
      7. Why do you want to perform this magickal operation?
      8. Is your will directed correctly?
         a. Do not influence another
         b. Do not influence in a negative manner
         c. Do a divination to check your plans
   C. To Dare
      1. Have the guts to change circumstances
      2. Have the guts to control your environment
      3. Take responsibility for your actions
      4. Choose the best course of action for the working to be done
   D. To Be Silent
      1. Learn to keep your mouth shut before you perform

2. Learn to keep your mouth shut while you are waiting for results
3. Learn to keep your mouth shut after the operation
   a. Protects your confidence
   b. Protects your reputation

❀ Your Work ❧

Project 1: Take a favorite spell and see how it fits into the outline above. Is there anything you would change, now that you have walked through the outline?

Project 2: Perform your spell with the outline in mind. Record your results.

Celestial Magicks

I know it is a pain, but let's start from square one and go through all the little nuances that make slam-bang-shoot-'em-up spell casting. Believe me, by the time you get through this chapter, and if you learn everything in here, there is no excuse for casting a lousy spell—unless your dog eats your notes, of course.

The ancients used the sun, moon, planets, and stars in their magick and religions. The working Witch follows in the footsteps of the Shamans before him or her by employing many of the same concepts. Normally, the first type of celestial magick employed by the working Witch is that of the moon and her phases. Is it necessary to learn this information? Yes, if you want to be an adept at spell casting.

I use four very important tools for celestial magicks:

1. *Llewellyn's Daily Planetary Guide*
2. *Llewellyn's Magickal Almanac*
3. *Llewellyn's Astrological Pocket Planner*
4. *Jim Maynard's Pocket Astrologer*[2]

Most magickal books give you a table of correspondences, throw a few paragraphs at you on how to use them, and leave you to your own designs. Here, we'll go through many of these various correspondences in more detail.

I mentioned before that most working Witches begin with the moon phase when planning a spell. First, of course, you have determined the who, what, when, where, why, and how. After the situation is clearly considered, take a look at the moon phases below and determine where your work should be done, if possible.

---

2. Available from Quicksilver Productions, P.O. Box 340, Dept. PAK94, Ashland, Oregon 97520. Phone: (503) 482-5343.

Lunar Magicks

This magick deals primarily with the timing and phases of the moon. Most Witches use the standard phases (full, new, waxing, waning, dark); however, these can be expanded for more advanced students in the following manner.

New Moon Magick

(Moon is 0-45 degrees directly ahead of the sun.) Sun and moon energies are combined in this phase to give great strength to new projects. Legend has it that in this phase, Diana, disguised as a cat, coerced her brother Lucifer into her bed of passions. The Queen of Witches, Aradia, is the result of this unusual union.[3] As the new moon signifies the conception of Aradia, she is always a willing participant in the magick of her children. Now is also the time to give thanks for workings (both long- and short-term) that have been successful. Banishments at the full and waning moons have most likely manifested by now. Offerings of milk and honey, or water laced with fertilizer for the plants outside (during the growing season), is appropriate. If in the season of sleep, then set out food for the small animals. Other Goddesses employed are Diana, Artemis, Astarte, and one of my favorites, Ana.

Timing: The moon rises at dawn and sets at sunset. For the best use of this energy, magick should be performed between dawn and sunset. This is not to say that you cannot work at night. However, to get the most punch for your magick, choose the correct timing. Also check the planetary hours to give added power to the working. Sun Goddesses such as Sekhmet, Vesta, and Heartha can be aspected with great success. This is a wonderful time for dragon magick, or rituals where the God and Goddess are balanced. Rituals focusing on the God are quite acceptable in this phase.

Conjuring: New moon workings can be done from the day of the new moon to 3½ days after. Naturally, the closer you are to the new moon, the better your chances of success.

Your work should manifest by the full moon or the next new moon. If it does not, repeat the working. Things to work for include:

Beauty, health, and self-improvement
Farms and gardens
Job hunting
Love and romance
Networking

Meditations: Work on bringing abundance into your life. Picture the harmony you desire, the current needs you have. Make a mind movie about how you want both short- and long-term goals to manifest. Concentrate also on parts of yourself (body, mind, or spirit) that need regeneration.

---

3. See *Ways of the Strega* by Raven Grimassi, Llewellyn Publications, 1995.

Crescent Moon Magick

(Moon is 45-90 degrees ahead of the sun. The crescent faces West, the home of the Calliech and the gates of death and rebirth.) The crescent is the symbol of the Goddess, a ladle of love, manifestation, and abundance. It is the holy cup of Her hand, containing the mysteries to be showered upon Her children. In the mundane world, you should be gathering information, ideas, and laying a foundation for the project you have set into motion through magick. Use small rituals and magickal techniques to help your mundane work along. Since the crescent faces West, the aid of Aphrodite, Marianne, Themis, or Tiamat can be aspected, as well as the ancient power of the Magdalens.[4]

Timing: The moon rises at mid-morning and sets after sunset. The crescent's greatest strength would be at the midpoint. Check an almanac for exact timing.

Conjuring: This phase lasts from 3½ days after the new moon through the seventh day. You can do some minor magicks each day to enhance your goals and projects. This is definitely a time for the Goddess and Her female archetypes, as the crescent energy is strong. Work for:
> Animals
> Business
> Change
> Emotions
> Matriarchal strength

Meditations: Continue to work on your mind movie for the manifestation of goals and projects, then slip into Goddess archetype meditations to cultivate a particular quality you would like to instill in your own life.

First Quarter (Waxing Moon) Magick

(Moon is 90-135 degrees ahead of the sun.) To most working Witches, waxing means the process of building up. Now is the time to put on a little extra steam, buck up a few things that are sagging, and push forward toward manifestation. Do a small ritual to continue success or bring it on a bit faster. If extra magickal guns may be needed, now is the time to use them.

Timing: The moon rises at noon and sets at midnight. Sunset is the prime time for waxing moon magick. Dusk is auspicious for fairies and their energy. Altar devotions and offerings for the fairy folk in return for a favor work especially well during this moon phase. A special trip to your outdoor shrine may be in

---

4. It is thought that many medieval cathedrals were dedicated to Mary Magdalen and not the Virgin Mary at all. The Magdalens were not street hookers as many would like us to believe, but temple priestesses to the Goddess in Matrifocal worship. The Magdalen, then, was the Holy Grail herself. It was not a mundane cup tossed from fortune hunter to fortune hunter. In this phase of the moon, the crescent represents the grail, who is indeed, the Goddess in her form of the Magdalen priestesses and elders. See *The Moon Beneath Her Feet,* published by Harper Collins, for more details on the Magdalens.

order, with a small ceremony to leave milk and honey, no matter the season. A wonderful time also to work with the triple Goddess aspect.

Conjuring: Moon is from 7 to 10½ days after the new moon. Check the planetary hours for spellworking or additional ritual performance. Do rituals for:

> Courage
> Elemental magick
> Friends
> Luck
> Motivation

Meditation: Meditate upon Gods and Goddesses of strength and success in pathworking exercises. Continue to use the mind movie. Instinct and intuition are valuable assets during this time. Program your mind both in and out of meditation to take advantage of these gifts.

Gibbous Moon Magick

(Moon is 135-180 degrees ahead of the sun and is mistaken by laypeople as the full moon, especially in the last day.) Time to catch loose ends or make any changes necessary. If the working appears to have stalled, don't panic. Often a gestation period is needed where no change is immediately visible. You may wish to relax a bit and begin planning any working you choose to do with full moon energy.

Timing: The moon rises at mid-afternoon and sets about 3 AM. This is a wonderful time for workings around 10 or 11 PM, if you are inclined. Goddesses of the night, such as Nuit or Star Goddesses, do well in this phase.

Conjuring: The moon is 10½ to 14 days after the new moon. Work for:

> Patience

Meditation: Continue your mind movie to bring both small and large goals closer to you. Mentally prepare yourself for the full moon energy yet to come.

Full Moon Magick

(The moon is 180-225 degrees ahead of the sun. At this point, the moon is directly opposite the sun. Here, you can create an arch of energy between the moon and sun.) All rituals of balance in life or a situation are done at this time. Full moon magick is like a white candle—all-purpose. If you follow lunar phases for most of your magick, you know that prophecy and protection are the biggies here. Totems like the raven are called to bestow their gifts of divination. Goddesses like Isis, Ashera, and Selene are called, as well as the Sisters of the Wyrrd, the Norns, and other Goddesses and Gods of fate. Short-term projects may have concluded now and it is time to give thanks for the blessings that have come your way. The full moon is also the time of legends—reading them, studying them, and making your own. You are a legend and have wonderful lessons and memories to offer. Individuals talented in the arts (dance, music, painting, pottery, metal work, etc.) find the full moon a most auspicious time for creativity. Power, of course, is generated, regenerated, and used by the working Witch. Any working that needs a major punch, such as a divorce case, help in finding a satisfactory job, healings for major conditions, can all be done now with excellent chances of success.

Timing: The moon rises at sunset and sets at dawn, therefore a midnight working (or when the moon is directly overhead) is best.

Conjuring: The moon is from 14 to 17½ days after the new moon. Work for:
    Artistic endeavors
    Beauty, health, and fitness
    Change and decisions
    Children
    Competition
    Dreams
    Families
    Health and healing
    Knowledge
    Legal undertakings
    Love and romance
    Money
    Motivation
    Protection
    Psychism
    Self-improvement

Meditation: Meditations involving prophecy and power in occult skills should be done now. Dream work is at its height. Don't forget to keep that notebook by your bed to record those important messages.

Disseminating Moon Magick

(Moon is 225-270 degrees ahead of the sun.) Banishing work starts now. If you want to get rid of a bad habit, banish illness or negativity, this is the time to begin. A good time to take things apart, whether it is old modes of thought or that radio you wanted to fix six months ago. This is the time of the Goddesses Bast, Kore, Ceres, Demeter, or other Earth Mothers.

Timing: The moon rises at mid-evening and sets at mid-morning. The time of souls (3 AM) would be the midpoint here. Check planetary correspondences if you aren't inclined to wakefulness in the wee hours of the morning.

Conjuring: The moon is 3½ to 7 days after the full moon. Workings should focus upon:
    Addiction
    Decisions

> Divorce
> Emotions
> Stress
> Protection

Meditation: Meditations involve removal of outmoded thoughts, bad habits, or anything that bothers you. Continue to work on thoughts of abundance and joy in your life. Keep working on that mind movie for short- and long-term goals.

Last Quarter (Waning Moon) Magick

(Moon is 270-315 degrees ahead of the sun. The crescent shape here turns eastward, opening Her arms toward the rising sun.) Release of any negativity around us, continued banishing work or minor magicks to support a banishing ritual begun during the disseminating moon. Continued banishing in the realm of healing (especially cancers and tumors, and other things that grow and aren't supposed to).

Timing: The moon rises at midnight and sets at noon.

Conjuring: The moon is 7 to 10½ days after the full moon. Work involves:
> Addictions
> Divorce
> Health and healing (banishing disease)
> Stress
> Protection

Meditation: Practice meditations to disentangle yourself from sticky situations, bad interpersonal affairs, healing (with regard to banishing illness), and removing bad habits. Again, keep working on the mind movie for short- and long-term goals. Reaffirm the positive things in your life.

Dark Moon Magick

(The moon is 315-360 degrees ahead of the sun.) Most famously known, of course, for cursing, chaos magick, and bringing justice to bear. Goddesses here are Kali, the Morrigan, the Calliech, Lilith, and Hecate. It is also a time to move within self, to explore our darkest recesses and understand our angers and passions, steering them to work for us in a positive way. Dealing with attackers is best begun during the dark moon.

Timing: The moon rises at 3 AM and sets at mid-afternoon. Despite the oddity, around 10 AM is the strongest pull of the dark moon. Close the drapes or use room-darkening blinds and meet the Dark Goddesses face to face. Check planetary hours for evening workings.

Conjuring: Moon is 10½ to 14 days after the full moon. Workings involve:
> Addictions
> Change

Divorce
Enemies
Justice
Obstacles
Quarrels
Removal
Separation
Stopping stalkers and theft

Meditations: Reach within yourself to pull out unwanted thoughts or desires. Examine them and dismiss them. Pathwork with the Dark Goddesses to receive their most exquisite gifts. Continue the mind movie for positive workings in your life.

Lunar Eclipses

There are two types of lunar eclipse:

1. Partial eclipse
2. Penumbral eclipse of the moon

You will need your *Planetary Guide* to check dates and times during the year when these two occur. Choose long-term goals you wish to work on well ahead of these events. Eclipses represent the perfect union of sun and moon, therefore practically any type of magick is acceptable. Many working Witches prefer to work with the Dark Goddesses during this time, correcting long-standing problems. Others lean toward the Shining Ones and fairy magick.

Moon Void of Course

The rule of thumb is to avoid doing anything important while the moon is void of course. If what you have done during this period works, consider yourself lucky. Call me stupid, it took me a long time to understand the concept of void of course. I don't know why. It was one of those "thangs" that wouldn't gel in my mind. In fact, it wasn't until I was studying horary astrology that I finally got the point. In horary astrology, the chart is not considered readable if certain circumstances are present. The chart has to be thrown out, and the question asked at another time. If the moon is void of course on the chart, the whole thing should be pitched.

Before the moon enters a new sign (Leo, Virgo, Cancer, etc.), there is a sort of dead space. The best way I can explain it is through Wiccan terms. The moon is between the worlds, in a time that is not a time, in a space that is not a space—it is in a celestial void where neither positive or negative energies behave as they normally do. To make this circumstance more irritating, it never lasts the same length of time. For example it could last only ten minutes, or as much as a day and a half. It isn't a phenomenon you can set your watch by, so you need to check either your planetary datebook or pocket astrologer.

The effects of the void moon vary. Some people manifest scattered energy, or that "I don't feel like myself today" position. Decisions have a habit of bordering on the illogical. Individuals under psychological counseling or drug therapy swing toward the irrational. Of course, those who need counseling and refuse to get it move toward more violent behaviors. The general rule during this time revolves around stuff you shouldn't do:

Don't do magick

Don't make major decisions

Don't make major purchases

Don't begin or complete any magickal operations

Don't make any major repairs

The void of course moon is a good time for relaxation and more spiritual pursuits, such as studying or taking a walk in the woods. It is like a cosmic time-out and can be very advantageous if used properly.

❀ Your Work ❁

Project 1: Learn the phases of the moon. Write down each phase; beside the phase, explain, in detail, how you feel the phase could be used in the life of any working Witch.

Project 2: Compare each phase to your life. What sort of phase are you living in right now?

Project 3: With both spell outlines, sit down and design a spell to match each of the phases of the moon. Perform all of them throughout the next three lunar cycles.

Those Magickal Days

The next thing a working Witch checks are the magickal days. Which day would be most auspicious to perform the working? The days are equated with the sun and six of the planets.

Sunday (Sun—yellow, gold, orange): Health, success, career, goals, ambition, personal finances, advancement, drama, fun, authority figures, law, fairs, crops, totem animals, volunteer and civic services, promotion, the God, men's mysteries, children, buying, selling, speculating.

Monday (Moon—white, silver, grey, pearl): Psychic pursuits, psychology, dreams/astral travel, imagination, women's mysteries, reincarnation, short trips, women, children, the public, domestic concerns, emotions, fluids, magick, spirituality, nursing, all things pertaining to water and bodies of water, antiques, trip planning, household activities, initiation, astrology, new-age pursuits, archetypes, totem animals, shapeshifting, religious experience.

Tuesday (Mars—red, pink, orange): Passion, partnerships, courage, swift movement, action, energy, strife, aggression, sex, physical energy, sports, muscular activity, guns, tools, metals, cutting, surgery, police, soldiers, combat, confrontation, business, buying and selling animals, mechanical things, repair, gardening, woodworking, hunting, beginnings.

Wednesday (Mercury—purple, magenta, silver): Wisdom, healing, communication, intelligence, memory, education, correspondence, phone calls, computers, messages, students, merchants, editing, writing, advertising, signing contracts, siblings, neighbors, kin, accounting, clerks, critics, music, editors, journalists, visual arts, hiring employees, learning languages, placing ads, telephone calls, visiting friends, legal appointments, astrology.

Thursday (Jupiter—blue, metallic colors): Business, logic, gambling, social matters, political power, material wealth, publishing, college education, long-distance travel, foreign interests, religion, philosophy, forecasting, broadcasting, publicity, expansion, luck, growth, sports, horses, the law, doctors, guardians, merchants, psychologists, charity, correspondence courses, self-improvement, researching, reading, studying.

Friday (Venus—green, pink, white): Romantic love, friendships, beauty, soulmates, artistic ability, harmony, affection, relationships, partners, alliances, grace, beauty, luxury, social activity, marriage, decorating, cosmetics, gifts, income, growth, gardening, architects, artists, beauticians, chiropractors, dancers, designers, engineers, entertainers, fashion, music, painting, poetry, courtship, dating, decorating homes, household improvements, planning parties, shopping.

Saturday (Saturn—black, grey, red, white): Binding, protection, neutralization, karma, death, manifestation, structure, reality, the laws of society, limits, obstacles, tests, hard work, endurance, real estate, dentists, bones, teeth, farm workers, sacrifice, separation, stalkers, murderers, criminals in general, civil servants, justice, math, plumbing, real estate, wills, debts, financing, joint money matters, discovery, transformation, death, relations with older people.

Now that I've given you all this information, what is the point? Take the most important aspect of the purpose of your working and check through the days. Which day would be most appropriate? Can you do your working on that day? Does it match your moon phase chosen? Which is the most convenient for you to use, the day or the moon phase? Can you possibly wait (like in long-range goal planning), or is this an emergency?

Planetary Hours

Finally, planetary hours can be beneficial, especially if you can't make it to the right moon phase or even the right day, though you can wait for both the appropriate day and planetary hour.

Planetary hours are divided into two parts:

Sunrise to sunset

Sunset to sunrise

Each hour of the day and night is matched to a planetary influence. Because only the sun and six planets are used as correspondences, you have a chance to use those influences either during the day or during the evening. The influences can either help or dissolve our magickal efforts. Planetary hours are calculated with reference to the rising sun, so each time you wish to use a planetary hour, you must first know precisely when the sun rises where you are living.

Here is how the working Witch discerns the planetary hour:

1. Find out what time the sun rises in your locality. This is not difficult. Use the Weather Channel on television, check the daily newspaper, or look in an almanac.

2. Get out the sunrise/sunset planetary hour charts provided at the end of this chapter.

3. Check the type of working you wish to do, and consider which planetary influence is best suited for your work. Write that down.

4. Choose which chart to use. Do you prefer working during the day or after sunset? On the chart, find the appropriate day you wish to use. If it is an emergency, it would be today, of course.

5. Divide the number of minutes of daylight by twelve. For example, if the sun rises at 7:00 AM and sets at 4:00 PM, you would divide the nine hours of daylight by twelve to calulate when the hours fall. That means that although we call them "planetary hours," the planetary hours will equal more or less than the normal sixty minutes we associate with one hour. In this example, the nine hours of daylight equals 540 minutes; 540 divided by twelve means each hour equals forty-five minutes. Therefore, Hour 1 would be from 7:00 AM to 7:45 AM. Hour 2 would be from 7:45 AM to 8:30 AM, and so on until sunset.

6. In Step 3, you wrote down the planetary influence you needed for the working. Find that planet under the day you chose. Run your finger over to the hour column; what hour does it fall under? In Step 5, you determined when the hours fell today, by using the sunrise (or sunset) of the day. What does the planetary hour you chose in the first column equate to today? This is the most auspicious time for you to do your working.

Let's say the first time chosen is impossible for you. You'll be at work. Go back to your chart to the correct day, and look for that planetary influence again. Run your finger back to the hour column, and calculate in today's time. Is this better? No?

Let's take this example further. If you can't perform magick during the daylight hours, you will probably prefer to take your time and plan the working at night. Use the table for the sunset planetary hours. Sunset is at 4:00 PM and the sun rises the next morning at 7:00 AM. The planetary hour calculations you did for the daylight hours would not be accurate here, since you have fifteen hours of darkness (as opposed to nine hours of daylight). Fifteen hours equals 900 minutes, which means that each hour equals seventy-five minutes (900 divided by twelve). Therefore, each Hour one would be from 4:00 PM to 5:15 PM, Hour 2 would be from 5:15 PM to 6:30 PM, and so on.

Finally, if none of these hours will work for you, either wait until the next available correct day and time or find another planetary influence that is close to what you need. You will find there are duplicates on many of the lists, so it shouldn't be too difficult.

Why all the fuss and bother, anyway? Calculating planetary influences puts you one step closer to a successful working, especially if other things can't, don't, or won't fall into line for you. It adds extra punch to the minor magicks explained earlier in this chapter and could give you success if you are feeling under the weather but must perform anyway. The hours are excellent for planning rituals as well.

❀ Your Work ✿

Project 1: Take ten of your favorite spells and calculate the appropriate lunar phase and magickal day. Perform at least three of these spells during the correct phase, and record the result.

Project 2: Take the same ten spells and add the planetary hour calculations. Perform three of these spells using the new data, and record the results.

Advanced Celestial Workings

When you are considering the celestial correspondences, you must also be aware of not only the phase of the moon, but the placement of it in relationship to the other planets in the heavens at the time of the proposed working, and what astrological sign the moon can be, will be, or should be in.

The moon is empathic. It can pick up the influences of the astrological signs as it travels through them. If this is not believable to you, think about yourself. Have you ever picked up bad or good habits when spending a great deal of time with another person who has those habits? I can remember going to camp when I was fourteen years old. My bunkmate was a girl from Georgia. Naturally, she had a thick, southern accent that dripped images of southern belles, white parasols, and pink lemonades. I was entranced. By the end of our two-week stay I subconsciously picked up a great deal of her accent, incorporating it into my own speech patterns. Upon my homecoming, my mother thought I might be a changeling. (Well, you never know.)

The moon, then, getting back to the topic at hand, is much like an open vessel. Of course she has qualities and energies of her own, but she is quite capable of reflecting the energies of the other bodies in the heavens around her as well as picking up on whether or not various planets agree with each other. Here is where your little pocket astrologer comes in. When planning magick, check to see where the moon is around the time you wish to do a working. What sign is she in? What planets are socializing with her at the time, and what sort of conversation they are having (called aspects)? In your pocket astrologer, the definitions of the aspects are given. It will only take you a few moments to figure it out. The following list will be of assistance to you.

Moon in Aries: Beginning of things, matters of self and your personality.

Moon in Taurus: Financial matters of a personal nature, vehicles, benefits, possessions.

Moon in Gemini: Relatives, communication, studies, writing, street smarts.

Moon in Cancer: Home environment, mothers, end of life, family.

Moon in Leo: Pleasures, hobbies, love affairs, entertainment, sports, your pets.

Moon in Virgo: Working environment, health, service extended, clothing.

Moon in Libra: Marriage, partnerships, legal matters, small animals.

Moon in Scorpio: Death, sex, taxes, inheritances, transformation.

Moon in Sagittarius: Religion, metaphysics, long-distance travel, in-laws, higher learning.

Moon in Capricorn: Business, career, reputation, father, honors.

Moon in Aquarius: Friendship, acquaintances, hopes and dreams, groups and organizations.

Moon in Pisces: Inner development, karma, restrictions, secrets revealed.

Planetary Aspects

Aspects are the socialization of planets with each other. By this time, you know what a planet is (if you do not, we are both in serious trouble). Some of the heavenly bodies get along, others don't—like people. Sometimes they can tolerate each other better than others (again, like us good ole humans). Other times, they have absolutely no patience and would prefer spitting at each other.

What happens in the heavens, say the experts, is a direct mirror of what is happening on the earth. Both movements, on heaven and earth, occur simultaneously. The working Witch needs to be aware of the big picture. Remember? The big picture here includes heavenly events and earthly events.

For years I had no interest in astrology. This doesn't mean I didn't believe in it. I simply didn't have the time or inclination to deal with it. Besides, I'm lousy at math. I would spend hours to get that correct slice of time and later find out my slice was soggy with errors. With the advent of the computer in my home, I got my little Witchie paws on a cheap chart-casting program. My life changed forever. While I was ferreting out the meanings of my own natal chart, I was also in the process of converting from eclecticism to an old Wiccan tradition. There was a great deal of work involved in it and I found myself talking to several elder Crafters for insights, suggestions, and ideas.

I happened to mention to one of these individuals about my new, great, marvelous, wonderful discovery of astrology and how, if used properly, it could be an asset to every being on the planet and should certainly be used by group leaders and elders, right? My acquaintance snorted in contempt. "Well, I don't use minor magicks and I certainly don't get involved in that astrology stuff. It's an excuse for people to behave badly."

Well, bust my bustle, I was a bit surprised at this outburst. It was obvious to me this person was condemning an entire mystical study because of something that had happened in the past. I was right.

In the next breath my acquaintance began a tirade of the ills of individuals who follow astrology. The largest complaint was one I'd seen myself. People who blame their shortcomings and bad behavior on the aspects of planets, glitches in their natal chart, or what sign the moon happens to be in at the time of their inexcusable behavior, have a problem that has nothing to do with astrology or the practice thereof. People who rationalize their bad behavior on the movement of the heavens are like anyone else who is trying not to take the blame for their own actions. In this case, the scapegoat is astrology. It isn't fair, especially when we understand that the heavens reflect earthly movements. Responsibility lies with the human who creates the action, not the heavens that reflect it. No matter what celestial energy is floating around at any given time, all humans have free will and can choose to behave badly or not.

Because I am associated with a lot of card readers and astrologers, I know of one client who used to call an astrologer now and then and tell her, "This isn't a good day for me. The moon is in Cancer and I'm always such a bitch." Then she would proceed to act like an utter, nasty idiot. My friend didn't buy it, and I agreed with her.

I was also disappointed in the acquaintance, because she prejudged an entire system of study for one silly reason. I would have respected this person more had she said, "I don't understand astrology. The concept escapes me, but I am sure there are many people who benefit from it." As it was, it made me wonder about her judgment on other matters, and I eventually distanced myself from that person.

Back to checking out the aspects when contemplating magickal operations. Use your pocket astrologer to see which planets are having a pleasant conversation on the day in question and which ones have declared all-out war. The following will help you in your determinations with moon energy and assist you in understanding how aspects can be read.

Moon Conjunctions

Moon conjunct the sun: Good. This happens during the new moon. Lots of growth, harmony, and intellectual stimulation.

Moon conjunct Mercury: Good. High level of intellectual activity. Both the head and heart are working together rather than fighting with each other. High level of communication as well as intuitive strength.

Moon conjunct Venus: Good. A great time for romance. Emotions are balanced. There is heightened sensitivity in anything creative. Social activities are in full swing here and will be a success.

Moon conjunct Mars: Challenging. A high level of aggressiveness. Impulses reign from violent to merely moody. Outbursts of temper tantrums to all-out knock-down drag-outs. A good aspect for courage.

Moon conjunct Jupiter: Good. Generosity is the keynote here. Health is revitalized and individuals normally have a good outlook on life.

Moon conjunct Saturn: In between. Although opportunities present themselves and hard work will be rewarded, there is a strong predilection to stinginess, timidity, and inadequacy. Self-esteem is not at its high point.

Moon conjunct Uranus: In between. Impulsiveness is sailing here. Sudden changes and unexpected events may rock or right the boat. Emotional tension could be high, as well as a need to step out and do something different.

Moon conjunct Neptune: Good. Excellent psychism here; religious revelations, harmony, but may lead to gullibility.

Moon conjunct Pluto: In between. Another line of impulsiveness, though perhaps more subtle. A need, perhaps, to build walls.

Moon Sextiles and Trines

Moon sextile/trine the sun: Good. Harmony and a sense of floating through the Universe. Strong desires do not occur here.

Moon sextile/trine Mercury: Good. Down-to-earth communication. Horsesense is most evident. Excellent timing for media, sports, business, etc.

Moon sextile/trine Venus: Good. Harmonious energies afoot. Increased interest in romance and the arts.

Moon sextile/trine Mars: Good. Lots of get-up-and-go. High energy and much activity. Opportunities both in business and home.

Moon sextile/trine Jupiter: Good. Nice, peaceful energies both in business and at home.

Moon sextile/trine Saturn: In between. Benefits available, but duties must be fulfilled and promises kept. Gains made through keeping things in order.

Moon sextile/trine Uranus: Good. Excellent time for psychism, spirituality, religion, and power. Ambition is strong. Inventiveness is high. New friends are now available.

Moon sextile/trine Neptune: Good. A imaginative time, sort of dreamy. Good time for pathworking meditations, dream recall, using the imagination in the arts, and problem-solving.

Moon sextile/trine Pluto: In between. Strong emotional conflicts will bring better results.

Moon Square or Opposite

Moon square/opposite the sun: In between. Full moon. How you handled yourself in the new moon phase determines how this aspect will affect you or your magick. You could be on the ultimate high or wading through the epitome of low.

Moon square/opposite Mercury: Challenging. Poor time for matters of communication. People's brains aren't connected with their logic. Reasoning is poor and emotional whims will become more important than they should.

Moon square/opposite Venus: Challenging. Domestic difficulties may arise. Moodiness, tendency to hold things inside rather than communicate. Possible difficulties with material things and purchases. Not a time to socialize.

Moon square/opposite Mars: Challenging. Tempers flare to violence. People are nasty, picky, and stingy.

Moon square/opposite Jupiter: Challenging. Overspending is likely. Stealing, poor financial investments made. Possibility of spiritual doubts and overindulgence in food, drink, or prescription drugs.

Moon square/opposite Saturn: Challenging. Depression possible. Bad judgment possible. Lack of flexibility.

Moon square/opposite Uranus: Challenging. Obsessions surface now, both odd and unusual. Possible accidents. Restless, uncommunicative energy afoot.

Moon square/opposite Neptune: Challenging. Deceptive energy weaving here. A tendency to run away from problems and be emotionally willful and stubborn—to be a pain.

Moon square/opposite Pluto: Challenging. Secrets abound when the moon hangs with Pluto. Jealousy is prominent and a sense of uneasiness prevails.

The Minor Magicks

Now that you know all this great stuff about the moon, let's begin with the little magickal procedures, which aren't really so little. The actual performance of minor magicks can take as little as thirty seconds, once you gain strength, ability, and confidence. However, like any good procedure, even minor magicks require some type of careful planning at some time. For example, although I can usually stop a bloody nose in less than thirty seconds (see *HexCraft*), it did take study and practice on my part. I worked up to this level of skill through a series of steps. And that's the point here. One of the major complaints I've heard is that modern magickal books do not carry advanced workings. What many fail to realize is that it is not the complication of the procedure, but the finesse with which it is done that makes it advanced or beginner in application.

I listed the minor magicks earlier in this book, but for sake of clarity, let's go over them, one at a time. As a reminder, before any magicks are performed, the working Witch checks his or her chosen divination system to inquire as to the results of the working and the extent of the situation.

Petition Magick

This is by far the easiest of the minor magicks. It requires, of course, a piece of paper, a sacred space, and your altar or altar stone. (You know, that big flat stone I keep telling you to drag around.) Petition magick is used alone for a minor magickal application and as an added procedure in full rituals. Petition magick can be used for a little problem or a whopper. The size of the difficulty has nothing to do with the ease of the spell. You can do this type of magick in sacred space or a magick circle, depending upon the severity of the problem or size of the need.

To Perform

Go to your altar and write down the problem or the needed result on a piece of paper. Burn appropriate incense to get your magickal self revved. Play some soft music, if you like. Verbally ask for guidance or the result you desire. Burn the paper. Wait for the result. Third-degree Witches use this procedure when asking to be blessed with the Eyes of the Spirit when dealing with clerical problems. Another variation is to place the paper on the altar in a spell box or jar until the desired result manifests. Then the paper is burned to seal and stabilize the result.

Petition magick is good for problems in which you do not feel the need, or do not choose to use any other type of magick. You may feel that throwing magick at a problem will not solve it, and seek the correct way to move. Sometimes we are so close to a situation that not even our divination skills serve us well due to our emotional involvement. Many working Witches forget the punch petition magick carries. Unlike other deities who are too busy to worry about their children, the Mother always listens. She may not give the expected answer, but She always cares for Her shining ones.

❀ Your Work ❧

Project 1: With the spell outline, perform a petition magick application. Record your results.

Project 2: Plug your work into a conjuration that includes your altar devotion, a circle casting, and quarter calls designed by yourself.

The Eight Gates of Light and Dark

The Gates were covered in the last chapter. Included also in this category are simple mind-programming techniques, neuro-linguistic programming, and hypnosis (both self- and guide-induced). Chants, too, are found in this arena, as is verbalizing to use the throat chakra. Pow-Wow artists use this type of magick, as well as the technique of sacred breath. Although you may snort, many packages on the market, such as the Silva program, are helpful to the working Witch. Valley of the Sun Publishing also carries an array of helpful tapes on topics from healing to past-life recall. Both I and my children have used them with success. My father, an alternative Christian, worked with me through the Silva tapes, and we have both enjoyed better lifestyles because of them.

Candle Magick

Working with candles is a simple or complex minor magick, depending upon the rite or ritual you perform along with it. Candle magicks can be used alone, in sacred space, or combined with folk magicks for practically any type of human situation. Candle magick works on the following principles:

The color of the candle
The type of oil you use to dress it
The sigils you carve (or do not carve) upon it
The sort of divinity you call as you light it

You can make candle magick complicated, if you like. This involves the array of colors, deities, oils, and the use of timing. There are five-day candle spells, seven-day candle spells, nine-day candle spells, Tarot candle spells, astrological candle spells, and planetary candle spells. Timed spells require a specific number of candles to be burned on a specific day or number of days, at the same time each day for a set period of time. A whole ritual can be written around a candle spell. In short, there is no end to your ingenuity in working with candle magick. It is fun, inexpensive, and it works.

Candle spells usually involve chanting or a poem-like charm, as well as raising energy. Most Wiccan students are taught candle magick early in their training in order to give them confidence when they continue to the more difficult aspects of various magickal operations.

Candle magick is versatile and is used by adepts to center and focus. Black, red, and white are the primary candle colors, and you will find that Witches who have been working for many years stick with these colors and don't worry about the others. Part of this is due to practicality and their excellent visualization skills, while still using the magickal colors of their ancestors.

In all fairness to the magickal community, I know a few working Witches who do not use candles at all and scoff at the interesting things you can do with them. What you believe is entirely your business. Remember that the Wiccan way is not to rain on someone else's magickal parade. If someone is tied to candles and their magick and you are not, so be it.

I've got another story for you. I pulled a fast one on my students. At the end of their first year, I gave them two massive tests—one on our traditional studies, and one on general Wicca 101. They had to pass both examinations with a ninety-six percent. If they failed, they had to do the whole year over again. To say the least, terror ran high in my dining room.

The Wicca 101 test takes four to five hours to complete, depending upon the individual. I spent a great deal of time grading the tests. When I gave them back, of course they compared their tests with each other, at which point I was greeted with a chorus of questions on the candle correspondence section. No one got any wrong, but many had different answers, which was supposed to be an impossibility since that part of the test was match the candle color to what it stands for in magick. A set number of colors with a set number of correspondences were given.

"You all got them right," I said, "because you need to experiment and find what works best for you." As an example, Bats may use orange for money because she sees money as something to earn, therefore it comes to her through tasks she performs, and not through a gift or a break in her taxes. Orange, then, to Bats, is the color of money. Black Isis sees healing as blue, because to her, all illness begins by an attack on the spirit. Blue is the spirit color.

The moral of this story is another Wiccan mystery: To each person the world of mundane and magick alike are singular in personal association. Because each person is different, things in books, or teachings from others, may not apply or work well for everyone. Uniqueness is the foundation of our religious belief and our magickal practices—to be different is an exalted state. If we all served alike, we all would not need to be on this plane at this time. Each must follow his or her own path and carve his or her own destinies. We are individuals, who in wisdom, learn to meld our differences into the One.

Unlike other Wiccan and magickal books, this one does not contain a color correspondence chart for you to refer to. It is time you experiment on your own and discover how and why each color vibrates for you, your needs, and your desires.

⚜ Your Work ⚜

Project 1: With the spell outline, perform an application of candle magick. Record your results.

Project 2: Plug your work into a conjuration that includes your altar devotion, a circle casting, and quarters calls designed by yourself.

A Candle Spell for Psychic Attack (by Diane McDonough)

My first instinct is to just charge and burn lots of black candles to absorb negativity and burn all trash-can energies away. My other choice is the "if momma ain't happy" spell. Grab a red candle, a black candle and white candle (or any three things that burn). Caress these, chanting "if momma ain't happy, ain't nobody happy, so make momma happy all the time." This is best performed alone or with people of similar understanding, because it seems to need that foot-stompin' wild-woman energy to really get the spell moving. While at first glance this may seem blatantly manipulative, it is a form of shielding, blocking negativity, and making the performer a focus for positive energy. Besides, it is fun to do. When this entertainment pales, put the candles someplace where they can burn undisturbed to send the energy out and about. Friday morning is a great time to do this spell, as it sets the framework for a great weekend under the astrological energies of Venus. The full moon also works well, if you would like to wait for a special moon phase. For longest effect, make this exercise a seven-day full moon spell. It will build a strong, positive shield of energy around you.

Cord Magick

Magick with cords is another simple magickal operation that can be used together with the Gates, candle magick, and petitioning. Cord magick entails the following:

Choice of cord color
Choice of cord length
Choice of a disposable cord or one you use over and over again
Choice of divinity

Standard cord magick uses a red, white, or black cord thirteen inches in length, with the intention of giving it away or disposing of it when you are finished. Of course, you can certainly work with every color of the rainbow or something in between—that is your choice and depends upon your own experimentation.

Cord magick requires the magickal operation of charging. Each knot is charged as a charm or chant is recited. Disposal of the cord depends upon the purpose of the spell. If it is to banish negativity, you would bury it immediately. If it is for healing or drawing something toward you, keep the cord until the job is done, then release the magick and burn the cord.

The knots are done in the following manner:

1------6------4------7------3------8------5------9------2

An example:

By knot of one, this spell's begun
By knot of two, my words are true
By knot of three, it comes to be
By knot of four, power in store
By knot of five, this spell's alive
By knot of six, this spell is fixed
By knot of seven, the answer's given
By knot of eight, I meld with fate
By knot of nine, the thing is mine!

There are three types of cord magick. The thirteen-inch cord, as indicated above, is explained above.

The second type of cord magick is used by traditional Witches. The Witch takes his or her cord of measure (which was given to him or her at the time of initiation—though sometimes it is kept by the High Priestess at the Hearthstone Coven) and uses it to access the group mind of the coven and tradition. This group mind can include lineage, ancestry, or the present group of people who make up the tradition or coven. The initiation cord is used to draw more power to assist the Witch in the task he or she is performing. This cord of measure is extremely important, as it is marked with the initiate's blood. When the initiate dies, the cord is to be buried with him or her. If this is not possible, the initiate is expected to have covered this in a will, stating that the cord should be sent back to the original High Priestess, who is then to ritually bury the cord. This cord of measure is white and slender in thickness (¼" to ⅛").

The third type of cord magick is also employed by the traditional Witch; however, a solitary Witch can use this type of magick, as I will explain in a moment. First, let's get the general information out of the way. When one enters a tradition with a degree system, often nine-foot cords in various colors are given to the initiatiates according to their station. For example, a first-degree Witch may wear a white cord, a second-degree wears a white cord and a red cord, and the third-degree wears the white cord, the red cord, and a black cord. Some third-degree Witches only wear the black cord. This is a matter of preference within the tradition.

The degree cords are knotted at three feet, six feet, and nine feet (at the end). A loop is then tied to the opposite end of the cord. If you were outside and needed to measure a three-foot circle, you would place your athame in the ground through the loop, making it easy to measure a perfect three-foot circle. The procedure is similar for making a six-foot (some traditions say seven-foot) or nine-foot circle. (The three-foot circle is for solitary work; the six- or seven-foot circle is for two to four people; the nine-foot circle is for larger groups.) As one moves through the stations (or degrees), the new cords are tied together at the three-foot, six- or seven-foot, and nine-foot marks, as well as wound together to make the loop for measuring. These cords are mich thicker than the cord of measure, and are worn at all traditional and open functions, unless clan law dictates otherwise.

Some traditional Witches link these initiation or station cords together in a ritual setting to manifest a desired end, as an asset for either the group as a whole or for a group member who is ill or needs special attention. When the result has been achieved or the rite done, the cords are taken apart and returned to their respective owners. This means that each cord must be marked before the technique is employed. Many traditional Witches mark their cords with amulets, talismans, or gifts from other magickal people. I have seen skull beads, animal claws, silver bells, equal-armed crosses, and Pagan rosaries used in this way, to give a few examples.

These station cords can also be used individually. To work with the Gates of the Underworld, only second- or third-degree station cords would be used, to access the properties that those stations represent. As another example, a third-degree Witch can use cord and knot magick to employ the eyes of the spirit with the third-degree cord. If it is a process of inversion, then the second-degree cords would be used. If it is an application of learning and study, the first-degree cord would be employed.

Can a solitary work this final type of cord magick? Yes. However, I would be very careful here as your cord will not denote a station in training or a degree level, but a link between yourself and the Universe. This cord should be nine feet long and fashioned by your own hand. It can be plain, multicolored, have thingies hanging on it—it doesn't matter, because it is your cord. Before using the cord, like any other tool, it should be cleansed, consecrated, and blessed. If you don't know how to do this, again, find a Wicca 101 book to show you how. This out of the way, what do you do with the cord? For starters I would work with this cord for personal fulfillment and self-esteem matters. The number of knots you employ should be an uneven number for banishing unwanted influences (or habits) in yourself, and an even number of knots to pull desired traits toward you. Remove the knots when the desired result is obtained, or leave them there to remind yourself that you have completed something wonderful.

❁ Your Work ✿

Project 1: With the spell outline, perform an application of cord magick. Design a rhyme. This makes the spell personal. Perform the magickal application, and record your results.

Project 2: Plug your work into a conjuration that includes an altar devotion, a circle casting, and quarter calls you design.

Gem Magick

Very popular in the eighties; the use of gem magick seems to have simmered down a bit with many working Witches in the nineties. Gem properties are easy for a beginner to master and help build both self-confidence and self-esteem. Gem magick includes work with crystals, gems, and precious stones. It can be used in conjunction with any of the aforementioned magickal operations, or alone in the form of jewelry for a variety of purposes.

Gem magick entails the following:

Choice of a stone to match the operation

Charging and programming the stone[4]

Experimentation is the key to gem magick, and this type of magickal operation is usually light. Workings for protection, continued health, self-esteem, confidence, ease in thinking, and gifts of refined speech and ideas are all small but good, solid foundations needed by the working Witch. Examples include creating a good environment (rose quartz); getting rid of negativity (amethyst); protection (smoky quartz); etc. You will have to study and experiment to determine what gems work best with your energies, which meld with you, and which are not in sync with your energy pattern. Certain gems can be mixed to make a tuned operation. For example, you could carry rose quartz and amethyst together. Be careful which stones you mix. They are like anything, people and animals alike, in that their energies may simply not attune to a need or desire.

Gem magick can be used with any of the previously listed magickal operations. Gems can have a mind of their own. If they feel they have no more to

---

4. If you do not know how to charge and program a stone, please refer to any Wicca 101 text that covers gem magick.

give to you, they will disappear. If they only needed a rest, they will come back. If they want to go to someone else, they will tell you.

Every working Witch should carry two lodestones: One to manifest the things he or she needs (or to draw things toward you), and one to dispel psychic attacks, break negative shields, and ward off unpleasant energies.

❀ Your Work ❀

Project 1: With the spell outline, perform an application of gem magick. Record your results.

Project 2: Plug your work into a conjuration that includes your altar devotion, a circle casting, and quarters calls designed by yourself.

Element Magick

This magick uses the five elements, as working Witches understand them: earth, air, fire, water, and Spirit. The pentacle is used here as the sacred symbol of commanding the elements and should appear prominently, either in your mind or on your altar when working with any (or all) of the elements. The magick of body, mind, and spirit are tied to both the pentacle and the energies it commands. All must be pure and working in unison for the operation to succeed.

Element magick can be physical or mental. For example, in Pow-Wow, the element of fire is represented by a healing stone you acquire yourself. Once cleansed, consecrated, and empowered, the candle flame and the energies it represents are instilled into the stone. No actual fire need be available when you are working with the Divinity stone (which is what the healing stone is called). It is now the Divine representation of the element of fire in its healing form.

Some working Witches argue that the pentacle is ceremonial in nature, and is not needed in the art of the Craft. The use of the star, however, dates back beyond Christianity, to the time of the stellar cults. Stars were also prominent in Egyptian magick (the Goddess Nuit). Stars symbolize sacred or celestial fire, and can be associated with the Craft need-fires and balefires (the representation of stars on earth—therefore melding the energies of earth and heaven together: heaven being the fire, earth being the wood used to feed the fire and sacred breath, oxygen, to grant continuance to both).

If you are uncomfortable with the star, it is okay. Try the triskele instead (see illustration), which has a compendium of meanings, including the three faces of the mother, the three faces of the father, or the three stars that collided to create our Universe. There are many more associations. Do some research and discover them for yourself. You will not be disappointed.

The Black Forest Clan Ritual of the Elements

Supplies: Your altar; an item representing each of the four elements (for example: salt, water, incense, a candle); illuminator candles (or simply use daylight); the center stone (a flat stone in the center of your circle); a small cauldron or bowl to contain the need-fire; oil for self-anointing.

Setup: Before the ritual, check all your props and supplies. Place the flat stone in the center of where your circle will be. Set the cauldron on the stone. Light the needfire, saying:

> *O creature of fire*
> *Wake this night/day*
> *To my needs.*
> *Shine forth through the Universe in protection and strength.*
> *By the essence of your eternal flame*
> *Link me to the power of my lineage.*

Ritual: Perform an altar devotion, a salute, and cast the circle with your athame. Say:

> *Elemental powers hear my call*
> *I pull in positive vibrations*
> *For protection and unity.*

> *North, East, South, West*
> *Come ye now*
> *At my bequest*

> *Circle round*
> *This sacred place*
> *By Witch's blade*
> *This circle's made.*

Call the quarters: set all the quarter items on the altar. Begin either in the North or the East (it is your choice). Pick up one item at a time. Go to the appropriate quarter, intone the call, raise the item before you, then move to

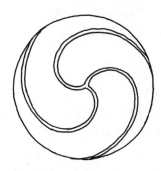

The Triskele

the center of the circle and place the item on your center stone. Repeat the procedure until you have called all the quarters.

> I, _____, son/daughter of the Shining Ones
> Raise this creature of earth
> To bring forth the stability and strength of my ancestors.
>
> I, _____, son/daughter of the Shining Ones
> Raise this creature of air
> To bring forth the wisdom and knowledge of my ancestors.
>
> I, _____, son/daughter of the Shining Ones
> Raise this creature of fire
> To bring forth the power and passion of my ancestors.
>
> I, _____, son/daughter of the Shining Ones
> Raise this creature of water
> To bring forth the love and intuition of my ancestors.
>
> I, _____, son/daughter of the Shining Ones
> Raise my arms to the essence of Spirit
> To bring forth communion with the positive forces of the Universe.

Attunement: sit in the center of your circle, next to your representation of the elements. Pick up the element representing the North (in this ritual, we chose salt). Shut your eyes and taste the salt. Allow your mind to wander into the realms of the North. Say the following:

> I open myself to the power of the North
> The enchantments earth
> I become one with the earth.
> I become one with the North.

Concentrate on the presence of the element of Earth in your circle. How do you feel? Anoint yourself with the element.

Move to the next element (East, air). Pick up the representative of the element and shut your eyes. Breathe in the incense, imagining that as it enters your body it is transmuted into the Divine essence of that element. If it helps, think of a corresponding color. Say the following:

> I open myself to the power of the East
> The enchantments of air
> I become one with the air.
> I become one with the East.

Concentrate on the presence of air in your circle. Anoint yourself with the element by passing the incense around your body. How do you feel?

Move to the next element (South, fire). Move your hand close to the candle flame (no accidents here, please). Shut your eyes and try to hold the image of the flame as long as possible. Say the following:

I open myself to the power of the South
The enchantments of fire
I become one with the fire.
I become one with the South.

Concentrate on the presence of fire in your circle. Anoint yourself with the element by passing the candle around your body. (Be careful.)

Move to the next element (West, water). Imagine the God and Goddess touching the bowl, infusing it with their Divine energies. Shut your eyes. Touch the water with your hand. Put a little of it on your tongue. Imagine you are the divine essence of the element. Say the following:

I open myself to the power of the West
The enchantments of water
I become one with the water.
I become one with the West.

Concentrate on the presence of Water in your circle. Anoint yourself with the water. How do you feel?

The last element, Spirit, does not need a prop. Sit quietly, shut your eyes, and envision the positive essence of the Universe descending slowly to the top of your head, then drifting down to your shoulders, covering you to your toes.

I open myself to the power of Spirit.
The enchantment of divine love.
I am one with love.
I am one with the Spirit.

Concentrate on the presence of Divinity in your circle. Anoint yourself with oil. How do you feel?

Conclude the ritual. Thank the elements for their participation. Do a closing salute, close the quarters, and draw up the circle. Clean up, and carefully record your experiences.

Trance and Magick

Throughout this text we have talked about trance, altered states of consciousness, self-hypnosis, and meditation in little swallows. I did this on purpose as these subjects do not go down easily all in one gulp. Let's plow away any confusion on the levels of the mind right now and be done with it.

Level number one is often called Beta. (Beta the name for a type of brain wave.) You are in Beta during normal, daily functioning. This is the turf of the conscious mind. You have normal motor control over your body when you are in Beta.

Level number two is called Alpha. Everybody talks about Alpha, to the point where you think it is a pet rather than a brain wave. Many occultists tell you that the best magick is done in Alpha; what they don't bother to tell you is what Alpha is and when Alpha occurs. They also don't tell you there are different levels of Alpha. When you are closer to Beta, you, of course, are more aware of your surroundings. When you are closer to Theta (the next level after Alpha, or level three), you are less aware of your surroundings.

When are you in Alpha? When you are daydreaming, when you are watching television, and get this one—when you are eating. That's right, your brain often slips into the Alpha state when you are eating. See, all this time you thought you had to be half-dead to reach the Alpha state or so magickally adept you don't even cast a shadow.

The Alpha state occurs when the following conditions are met:

The body is relaxed

The mind is relaxed

The spirit is relaxed

Most ritual magick is done in high-level Alpha (very close to Beta) because you need to walk around and do things. Most meditation and path-working is done at the lower end of Alpha and even into Theta.[5] (Theta is the state you experience right before you slip off to sleep. The sleep state is called Delta, for those of you who can't resist knowing that detail.) Theta, according to some experts, is where psychic activity is most prevalent. Many occultists believe that with practice, one can reach Theta as quickly as one reaches Alpha. I agree, but that is a discussion for another book.

Now, before a wonderful reader writes me a letter: Yes, I know that in hypnotherapy the levels of the conscious mind are alertness, daydreaming, moderate trance, and deep trance, moving into the sleep cycle. Those labels, however, are for hypnotherapy, not for magick.

Alpha is the turf of both the conscious and subconscious mind. The further down in Alpha you go, the more the territory is claimed by the subconscious mind. In Theta, the ground belongs purely to the subconscious, so it is logical that psychism would be at its height here.

It is true that the best performance of a magickal application is when you are in the Alpha or Theta states, but I wouldn't have an anxiety attack wondering what state you are in during a magickal application. The levels of the mind are natural—simply relax and let your higher mind be your guide.

Major Magickal Applications

Major magickal applications are called such because you must first know how to perform many minor magickal operations to mix with them or you must

---

5. If you find yourself "disappearing" when in meditation, then coming back and wondering where you went and what happened to you, don't have heart failure. You were not abducted by aliens, rather your higher mind took a trip to gather information for you. This information is often catalogued in your subconscious mind, ready to access when you need it by the use of your intuition or feelings.

have attained some degree of expertise in study related to the application. Each application requires a lesson. Some of the applications require months of study; others (such as Pow-Wow, herbal, Tarot, and runic magick) are best performed with at least a year's study and experimentation or when you are comfortable with your knowledge of that particular art.

Tarot Magick

Requirements: A Tarot deck; knowledge of the Tarot. Beginners should refer to Janina Renee's *Tarot Spells,* Llewellyn Publications. Advanced practitioners should develop their own correspondences.

The cards are used to create visual representations at various points in the spell. Although the energies of only one card can be employed, it is common to use from three to seven cards to draw a particular path to a desired outcome. Minor magicks employed are usually candles, chants, charms, petitions, and gems. Tarot magick is versatile. Everything from finding lost pets to getting money paid that is rightfully due you falls under the realm of this major magick. It can be done either in sacred space or employed in a ritual. The choice is yours.

Herbal Magick

Requirements: A working knowledge of both the medicinal and magickal applications of plants; a supply of herbs, both fresh and dried. Beginners should refer to *Cunningham's Encyclopedia of Magickal Herbs,* Llewellyn Publications. Advanced practitioners should develop their own correspondences as well as build a sizable library on the medicinal value of plants, for medicinal information lays the foundation for magickal applications.

A few interesting books on the subject are:

The History and Folklore of North American Wildflowers by Timothy Coffey, Facts on File

Garden Flower Folklore by Laura C. Martin, The Globe Pequot Press

Aromatherapy for Common Ailments by Shirley Price, Fireside

Rodale's Illustrated Encyclopedia of Herbs, Rodale Press

Culpepper's Color Herbal, Sterling Publishing Company

The Healing Herbs by Michael Castleman, Rodale Press

The Complete Aromatherapy Handbook by Susanne Fischer-Rizzi, Sterling Publishing Company

Herbs are used in conjuring bags, poppets, dream pillows, loose, in incense, and medicinally, in both fresh and dried forms. Knowledge of correct medicinal applications is extremely important and lays a framework for magickal work. Equipment such as storage containers, a mortar and pestle, and bags are necessary. Herbal magicks are used in conjunction with minor magicks, such as candleburning, chants, charms, and petitions. Plant application is a major magick because of the compendium of knowledge needed to use all resources available.

Herbal Invocation/Spell (by Autumn Raindancer)

> *Earth-born stone*
> *of brilliant hue*
> *Such energy makes*
> *dreams come true.*
> *Blend and grow*
> *with human desire*
> *amidst candles that*
> *throb with radiant fire.*
> *Herbs of life*
> *planted with passion*
> *mesh with these*
> *and begin to fashion*
> *realities just and*
> *understood.*
> *My magick*
> *for the highest good.*
> *And if my Goddess*
> *does agree,*
> *then manifest!*
> *So mote it be!*

Talismanic Magick

Requirements: A working knowledge of any magickal system, which may include Wicca, Druidism, ceremonial magick, etc. Any 101 book on the above subjects should have a short section on talismans for beginners. Advanced practitioners should see *The Lesser Seals of Solomon,* Samuel Weiser.

Talismanic magick, especially where ceremonial applications are used, is a definite art in and of itself. It takes patience and a mind for the meticulous. Knowledge of magickal alphabets, planetary correspondences, and angelic forces is needed, as well as familiarity with various sigils. Study is required to learn when, why, and how to create. Many minor magickal applications are often included as well, including colors, candles, elements, moon magick, drumming, and chanting.

Magickal Alphabets

Requirements: Knowledge of a particular magickal alphabet. Beginners should choose one alphabet and learn it thoroughly before advancing to others. Try *Buckland's Complete Book of Witchcraft,* Llewellyn Publications. Advanced practitioners should be able to write anything in their chosen alphabet, but don't expect to have your letters read by the recipient, should you be so adventurous to write to someone in your magickal language to show what you know. Your letter will most likely find itself trashed in quick order or burned, if the recipient is wary of its contents. In some Craft traditions, first-level students are required to learn one complete magickal alphabet and be able to translate their entire Book of Shadows into a secret, magickal tome.

Although magickal alphabets could be considered a minor magick, systems such as the runes (whether you are using the Witches' Runes or the German/Norman/British ones) can delve quite deeply into magickal applications and require a great deal of study. Magickal alphabets are used with minor magicks like petitions, candles, mental programming, and moon magick. (A small selection of these alphabets can be found at the end of this chapter.)

Sympathetic Magick

Requirements: Knowledge of the signature system. Beginners should check any Wicca 101 book or information on folk magick. Advanced practitioners should know at a glance what signature is to be used for any situation. Practice and study separates the beginners from the advanced practitioners here.

Many Witches these days overlook the value of sympathetic magick and become involved in ceremonial machinations, believing that because the latter contains more steps and length of time to conduct than the former, it makes it better. This is a mistake. Most situations that a working Witch faces, for good or ill, can be dealt with through sympathetic magick. Pow-Wow is a course in sympathetic magickal study, and takes time to learn.

> *It is an ancient idea that Providence has provided in the natural world, all the cures for man's and woman's ills. And the cure, usually a plant, but sometimes employed by other methods, can be recognized by its signature whether this be in color, shape, size, or smell ....*[6]

We can thank individuals like Albertus Magnus (fifteenth century) and Nicholas Culpeper (sixteenth century) and their interests in magick, astrological correspondences, and plant relations for keeping such folklore alive and kicking right into the twenty-first century.

---

6. *The History and Folklore of North American Wildflowers* by Timothy Coffey, Facts on File, Inc., 1993. Page 17.

Ritual Magick

Of course, both beginners and advanced practitioners are involved in ritual magick. Here, the advanced practitioner is not considered adept because he or she has more toys or steps, or a volume of words memorized to spring from his or her mouth at every moment. Not true. Advanced practitioners are well aware of the amount of advanced planning that is required. The actual performance may last five minutes, perhaps even less, but all the movements, timing, and whatever else is needed are accurate, with no mistakes (most of the time). Use minor magicks in ritual.

Cauldron Magick

This type is more a mixture of minor magicks and the knowledge of signatures rather than an application in itself. There are several types of cauldron magick:

Ategenos (regeneration)
Wisdom
Chaos
Plenty

Each type has its own deity attributes and signatures. We will discuss cauldron magicks further on in the text. Why? Because it's my favorite and I'm writing the book.

Now, I know what you are thinking. Can Silver do all these things she has written about? To paraphrase an author by the name of Sidney Hook: "Many challenges confront the working Witch, and I am confident I have not successfully met them all." No Witch worth his or her broomstick can claim to excel at each and every one of the minor and major magicks listed, though I've known a few who come pretty darn close.

Choosing the Right Spell for the Job

Let's face it, there are about as many spells and techniques for performing acts of magick as there are Witches. That's the fun and interesting part of magick, after all. There is a variety of means to meet an end and you need not be exceptional in every variety available—only a few will do. Your first consideration when gearing up for any type of magick is determining the size and particulars of the situation. Then you can decide what type of magick to use and how strong it has to be.

Unfortunately, most people, including Witches, are not very observant. One skill working Witches must practice is the willingness to watch what is going on around them—to take the time to see the big picture, rather than a close-up view. If you decide to be as closed as a clam, be prepared to be side-swiped by the biggest ocean liner in your sea. (Yes, I've gotten creamed on occasion.) In the mundane world, be more observant. Use all your senses. Be aware of global, national, and local news, as well as what is going on with your friends and family. Don't, of course, believe everything you hear, but do be aware. Whether you like it or not, you are a part of the human condition. You can contribute either positively or negatively, but you can't contribute at all if you don't know what the heck is going on. Listen to people. Keys to life and spirituality are everywhere around you.

All adept working Witches I have met use some type of divination system as a prelude to magick and ritual or to keep tabs on what is happening around them. There is nothing wrong with throwing the bones to find out why your sister has left her normal prim and proper lifestyle and has ditched her kids and nice husband in favor of a long-haired, double-tattooed, triple-nose-pierced dude in leathers. Especially since now you've got the kids. This is not poking into someone else's business. My motto is: If it affects you, find out what the heck is going on. Don't hide behind an ethical argument that doesn't exist.

Let's look at another outline. This one is for choosing and performing the right spell or working for the situation at hand.

A. Phase One
    1. Outline the problem on a piece of paper.
    2. Read it to yourself several times.
    3. Clarify, if necessary.
B. Phase Two
    1. Determine if this is a long-term or short-term situation.
    2. Throw the bones (cards, runes, peek into your crystal ball, whatever).
    3. Record the results.
    4. Do you need more clarification to continue? Probably, if the answer was negative.
    5. Throw the bones again if there was any doubt.
C. Phase Three
    1. What mundane work can be done in lieu of or in conjunction with magickal work?
    2. Write a list so you don't forget.
D. Phase Four
    1. Choose the appropriate magickal operation (minor or major).
    2. List other minor applications.
    3. Determine the correct phase and aspects of the moon.
    4. Determine the correct day of the week.
    5. Determine the correct hour of the day.
    6. Determine the correct deity energy.
    7. With all of these chosen, check how many of these can you employ together given the time you have available (is this an emergency?).

8. Will you perform the working in sacred space, or cast a circle?
9. Will you do a simple rite or a full ritual?
   a. What circle casting will you use?
   b. What quarter calls will you use?
   c. What sacred energies will you invoke?

F. Phase Five
   1. Gather all necessary tools.
   2. Ground and center.
   3. Perform the altar devotion.
   4. Move into the sacred space, ritual, or rite procedure.
   5. Perform the magickal operation.
   6. Close the operation.

G. Phase Six
   1. Ground and center.
   2. Clean up.
   3. Record what you did in your magickal journal.
   4. Wait for results (if this is a time spell, repeat if it is not successful).
   5. Deactivate (see Chapter 8) any magickal items with honor once the spell has come to fruition.

Let's put it all together. I'll use a real example so you can follow what I did and understand the outcome.

❀ Your Work ❧

Project 1: Employ the outline above in your work. Keep records of both your achievements and your failures.

Project 2: Perform the Black Forest Clan Ritual of the Elements. Record your experience.

Project 3: Choose a magickal application in which to excel. Go for it! Each full moon, note your advancements or difficulties. Do a small ceremony each month to enhance your progress. Write the ceremony yourself; make each one different. For example, the ceremony for the first month could be entitled "Beginning Gifts." In this ritual, you would ask for the appropriate knowledge to get you started, stamina, determination, intuition, and so forth.

The Case of the Questionable Boyfriend

"This is Naomi," burbled my answering machine at midnight. "We have a major problem here. I need to talk to you as soon as possible. Call me in the morning. My number is—"

I rolled my eyes at the answering machine, but did not move my lazy behind off the sofa. Lots of people call me at strange hours because I'm hard to get hold of. Although Naomi sounded stressed, I did not detect panic. It could wait until morning.

At 8:00 AM, I brewed a cup of chamomile tea—my all-time favorite stress reducer. I had a big day scheduled with several tarot readings and appointments. Besides, the children were home for the summer and four balls of human energy are hard to take on any given day. I called Naomi and scheduled an appointment for 8:00 PM (yes, my days are very long). Rather than listening to an explanation on the phone, I told her to wait until her appointment. It would give me a chance to do a reading without Naomi's emotions present.

Naomi Banister and her sister, Jessie, are regular Tarot clients of mine. Along the way, I've taught them various Pow-Wow techniques that have worked well for them. If they presently had a major problem, I knew they'd already done everything I'd taught them. (I like people like Naomi and Jessie; they aren't afraid to help themselves.)

The reading indicated general strife within Jessie's home brought about by a younger man. There was the possibility of drugs and bad mojo involved, as well as a connection to her daughter, who was planning a move soon. Deception webbed its way through the entire reading. That was enough to go on. I would let Naomi tell me the details when I saw her.

Precisely at 8:00 PM, the drama began to unfold. As I read in the cards, there was a disturbance in Jessie's home in the form of a 26-year-old boyfriend, unfortunately attached to Jessie's daughter. This young male was indeed unique. He had four protection from abuse orders out on him from four different women. Jessie's daughter knew about this, but she didn't care. She was in love. Personally, I thought there must not be a denser human being on the planet.

Once I picked my jaw up from the table, I began to throw the cards. We took a look at Jessie and how this relationship was affecting her both in the present and what the future may have in store. As the young man had taken up residence in Jessie's home, we had more leverage for magick.

Then we looked at our young buck. My, what a peach he wasn't. Psychologically unstable, bordering on dangerous for everyone in the home. He was also playing with negative magick, the little bugger.

Even Witches are capable of hatred, and I am no exception. Point me in the direction of an abuser or an idiot who tries to harm others through magick, and I'm the dark Goddess incarnate, no aspecting necessary. I know this about myself, and have learned to corral my emotions before they get out of hand.

To double check, I threw the cards again to determine where the little devil was aiming his magicks. Enchantments were the name of his game, spun toward any family member he could get. My first order of business was to deactivate the enchantment.

Here's how I did it:

The day: As luck would have it, it was a Mars day. That was fine. I would have preferred a Saturn day, but Mars would do. Mars, of course, is aggressive, full of action, strength, and courage, all the things needed to break an enchantment.

The moon phase: Again, I lucked out. We were midpoint in the disseminating moon. Perfect timing for banishing.

The moon was in Pisces: Karma and the revelation of secrets were definitely in place here.

The moon was opposite Saturn: Ah, this was tricky. Obsessions, especially weird ones, are revealed in this aspect. An opposition shows there is a need to balance forces. Energies need to be pushed and pulled. Attack, on the part of the Witch, was not the key. Positive magick was called for. The fact that the moon was trine the sun pushed a speedy resolution. Harmony was possible, but this particular trine was not as strong as I would have liked.

The moon was *not* void of course: This was good.

Sunset was at 8:30 PM. Hour 1 on Tuesday was Saturn.

I work a great deal with herbs. While my clients were present, I chose the following tools:

1 empty bottle
2 oz. vinegar
1 teaspoon aseyfatida (stinky stuff to break hexes and bust enchantments)
1 teaspoon nightshade (a poisonous garden creeper)
1 teaspoon vervain (to make it go)
1 teaspoon dragons' blood (more power)
a small piece of paper with the fellow's name on it
1 black candle to drive away negativity
1 pin
1 nail
1 screw
1 rattle

My clients were most familiar with Pow-Wow magick, therefore I worked within that system while they were watching. In my mind, I cast a personal circle around myself, then I put all the ingredients in the bottle, finishing by saying:

A pin to prick your conscience
A nail to nail you with justice

A screw to screw you with your own evil
May you not harm another soul.

I left the bottle uncapped and took it, the black candle, and the rattle over to my altar.

My clients would be in attendance for the first magickal operation. Therefore, I carefully chose a circle casting that was not a part of my tradition.

Altar devotion

Salute

MorningStar's Earth circle casting

Calling the four quarters to guard and participate

Invocation to the Goddess Ana

Charging the Witches' bottle to aid in breaking the enchantment and dispelling evil

Offering the bottle to the quarters for their assistance in expelling evil from Jessie's life

Capping the bottle and sealing it with black wax

Raising energy

Directing/expelling energy

Offering thanks to the Goddess

Dismissing the quarters

Winding up the circle

I knew the working was successful before it was finished. During the direction of energy, I felt a big *pop.* The minor enchantment was broken. After the ritual, Jessie remarked that she felt much better, as if a weight had been lifted off her shoulders. Jessie agreed to take the bottle and bury it at a cross-roads in the name of Ana that very night.

Before I go any further, let me assure you that people throwing black magick around (who are good at it) are a rarity. Even sickies who think they are good at it, usually aren't. This guy was a dabbler. He was playing at magick, nothing more. Like a flea on a dog, he was an irritation. It was his physical actions, his predilection toward violence, that worried me the most.

By now you are wondering, "Well, what about free will?" Yes, this was tricky here. Jessie's daughter, for whatever misguided reasons, did not give permission for this yo-yo to be removed from her life. Perhaps there was a lesson here for her to learn. On the other hand, any elder of the Craft can intervene when magick is used irresponsibly; that's one of the reasons they are elders. Finally, Jessie had given her permission to work for herself and her husband (who was aware of her appointment with me). They wanted the young man out of their house. That, we could certainly do.

I encouraged both Jessie and Naomi to continue their own Pow-Wow workings on the situation and agreed to do something about the unwelcome house guest. Now you are probably saying, "Why didn't she kick him out?" Because the daughter would trail along after this scumbag and Jessie feared for the girl's life. Jessie thought that as long as the guy was under her roof, she could keep an eye on him until the girl lost interest or saw him for what he really was.

It took three months for this drama to come to a close. Jessie's daughter and the boyfriend moved out within twenty-four hours of the spell; however, she returned home one moon cycle later, disgusted and disgruntled. The boyfriend was accosted by some unfriendly motorcycle types and disappeared, exactly three months to the day the spell was cast.

The key here, then, was revelation of the truth.

❀ Your Work ✿

Project 1: Apply the information in this chapter. Before attempting to put all the information together for a project of your own, consider carefully the spell outlines, the lunar phases, the magickal days, etc. Do a few dry runs by thinking of situations at random, considering what you could or could not do in a magickal working.

Project 2: Put it all together, complete with circle conjuration and quarter calls. Design a ritual using all the lessons learned in this chapter. Perform the magickal application. Record your results.

Magickal Alphabets[7]

English	Daggers	Passing the River	Celestial	Writing of the Magi	Old Persian Cuneiform
A					
B					
C					
D					
E					
F					
G					
H					
I					
J					
K					
L					
M					
N					
O					
P					
Q					
R					
S					
T					
U					
V					
W					
X					
Y					
Z					

7. This is not meant to be a definitive list of these magickal alphabets. Interpretations may vary.

Planetary Hours

Sunrise

Hour	Sunday	Monday	Tuesday	Wednesday	Thursday	Friday	Saturday
1	Sun	Moon	Mars	Mercury	Jupiter	Venus	Saturn
2	Venus	Saturn	Sun	Moon	Mars	Mercury	Jupiter
3	Mercury	Jupiter	Venus	Saturn	Sun	Moon	Mars
4	Moon	Mars	Mercury	Jupiter	Venus	Saturn	Sun
5	Saturn	Sun	Moon	Mars	Mercury	Jupiter	Venus
6	Jupiter	Venus	Saturn	Sun	Moon	Mars	Mercury
7	Mars	Mercury	Jupiter	Venus	Saturn	Sun	Moon
8	Sun	Moon	Mars	Mercury	Jupiter	Venus	Saturn
9	Venus	Saturn	Sun	Moon	Mars	Mercury	Jupiter
10	Mercury	Jupiter	Venus	Saturn	Sun	Moon	Mars
11	Moon	Mars	Mercury	Jupiter	Venus	Saturn	Sun
12	Saturn	Sun	Moon	Mars	Mercury	Jupiter	Venus

Planetary Hours

Sunset

Hour	Sunday	Monday	Tuesday	Wednesday	Thursday	Friday	Saturday
1	Jupiter	Venus	Saturn	Sun	Moon	Mars	Mercury
2	Mars	Mercury	Jupiter	Venus	Saturn	Sun	Moon
3	Sun	Moon	Mars	Mercury	Jupiter	Venus	Saturn
4	Venus	Saturn	Sun	Moon	Mars	Mercury	Jupiter
5	Mercury	Jupiter	Venus	Saturn	Sun	Moon	Mars
6	Moon	Mars	Mercury	Jupiter	Venus	Saturn	Sun
7	Saturn	Sun	Moon	Mars	Mercury	Jupiter	Venus
8	Jupiter	Venus	Saturn	Sun	Moon	Mars	Mercury
9	Mars	Mercury	Jupiter	Venus	Saturn	Sun	Moon
10	Sun	Moon	Mars	Mercury	Jupiter	Venus	Saturn
11	Venus	Saturn	Sun	Moon	Mars	Mercury	Jupiter
12	Mercury	Jupiter	Venus	Saturn	Sun	Moon	Mars

Conjuring by Circumstance

Keep my words positive, words become my behaviors.
Keep my behaviors positive, behaviors become my habits.
Keep my habits positive, because habits become my values.
Keep my values positive, because values become my destiny.[1]

This chapter covers various religious and magickal circumstances that may occur in the working Witch's life. I have provided a mix of techniques, spells, and assorted conjurations. All conjurations are a result of my own studies, or from the experiments of my Wiccan friends. Everything listed has worked for us at one time or another. Although I believe I have banged the following ideas into your head throughout this book, let's take one more look at some pointers:

Magick follows the path of least resistance.

Magick cannot be turned on and off like tap water. Sometimes you've got it, and sometimes you don't. Failure should lead to solution, not to depression. Learn to pick your magickal self up and try again, or perhaps try something different.

Never work magick for ill or harm to anyone, including yourself.

---

1. *The HeartBeat Magazine*, August 1994.

You need not follow the conjurations in this chapter precisely. In fact, I encourage you to use your own judgment. All I ask is that you carefully choose the changes you make, and double-check yourself before performance.

At the end of this chapter you will find four types of altar set-ups. By this time in your studies, you should be well-schooled on how to set up an altar. However, I thought it might be nice to share both traditional and eclectic set-ups for you to try, should you be so inclined.

Ategenos

To conjure transformation within yourself.

Moon phase: New, crescent, or first quarter.
Moon signs: Aries, Scorpio, or Pisces.
Day: Saturday.
Planetary hour: Saturn.
Deity: The Calliech.[1]
Colors: Purple and silver or grey.
Totem animals: Stag (East), bull (South), horse (West), bear (North).
Tools: Hearthstone or altar; cauldron; cup that fits in cauldron; one seashell necklace; one candle (your choice of color) for illumination.
Tea: Valerian and chamomile, ½ teaspoon each in teaball.
Incense: Patchouli.
Circle: Full ritual.
Quarters summoned and stirred: Guardians to protect/Ancients to assist.
Quarter opened: West only; acknowledge the others clockwise but do not open.

Conjuration

> *Ancient Ones draw nigh this night*
> *Circle around, assist my sight*
>
> *Guardians of the quarters, round I go*
> *East, South, West, North*
> *Help the energy flow*

---

1. The Calliech, should you not have met her before, is quite an interesting character. She is Scottish in origin, wears flowing grey robes, and has a blue face and long white fangs. She is the Keeper of the Gate of Ategenos (in Celtic lore) and a force to be reckoned with. Don't conjure Her unless you are strong of heart and pure of intention. According to Murray Hope in *Practical Celtic Magic,* 1987, page 49: "The worship of Cailleach covered the whole of the Highlands of Scotland where Her people were the Caldones or Kalendonioi. The Cailleach has a blue-black face, one eye in the middle of her forehead and projecting teeth, somewhat after the style of the Indian Kali. She carries a hammer and thunderbolts, and is protectress of horses, deer, pigs, goats, cats, snakes, and can be considered a sort of female Thor..."

Protectors of Witches, round once more
To seal this circle
I walk
I conjure
'Tis done.

Quarters

North, the Earth, the wind, the rain
Assist me now, upon earth plane

East, the sun, the wisdom, the sight
Assist me now, this sacred night

South, the power, the passion, the gift
Assist me now in this energy shift

West I open, the gates swing wide
I seek the answers that lie inside.

Invocation

Oh Mighty Calliech, Queen of the Underworld
I,_____, seek the transformation of self.
I feel that I am prepared to make this transition in my life
I am ready to assume the responsibility of the chosen.

Meditate for as long as necessary on precisely what you have chosen to change within yourself.

Dark Lady, Ruler of Rebirth
I fully accept the responsibility of my own actions in this lifetime.
I,_____, ask for the enlightenment needed to
(specifically state the transformation).

Meditate for as long as necessary again. The Calliech will appear in the circle or in your mind and give you the advice you need on your spiritual journey.

Working

Trace a banishing pentagram over the cauldron in which the cup of tea is placed. Place your hands over the cauldron and say:

I am the tool
You are the fire
Fill this cup
With all I desire.

Drink the contents of the cup, imagining the desired change flowing through your body.

Draw energy from the West, imagining the Calliech is sending it to you.

Chant:

> *Center and circumference*
> *Throughout and about*
> *Transcendence*
> *Transformation*
> *Change*
> *Everywhere and nowhere*
> *Within and without*
> *The void*
> *Immanence*
> *Beyond time*
> *the turning wheel*
> *Red, white, and black*
> *The cauldron*
> *Changes me.*[2]

Ground and center.

Closure

Thank the Calliech.

Close the West.

Thank the remaining quarters.

Pull up the circle.

Ground and center.

Clean up.

Banishing

There are many types of banishing, which will certainly affect what magick you choose to perform. Banishing bugs from your yard is not the same as banishing an unwanted person from your life. One need not do a full ritual to banish small things. As your skills grow, there will be fewer things in your life you will need to, or choose to, banish. Your studies move you into a more harmonious environment where many difficulties are banished as a result of your positive endeavors.

There are times, however, when a situation arises, and something must be done. For small matters, folk magick works well. An old Pow-Wow trick is

---

2. Spirit/Ether from *The Spiral Dance* by Starhawk.

to weave nettle and thistle together and throw it on the porch step of the individual who is bothering you. Often, the person will move.

Minor magicks such as the cord and knot, candle, and petition should serve your needs for little banishings.

Using meditation is also beneficial. Concentrate on banishing the negativity that has entered your life. Lock it in an imaginary chest. You can banish unwanted associations in the same way by sending your totem animal to ward a person away from you or your home. This technique works well for me. I call it the manifest spell, but it really is a matter of concentrated thought and a message carried by your totem animal.

To banish negativity from your home or work site without being obtrusive, there are stones you can either purchase or empower yourself, called spirit stones. These stones are said to carry the spirits of the ancestors (in general or in particular), such as lineaged ancestors. Sometimes the stones are taken from family grave plots to pull in the energy and assistance of those who have loved you or who were magickally inclined in your family.

Symbols, such as the banishing pentagram, are extremely useful and can be used in every banishing regardless of its complexity.

In folk magick, things to be banished are often anointed in vinegar, or a formula is made where specific herbs are steeped in vinegar.

Talismans[3] can be designed to banish things; Tarot cards or runes can also be used.

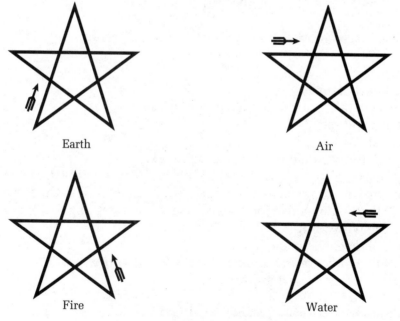

Earth Air

Fire Water

Banishing Pentagrams

---

3. A talisman is an object that has been magickally charged in order to bring something to the bearer. Such an item could be a gemstone to win a court case, or a drawing to put in your pocket that is designed to bring good fortune.

Remember to match the magick to the level of difficulty or persistence of a problem. If you try to banish something and it doesn't go away, you have a few things to consider:

This is a lesson, and you aren't getting it. Do a little meditation.

You are hitting the problem from the wrong direction. Try a new tactic.

The problem may be more deeply rooted than you first thought. Do a thorough divination. Call a magickal friend for some advice or a reading on the situation.

You may not be seeing the proverbial forest for the trees. You may be missing the problem. Look beyond the obvious.

Psychic blocks are in place, either created by yourself or by someone else. Remember, someone doesn't have to be magickally gifted to create a block. Everyone is psychic, some more than others, but many don't realize it. Even that creep at work who harasses you can have psychic blocks in place. Psychic blocks are not only created by the demented. Extraordinary individuals in their field or very spiritual people build psychic canopies around themselves, too.

Banishing Stalkers

Moon phase: Dark moon, full moon, last quarter, disseminating.
Moon signs: Scorpio, Pisces, or Libra.
Day: Saturday.
Planetary hour: Saturn.
Deity: Morrigan (a Celtic triple warrior goddess).
Colors: Black and red.
Totem animal: Wolf.
Angels: Most are acceptable for banishing work.
Tools: Spirit rattle;[4] bottle with cap; vinegar; garden nightshade; morning glory vines; garlic; dragons' blood; staff; two black candles; a piece of paper with the stalker's name on it (or "the person who is stalking me").
Circle casting with staff:
> *I conjure thee, O circle of art*
> *That you will be for me a place of fulfillment and power*
> *A fortress of strength and protection*

---

4. This particular rattle is a hollow gourd with a large hole in the top, with a netting of snake vertebrae or hard nuts around the outside of the gourd. Normally considered a tool of the elders, one used only by the mothers and fathers of a clan or the high priestess/priest of a coven. It is akin to the silver bough used by Druid clerics or clan leaders in Celtic traditions. The purpose of the spirit rattle is to call the Ancient Ones. It should not be held or touched by anyone other than its master or another elder.

Containing the necessary energies therein until I release them.
I move
in harmony
and in strength.

Quarters

Call them all; you are going to need them.

Self-blessing:

> *Earth my center*
> *Air my wisdom*
> *Fire my power*
> *Water my energy*
>
> *Ground me*
> *Guide me*
> *Empower me*
> *Move me*
> *To do what must be done.*

Call to totem animal:

> *Hellish howl*
> *Sharpened tooth*
> *Power of clan*
> *Now appear.*
> *Wolf of Silver*
> *Draw thou near.*
>
> *Welcome pet*
> *My dearest friend*
> *With snapping jaws*
> *My sign of kin.*
> *Bound forward beast*
> *In strength in truth*
> *The hunted turns to hunter.*
>
> *This night the ancients stalk their prey*
> *In protection of the innocent.*
> *My will be done by break of day*
> *and evil will be spent.*

Invocation

> *Great Morrigan, Goddess of Life and Death, Mistress of Clan justice.*
> *Wake now, my mother of trembling, and hear the chant of thy*

sister/brother who calls you from your slumber. Come forth and bring thy warrior spirit.

Put the dragons' blood, garlic (crushed), nightshade, morning glory vines, and the stalker's name in the bottle.

Pour vinegar over the contents of the bottle; empower the bottle and contents.

Working

Dark Morrigan on a Dark Horse
Ride with me tonight
Swirl thy soft cloak around _____
So he turns from me in fright.[5]

Chant with rattle:

Move away the evil
Move without a sound
Send back his nightmares
Morning glory bound.

Seal the bottle with black wax and inscribe your personal sigil in a wax puddle on the top.

With this sign I seal your fate
Back you go
To evil's gate.

Close ritual in the normal manner.

Clean up.

Bury the bottle off your property with an equal-armed cross inscribed in the dirt or at the foot of a black locust tree. (I do know a few ladies who keep the bottle around to shake every once in a while to make certain the stalker never returns.)

Chanting

Almost every spell book gives you a few chants, but no one ever tells you how you are supposed to feel or what you are to be doing while chanting. After all, you are only uttering words, how difficult is that?

There is an art to chanting, but you must find the art within yourself. Do you feel more energy when you chant fast or slow, soft or loud? Perhaps you like to start softly and end with a lusty note. Do you have the courage to let go while chanting, to let the rhythm vibrate? Relaxing into the beat will raise

---

5. You can find a spell for binding using the Dark Woman on a Dark Horse and her swirling cloak in *The Holy Book of Women's Mysteries* by Z. Budapest, Wingbow Press, 1989.

more power. Concentrating on the words will break the focus. Your mind must go beyond the language and into the Universe, which is why many students are taught chants in a foreign language. That way, they can't concentrate on the words once they learn to pronounce them.

The act of chanting uses the throat chakra. Divine energy can be reached through your transmitter, your voice. It is a call to the Universe for assistance. In magick, sometimes we get so wrapped up with mental and spiritual pursuits that we forget our voice can be heard and understood by the Universe, as well as by many positive entities within that Universe that we cannot see with the naked eye. Chants should be memorized for their maximum benefit and best performance. If you like to stick with small ones, that's fine. If more elaborate chants entice you, that's terrific. Use what raises the most power and the most self-confidence for you.

Along with chanting comes breathing. A natural thing, don't you think? Nope. The key is to relax through deep breathing before you begin the chant and to continue that breathing pattern while you are chanting. You become a balanced conductor, capable of pushing more power. This takes a bit of practice, but it can be done. Group chanting is extremely powerful, whether you are on the playground with your kids and don't like the looks of those fellows hanging around over there, or in a ritual setting with your brothers and sisters. The place is not important when it comes to chanting, the tuning is the ticket.

Chant For Inner Strength or When Faced With a Stressful Situation (by Autumn Raindancer)

I call the light of
golden rays
I seek protection
thus, I pray.
for heavenly forces
at my side
angels, sages,
spirit guides
or wolves who walk
with cunning skill
Come to my aid!
Come at my will!
Black bird soaring
light my path
so I am victim
to no one's wrath!
And when my
journey knows success,
all those who aid me
Goddess bless!

Cauldron Magick

From our sisters perched on their porches along the winding Appalachian Trail to our kin in Louisiana, magick in the Americas traveled along the Mississippi River, branching in every direction. I often urge my students to attend family reunions, chat with their grandparents and their friends, and delve deep into those family trees. You have no idea what kind of magicks are lurking there, dormant, waiting to flower in your hands.

In practically all Craft traditions, there is an item that is considered the focal point. Its meaning encompasses the core of the tradition. I've mentioned this information earlier under a footnote, but I want you to review it again, and consider its importance. Although repeated information can be boring, this is important for you to remember. The focal point for the British Traditional Witch is the wheel, and one is normally placed in the center of the altar. In Alexandrian and Gardnerian Traditions, you will usually find a pentacle, which has been adopted by most eclectic groups as well. In some traditions, such as the Caledonii, few props are used. You will not find their altars brimming with too many goodies. Other traditions, usually those born of eclectic groups, rely heavily on astrological symbolism. A disk of the zodiac may be found in the center of their altars. In the Black Forest Clan, our focal point is the cauldron, much like the need-fire of the Caledoniis. (As it should be, since that is where we originally came from.) Our unusual twist, of course, is that all of our elders practice Pow-Wow right along with our Craft techniques. For us, the cauldron encompasses the majority of our magick and is the foundation of our religious practices.

I mentioned before that in Celtic mythos, Dagda had the "cauldron of plenty" while Cerridwen had the "cauldron of knowledge, intuition, and wisdom." The Calliech, one of our primary Goddesses in the Black Forest, holds rule over the cauldron of change and transformation. The Morrigan carries the cauldron of passion and war, from whence she mixes and draws victory and all such matters of attainment.

In a ritual, quarters are represented in the following manner:

Dagda: North—Plenty, prosperity, stability

Cerridwen: East (some put her in the South)—Knowledge, intuition, wisdom

Morrigan: South—Passion, creativity, strategy

Calliech: West—Transformation, flow

Ana: Center—first mother of all

If you prefer more balance, then you can exchange Kernunnos or Herne for Cerridwen in the East, in reference to the Gunderstrup Cauldron.

The symbols at each quarter would have the cauldron as the primary base along with a secondary symbol, indicating the God or Goddess or element for which the cauldron stood. Dadga's cauldron can contain food or the fruits of harvest; Cerridwen's cauldron could contain feathers, ink pens, a holy book, or incense. The Morrigan's cauldron normally contains fire and the Calliech's cauldron contains water and ice—ice representing the crystallization of change or the normal refusal of humans to change, representing the idea that most change takes place slowly and deliberately. If you live near the sea, then seawater in the Calliech's cauldron would also be appropriate.

Casting the Cauldron Circle

Stir the air (with your hand, athame, wand, or staff) in front of you in a clockwise motion at any speed you like until you naturally stop. Remember that your visualization is the key.

I stir the magick cauldron
The circle bubbles
Into existence about me.

This Witches' pot
Stops time on the dot
The energy waits upon my command.

I call protective wolves to surround the circle.
I stir the Ancients to assist.
I summon the energy of the elements.

This circle is sealed.

Quarters

Greetings, Father Dagda
Spirit of Earth and plenty
Element of North
Please join with me this night/day.
As I stir thy cauldron, I request thy blessings.

Greetings, Mother Cerridwen
Spirit of wisdom and intellect
Element of East
Please join with me this night/day.
As I stir thy cauldron, I request thy blessings.

Greetings, Mother Morrigan
Ancient One of passion and might
Element of South
Please join with me this night/day.
As I stir thy cauldron, I request thy blessings.

Greetings, Mother Calliech
Ancient One of transformation and rebirth
Element of West
Please join with me this night/day.
As I stir thy cauldron, I request thy blessings.

Greetings, Grandmother Ana
She of a thousand names
The beginning with no end
Please join with me this night/day.
As I light thy need fire and request your blessings.

Invocation

The cauldron churns
It boils
It moves
Magick builds.
Come, Mighty Goddess
Ruler of all worlds
Join with me tonight/today
In the cauldron of my life.
So mote it be.

The focus of cauldron magick is, of course, the cauldron. Here is how I prepare my spell cauldron:

Cleanse, consecrate, and empower the empty cauldron. Draw a pentacle in oil, holy water, and salt on the inside bottom of the cauldron.

In a ritual you design, ask the Goddess and God to bless the cauldron.

Sprinkle a teaspoon of vervain (to make it go) and a teaspoon of dragon's blood (more power) at the bottom of the cauldron. Fill the cauldron three-quarters full with, yes, packaged kitty litter. It says non-flammable on the package, smells good, and is easily disposed of. It is also environmentally acceptable.

At this point, there are several directions you can take your cauldron magick. There are times when I will put a second, smaller cauldron in the big cauldron. This smaller cauldron could hold the following:

A tea candle
A selection of herbs
A potpourri burner
A poppet
Gifts to the Devas, Fairies, or Divinity
Water for divination

Around the smaller cauldron, I may place candles, flowers, knives, stones, runes, or tarot cards, all of which can be supported by the kitty litter. If someone comes to call at the wrong moment (which hasn't happened yet, but a working Witch thinks ahead), I can pick the whole thing up by the handle and put it somewhere out of sight. You may wish to use this type of cauldron in a magick circle and take it to each quarter, asking the blessings of the contents. As I said, use your imagination and I am sure you will have delightful results. If you are doing the same types of magick over and over again, such as abundance, harmony, etc., you do not need to dispose of the contents of the entire cauldron. However, if you need to stop gossip, for example, the large cauldron should be prepared again.

Stopping Gossip

1 cauldron, prepared and filled with kitty litter
1 black candle
1 small fire bowl
1 teaspoon yew berries[6]
1 teaspoon lobeila (gag root)[7]
1 teaspoon rosemary
the name of the individual causing the problem on a piece of paper
a few drops of alcohol

In the small bowl, mix the yew berries, lobeila, and rosemary. Beside the small bowl, in the kitty litter, place a dressed black candle to dispel negativity. Hold the paper with the evildoer's name on it and envision the person with his or her mouth sewn tightly shut and removed from your life. Put the paper in the bowl, sprinkle with a few drops of alcohol, then stand back and drop in a match. Poof! The problem is gone. Of course, you will need to raise energy by chanting, drumming, etc., and don't forget the magick circle or grounding and centering.

To Bring Love into your Life

1 cauldron, prepared and filled with kitty litter
1 red candle (for passion and to represent your life blood)
1 small fire bowl
1 teaspoon rose petals (for love)
1 teaspoon marigold (for strength)
1 teaspoon vervain (to make it go)

---

6. Yew is the tree of death. The berries are poisonous and should not be ingested.

7. Lobeila is a poisonous plant and should not be ingested. (See discussion of poisonous plants further on in the text.)

your name written on a heart-shaped piece of paper
a few drops of alcohol
1 drop of your blood (optional)

In the small bowl, mix the rose petals, marigold petals, and vervain. Beside the small bowl in the kitty litter, place the dressed red candle to bring love to yourself. Hold the heart with your name on it and imagine it is your heart, happy, safe, balanced, and filled with passion for life. You can put a drop of your blood on the paper. (This is an old practice to ensure sympathy, but is not necessary.) Put the paper in the bowl, add a few drops of alcohol, stand back, and set the mixture aflame.

Divination

Moon phase: Full moon.
Moon signs: Gemini, Sagittarius, Pisces.
Day: Sunday or Monday.
Planetary hour: Moon.
Deity: Diana.
Color: Silver.
Tools: Your divination tool, one candle (your choice of color) for illumination.
Tea: Valerian and chamomile, ½ teaspoon each in teaball.
Incense: Patchouli.
Quarters summoned and stirred: Guardians to protect/Ancients to assist.
Quarter opened: Your choice, depending on what type of divination you are doing—acknowledge the others clockwise, but do not open them unless you feel it is necessary.
Circle casting: Raise one hand over your head to the sky.

Lower one hand to your side, palm up.

Pull down.

Pull up.

Bring your hands together while you speak the following:

> *The circle appears*
> *It grows*
> *It encompasses*
> *It protects.*
>
> *Celestial Ancients*
> *Form a link between us.*

Star Bones

You will need nineteen bones. You can use animal bones (small ones), or create your own out of Fimo® or clay. Paint one of the following symbols on each bone.

- ☽ **Moon:** mysticism, dreams, intuition, psychic signs, inner self
- ☉ **Sun:** family, good health
- ☿ **Mercury:** communications, conversations, meetings, letters, phone calls, speed
- ♀ **Venus:** love, beauty, gifts
- ♂ **Mars:** conflicts, disagreements, powerful events
- ♃ **Jupiter:** money, possessions, property
- ♄ **Saturn:** spirituality, death, transformation, change
- ♅ **Uranus:** creativity, doubles the intensity of any bone it is near
- ♆ **Neptune:** subconscious, secrets, mystery,
- ♇ **Pluto:** groups, friends, socialization, parties
- ⚳ **Ceres:** the feminine principle
- ⚴ **Pallas:** keen insight and creativity of the mind
- ⚵ **Juno:** compatibility, partnerships, friendships, soulmates; also a mirror of events
- ⚶ **Vesta:** dedication, focus, goals, hard work
- ⚷ **Chiron:** modes of teaching, a key to knowledge, turning point of an issue
- ℞ **Retrograde:** a situation that appears to stand still, is declining, or going backward
- ? **Unknown**

One for the querent

One for the reader

On a large piece of poster board, draw a circle and split it into twelve equal parts (see illustration). Each pie slice will be labeled with an astrological house from One to Twelve.

First House: house of self

Second House: house of moveable possessions

Third House: house of streetwise smarts

Fourth House: house of family

Fifth House: house of pleasures

Sixth House: house of service to others

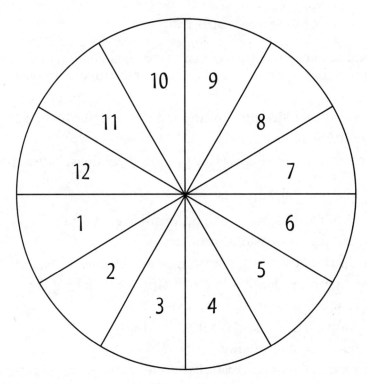

Star Bones Chart

Seventh House: house of partnerships
Eighth House: house of death and transformation
Ninth House: house of higher learning
Tenth House: house of career
Eleventh House: house of social business
Twelfth House: house of hidden secrets

Shake the bones and cast them onto the poster board. Use your intuition to interpret your past, present, and future.

Funeral: A Rite of Parting

Moon phase: Full moon.
Moon sign: Scorpio.
Day: Sunday or Monday.
Planetary hour: Moon.
Deity: Gubba.[8]
Colors: Blue, white, and silver.

---

8. What? You think I'm going to do all your work for you? Nope. Research this one.

Tools and supplies: Athame; bowl of water; hand towel; flowers; tissues; white floor covering; a picture of the loved one and something that belonged to him or her.

Tea: Valerian and chamomile (equal parts) ½ teaspoon each in teaball.

Incense: Frankincense.

Quarters summoned and stirred: Guardians to protect/Ancients to assist.

Quarter opened: West, the Gates of Death—acknowledge the others clockwise, but do not open them unless you feel it is necessary.

This is not a funeral as in body lying before you, tons of weeping, and psychological shell-shock. In our present society, Pagan funerals are not the norm. Many Pagans have loved ones who are not of the magickal persuasion, yet have been very close. Unfortunately, most services held for the dead in our standard religious structure do not nurture the one who grieves, but they complete a passing with concentration on the deceased or take advantage of the situation and scream hellfire and damnation to those living, and grieving, in the pews. (I've been to one of those—a disgusting display, let me tell you. Had I been the dead person, I'd have gotten up and walked out.) This leaves the magickal individual stuck without a proper grieving process.

I designed this ritual several years ago to assist grieving Pagans. It does not require the presence of the deceased body or ashes, and is normally done at least three weeks after the standard funeral. By this time, the grieving one has gotten over the initial shock and is beginning to come out of the daze of grief. Please note that the full grief processes lasts far longer than three weeks, but by this time the person is capable of sitting in ritual and is usually ready to say his or her final good-byes.

The prime focus of this ceremony is you—I kid you not. It is your strength, your compassion, and your soft words that will allow your friend to pass through this phase of his or her life and deal with the loss with the nurturing of the Mother and Father. To do this ritual effectively, you must be mentally balanced and healthy.

Before the grieving person arrives, you need to set up a special room where you will not be disturbed. Everything should be soft and comfortable. I decorate my altar in white, blue, and silver. I buy a vase of cut flowers for the occasion. Both the flowers and the vase will leave with your friend, therefore the vase should be new, cleansed, and consecrated. A bowl of consecrated water should be at the foot of the altar, along with a snow-white hand towel. A box of tissues needs to be nearby. (I often stick it under the altar, within easy reach.) In front of the altar I spread a large, soft comforter of white and blue, along with several large pillows. I choose soft music, often something by Enya, to set a peaceful, protected mood.

When your friend arrives, ascertain his or her energies. Your friend may be frightened, nervous, or even deadpan. You will need to regulate your energies accordingly, resonating to give what is needed at this time. Before you begin, sit and chat a while. Give your friend a cup of ritual tea to calm his or her nerves.

The ritual is simple. Begin with the altar devotion, cast the circle, acknowledge the quarters, then open the West quarter. Have your friend sit in front of the altar, supported by the pillows. Make sure the individual is in total comfort. You sit across from him or her.

Have the person hold his or her hands over the bowl of water and begin to gently scoop the water with your hands over the person's skin. As you do so, say that you are washing the pain and grief from your friend's body. Tell your friend to let go and feel the spirit of the Mother move within—feel Her nurturing energy. Your friend may cry at this time. That's okay. Keep going. When you feel you are finished, dry your friend's hands with the white towel. Draw in the energy of the Mother, then hold both your friend's hands in yours and place them on your chest. Allow the loving energy of the Mother to enfold you both. Again, your friend may begin crying, but that's what the tissues are for.

Ask the individual if he or she is now ready to say good-bye. If the answer is yes, then continue with the ritual. If your friend says no, then ask if he or she would like to meditate first. There may be a time when your friend says he or she does not want to continue. That's okay, too; just close it up in the usual fashion.

Check the soft music. It should continue through the next phase of the ritual. If you think there is a possibility of the tape running out, pop in a fresh one—don't take the time to fiddle with the rewind.

When you both are ready, you stand, then move to the West quarter. Your friend is to remain seated. Call upon Gubba and ask Her to open the Gates of the Dead and allow the deceased one to pass through to say good-bye to the loved one in your circle. Strange things may happen here, so you will have to be strong. Candles may gutter, it may get cold, things could go bumpity-bump, etc. Keep your cool and act like you have not seen anything. Turn to your friend, hand him or her the box of tissues, and say that it's time. Walk to the East, cut a door, and step out of the circle. Close the door and leave the room.

Give your friend ten minutes.

Return to the room, and wait patiently outside the circle until your friend acknowledges you. Ask him or her to cut a door to let you in. Although you could do it yourself, this is a signal from his or her subconscious that the rite is almost over and you are back to close the West quarter. If the person asks for more time, turn silently, leave the room, and return in another ten minutes. If your friend cuts the door, you know that he or she has has acknowledged the last good-bye.

Thank Gubba, ask her to take the deceased one back to his or her appropriate place, and close the West quarter. Sit with your friend awhile. Idle chatter is acceptable. When you are ready to draw up the circle, hand the flowers and vase to your friend. Say that these are to be placed on the deceased's grave. If your friend cannot get to the grave site, then tell him or her to throw the flowers and vase into a living body of water—save for one flower, which your friend should dry and put in his or her Book of Shadows.

Don't let your friend leave directly after the closure of the ritual. Sit awhile and talk about other things. Make plans to do something special together within a week or so (so you can check on your friend and make sure everything is percolating well in his or her life).

I wasn't kidding when I said you need to be of strong stuffings to do this ritual. I have had some truly bizarre visualizations and power surges when opening the Gates of Death. Be prepared. Your friend in the circle will not know what you are going through. Grief has a habit of deadening psychism and empathy. It is during his or her time alone that the person may (and this is a big may) experience otherworldly occurrences. One young woman told me that something kept tickling her feet. Another said she felt a gentle hand on her shoulder while she was crying. It wasn't me; I was in the other room with the kids watching television.

The Council of Elders

One sticky summer afternoon, I received a phone call from a very dear friend of mine who lives on the California coast, light-years from my little country town.

"There is a problem," he said. "I'd like to talk to you about it."

Whenever I get a phone call like this, three things happen: I grab a drink, sit back, and shut up.

"There is a group," said my friend, "that purposefully caused a great deal of discomfort with the city council. They stirred up a terrible fuss, and as a result a Wiccan group was harassed, threatened, and forced to appear in a council meeting."

"Give me the details," I replied. "First, who is the group with the hatchet?"

"Another Wiccan group."

"How disgusting!"

Sad, but true. Over the past several years, some Wiccans have managed to run amok. Of course, let's not get hysterical. In every religious structure, bad guys will lurk. Why should we be so different? I do admit, we get more than our share of drifters—those who are interested briefly, puff up and proclaim all sorts of things, then wander back into the mist of seekers. That's okay. Perhaps we had something to learn from each other.

It is not okay if those whose acts are in question commit a crime or purposefully hurt others for the joy of it, or to increase their personal popularity or pocketbooks. This is not acceptable in any positive religious structure. What can we do?

There is a great deal we can do. First, if you feel a Wiccan or Pagan has committed a crime, report it. Let the laws of our country do their work.

Second, if the individual is part of one of the old traditions, contact the person's Council of Elders and fairly indicate the problem. Don't be petty or sniveling.

Finally, if the individual is an eclectic, don't feel there is no one to turn to. There is, and here is how you do it.

Ceremony of the Ancient Ones

Gather all the facts and place all written information at the foot of the altar. Prepare yourself for a full ritual, including ritual dress.

If you are a traditional, follow your tradition's guidelines on altar set-up and ritual form. If you are an eclectic, use the basic Wiccan altar set-up, nothing more.

Moon phase: Full moon.
Moon signs: Libra, Virgo, or moon conjunct the sun (the new moon).
Day: Sunday, Monday, or Saturday, depending upon the issue.
Planetary hour: Moon, Sun, or Saturn (again, depending upon the issue).
Deity: Generic Lord and Lady, unless you belong to a tradition.
Colors: Black and white (denoting balance).
Supplies: Your staff (elders will use their appropriate tools).
Tea: Valerian and chamomile, ½ teaspoon each in teaball.
Incense: Frankincense.

Circle Casting and Quarter Calls

If you are traditional, follow the casting and call of your tradition. If you are eclectic, do the following:

> *I open my hand*
> *the circle*
> *grows*
> *encompasses*
> *protects.*

Throw it out to encompass you and stamp your foot.

> *Ancients of the North*
> *I call ye forth to sit in a circle of High Council.*

Be very patient and wait for their appearance. They will come.

> *Ancients of the East*
> *I call ye forth to sit in a Circle of High Council.*

> *Ancients of the South*
> *I call ye forth to sit in a Circle of High Council.*

Ancients of the West
I call ye forth to sit in a Circle of High Council.

Ancients of the Center
I call ye forth to sit in a Circle of High Council.

Stand in the center of your circle and light a need-fire[9] to represent the hearth and home of the Ancients.

Sit in the center of your circle.

I have convened this High Council to set before you a problem of serious nature.

Outline the problem.

Ground and center.

Close your eyes. Listen to the words of the Ancients. They will not fail you.

When you are through, bid the Elders good-bye, close up the circle, and ground and center. Rest assured that your problem will be dealt with fairly.

Obviously, contacting the High Council/Council of Elders is not a flippant thing to do. Only matters of the gravest concern, when you have nowhere to turn, are subject for these supreme beings. Through these council sessions, I have learned two important things:

1. We are not obliged to suffer the foolishness of others.
2. The world, despite its appearance of chaos, is quite ordered.

Modern Version of the Hand of Glory Spell

In Chapter 5, I told you about the Hand of Glory spell, originated by Albertus Magnus during the Middle Ages. Here is a modern version to use to stop criminals or criminal intent.

This is a heavy-duty working. This spell is not for the faint of heart or foolish Witch. If you use the working to harm someone, you will pay dearly. This magickal practice should be used only to control, then banish negative energies. This spell is said to be one of the most powerful sympathetic workings still in use today.

Moon phase: Dark or full moon.
Moon sign: Scorpio or Pisces.
Day: Saturday.
Planetary hour: Saturn.
Deity: The Hooded God.

---

9. Use a small cauldron or candle. If you are outside, you can build a small bonfire.

Color: Black.
Supplies: Five pounds of modeling clay; an item in sympathy with the criminal, or a photograph (if neither are available, write the criminal's name on a piece of paper); modeling clay tools; holy water; a black votive candle.
Tea: Yarrow.
Oil: Frankincense.
Incense: Musk.

Cleanse, consecrate, and empower all tools. Form a hand from clay. The model should be large enough that you can make an indentation in the palm to support a votive candle. Model the hand around the sympathy item.

Wipe the hand with holy water to smooth it. Let the hand dry.

Perform your normal altar devotion. Use the circle casting and quarter calls of your choice. Dress the black candle with your favorite oil. Light the candle and place it in the palm of the Hand of Glory. As you stare at the flame, concentrate on the criminal being caught by the proper authorities without harm to anyone. Burn the candle for about ten minutes each night for seven nights. Each time you light the candle in your protective circle, you are to visualize the perpetrator being apprehended by the proper authorities.

Hatred

We all experience it. Even Witches hate. The emotion is not easy to deal with. There are times when conflict arises because we force the issue. In other situations, we are swept up in the fray, not responsible, but somehow involved.

Working with hatred is a step-by-step process. Nothing you do for a few minutes, or even half an hour, is going to make you stop hating someone. Hatred is emotionally crippling if not dealt with properly. Often, one of the foundations for this emotion is fear. What will that person do to me? Why did he target me? How could she have insulted me like that? Hatred lowers our personal self-esteem. Hatred hurts.

Working Witches do not often experience pure hatred. Normally, they live balanced, peaceful lives, especially if they have been practicing their religion for awhile. All the worse, then, when hatred slithers, surrounds, and strikes. When one has gone quite a distance in harmony, chaos can be extremely unsettling, and we revert back to the way we were before we learned all the nifty secrets of the Craft. The first order of business when dealing with hatred is to connect with your religious base. I am not talking about rules and regulations, I'm talking about becoming one with the world around you. Connect with the Earth and put some distance between your hatred and yourself. This way, you will be able to consider all the ramifications logically, not like a drowning person in a sea of emotions using a toothpick for a life preserver.

Next, do something creative as an outlet for the emotions you are experiencing. Draw a picture (you don't have to be Rembrandt), write a story, compose some music, sew something, clean off your altar, go bowling, spend an evening at the races, go to a movie, it doesn't matter as long as it is productive to you. To resolve stress, you need to find an outlet; if not, total meltdown and possible illness later on stare you directly in the choppers.

Finally, ask yourself the final, all important question, "Will anyone in a hundred years give a shit about my present problem?" If the answer is no, then it is solvable. If the answer is yes, you've got a problem and I suggest you channel Ghandi.

Now let's get that problem in perspective. Hatred is best dealt with if you feel you can do something about it. It is when we feel our hands are tied or that our actions will be ineffective, and we falter. Our first steps do not have to be big ones—a piece at a time will do. My advice is always to begin with magick and end with magick, but be sure there are mundane actions somewhere in between.

There are some magickal people who claim magick should only be used as a last resort. Fine, if they want to wait until the manure is so deep they're choking on it, be my guest. To begin with magick is life-affirming and self-confidence building. Start by releasing the anger in a magickal environment. If you like, transmute it into positive energy and watch it drift away or send it to Earth Mother. Use affirmations; create small magickal items like a dream pillow[10]—take it one step at a time. Work through the problem on a mundane level as well. Do you need to contact an attorney, begin paying a bill with what you can, actively stay away from the next-door neighbor, etc.? If you mix magick, religion, and mundane actions, success is likely.

What if the problem is in your face? This is not as easy, granted, but solvable. First, decide as fairly as you can what would be the perfect, ultimate outcome without interfering in another's free will (of course, we are not talking about criminal activities). Work immediately, in full ritual, for that goal. Not all things can be planned; everyone gets hit with spur-of-the-moment difficulties. When that happens, the most important time to do the ritual is when you can. If you don't have time, make time. Follow up the ritual with positive meditation and affirmation. You will be pleasantly surprised at the results.

Putting Problems or Situations on Hold

This is an old Pow-Wow practice. Before you stop the wheels, I suggest you carefully consider why you want to put a halt to things. If it is because you wish to delay the inevitable, this is not a good idea. If you wish to slow things

---

10. A dream pillow is a small pillow fashioned by you and filled with carefully chosen herbs to bring about the desired energies. Often used for sweet dreams, to ward off night terrors, etc., as the pillow is placed under your regular pillow, working its magick while you sleep. Be sure not to stuff your pillow with poisonous plants. I suggest consulting a copy of Scott Cunningham's book entitled *Magickal Herbalism*.

down to give you some time to think of the right action and there is no other way around it, then this is the magickal tidbit for you.

If tempers are high, the freezer is a very good place to chill them out. Write the situation on a piece of paper, wrap it in plastic, and put it in a small bowl of water. Put the bowl in the freezer. As the water freezes, the problem will go on hold, still circling, mind you, but in stasis. It is your responsibility to deal with the problem. When you are ready, melt the ice in a ritual circle and continue toward a positive working in ritual.

Separating Yourself from a Problem or Person

Small issues can be handled in a magick circle, whereas larger issues may need a full ritual. Think carefully which is best for the situation. You will need two black candles, a long black ribbon, black gloves, scissors, the cauldron containing a small amount of alcohol, and a silver bell. Cleanse and consecrate all items. Dress the candles to send negativity away from you, then light them. Hold each end of the ribbon and name the ends. Pass the silver bell over the altar several times, until you feel you are in tune with the Universal energies of love and peace. Anger is not a luxury afforded to you in this situation. Put on the black gloves and say:

> *I call upon the energies of Universal balance*
> *I call upon the ancient energies of my people*
> *I call upon the living essence of the Morrigan*
> *I call upon the mighty presence of Herne*
> *Underworld and heaven*
> *Land and sea*
> *I waken these energies unto me.*
> *Witness now that I renounce and sever*
> *Break bonds and connections with* _____
> *By all powers that are One Power*
> *May the great sisters of karma now weave anew*
> *And separate me from you*
> *As I will, so mote it be!*

Cut the ribbon:

> *It is so.*

Light the cauldron. Burn both pieces of ribbon.

The Magick of Poisonous Plants

Before you start kicking up a ruckus, let's talk a bit about poisons. Logically, everything you can't eat is poisonous. Should I consume my computer, it

222

would kill me. If I had a hankering for the bleach under my sink, that would kill me, too. So, if you think I'm giving you some cool information in order to hurt someone, forget it. That's not the point here. Because I am going to talk about toxic substances, I'm going to give you the standard disclaimer: Neither I nor the publisher are responsible for what you do with toxic herbs. Now, disclaimer out of the way, let's get down to business.

Why would we worry about poisons at all—isn't that walking the line of negative magick? No. Have you ever heard the old adage, fight fire with fire? It is the same case in a poisonous situation. For example, in my Pow-Wow studies I found that lobeila (gag root) is a primary ingredient in a poppet for stopping gossip. There are several types of lobeila. The kind planted around the front walk of my house is very delicate, with tiny blue flowers. I would never be stupid enough to eat it, but it is planted there to keep nosy neighbors at bay. Its reaction time is one to several hours. Other magickal applications include assistance in divination if the herb is dried, put in a small pouch, and stored with the divination tool. Eyebright, also a member of the same family, can be steeped and painted on magick mirrors.

To the right of my property I have planted a line of yews. Yew is also poisonous. It is a tribute to the dying God. I would never be dumb enough to consume it. In late summer, red berries appear. These berries are excellent in bottles for stalkers (the blood of the God) or in magick where you are trying to banish a bad habit, or leave a sacrifice (as in the berries) at a household shrine. Everyone familiar with gardening knows not to eat these berries. Any magickal spell with yew should work within one hour, thus the major popularity of the plant.

Poisonous plants grow everywhere, often in wastelands, by super-highways, in fallow fields, and along the fence or garage. Garden-variety nightshade, a poisonous plant, grows practically everywhere in central Pennsylvania. I often use it in Witches' bottles. Any poisonous plant gathered at midnight during a full moon or during its native astrological sign gives the plant strong magickal connections.

In magick, how do you know which poisonous plant to use? First, you would check the plant's correspondences (See Scott Cunningham's *Magickal Herbalism*). Second, define your problem. Do you need something that works quickly or slowly? Now we get to the toxicity level of the plant. Just how deadly is it? Many plants are poisonous, but not fatal. For example, poison ivy only causes skin eruptions and itching. I once, very carefully, used a poison ivy leaf to give me the itch to finish a project on time. (Luckily, I am not affected by poison ivy. I suggest, if you are allergic to poison ivy, that you use disposable, rubber gloves to take a cutting. Remember, the oil of the ivy causes skin irritations, even after the plant has been disposed of. Anything the plant touches may cause a problem.) The spell did help me to complete the project ahead of schedule.

I cannot stress enough that you should be careful when working with any type of poison or mixture of poisonous substances. Don't eat it. Don't put it near children. Don't let it sit around without a label on the bottle, jar, or bag.

My rule of thumb at home is that once I make and use a poisonous mixture, I destroy what is left over. That avoids any mistakes or accidents.

Note: The reaction times given below for each herb are both physical and magickal.

Belladonna (deadly nightshade/garden (common) nightshade): Originally introduced as a drug. All portions, including the leaves, berries, and especially the root system, are extremely poisonous. Belladonna is Italian, meaning beautiful woman. During the Renaissance, women applied an extract of this plant to their eyes to dilate their pupils and give a wide and beautiful gaze.[11] Nightshade can be used in beauty magick (do not apply it to skin or ingest it). One could make a poppet with a touch of nightshade to enhance beauty, or place a tiny amount in a sachet and sew it to a ladies' garter. To banish, keep in mind the toxicity level. Nightshade's reaction time is several hours to several days. At one time, it was used medicinally to treat ringworm and running sores, or to cool inflammations. It is not recommended for this sort of use today. Astrological correspondence: Saturn.

Hemlock: The demise of Socrates. This plant grows along the roadside in the United States. It looks a little like a cross between a delicate fern and a hemlock tree. All parts of the hemlock, especially its fruits, are considered lethal. It works to paralyze muscles, therefore, in magick, should you wish to paralyze a situation, a bit of hemlock would be added (not ingested, of course). Reaction time is a few hours, therefore this is a fast-acting banishing plant. At one time, hemlock was used as a sedative and is not recommended for domestic use (that means us, guys). Astrological correspondence: Saturn.

Lily of the valley: This beautiful spring plant that we often consider being in a faery-tale garden is actually a deadly beauty. Found in North America, Canada, and Britain, its bell-shaped flowers are familiar to most gardeners. Causing intense irritability, it is used magickally to stop harassment (and never, of course, ingested). Reaction is immediate. If you have someone who is really raking you over the coals, put a sprig of lily of the valley on your desk or dining room table and ask its Deva to stop the negativity coming your way. According to *Culpeper's Color Herbal,* the plant is used by drug companies for medicinal purposes. Lily of the valley has a long and colorful history. It is mentioned in medieval Christian legend as the result of Mary's tears at the foot of the cross. Lily of the valley is the flower of Ana, the first Goddess, and was at one time used extensively in medicinal cures. Pennsylvania Dutch couples plant the lily of the valley in their first garden to promote longevity of the marriage, and you will find a touch of this flower in many bridal bouquets across the nation. Astrological correspondence: Mercury.

Wolfsbane (monkshood): Several varieties are found in the United States and Canada. When wolfsbane blooms on a full moon, beware. Wolfsbane is excel-

---

11. *Deadly Doses: A Writer's Guide to Poisons* by Serita Deborah Stevens, Writer's Digest Books, 1990. Page 43.

lent for redirecting predators coming after you. Reaction time for this plant is ten minutes to several hours. A very magickal plant, even the old werewolf movies featured its legend. The entire plant is poisonous, especially the leaves and the roots. When drying, the roots give off fumes that cause giddiness. It is suggested to use only the flowers in magick. Astrological correspondence: Saturn.

Rhododendron, azalea, mountain laurel: You will find these plants everywhere. These bushes have a reaction time of six hours. The Greeks found the honey from bees that fed on azaleas and rhododendrons to be poisonous.[12] These plants are great for protection. My husband bought me an azalea bush for the birth of each child, asking the Deva to protect our children from accidental poisoning and watch our property as they play. Astrological correspondence: Venus.

Elderberry: Although cooked elderberries are fine, the leaves, bark, roots, and raw berries are considered poisonous. The American Medical Association says it has found no documented cases of poisoning from this plant.[13] Reaction time is several hours. Elderberries are great for "elder" magick, times in which you wish to call the Ancients. An offering of elderberries on the altar is an appropriate form of magick here. There is a difference between the elder and the dwarf elder, the latter which is most poisonous. Astrological correspondence: Venus.

Black locust: Oral legend in my state cites the black locust as the burying place for things of evil—and the protector of the Dark Goddess. If someone has done you wrong, say the oldsters, bury the person's name at the foot of a black locust. This is a very messy tree. If you are in a messy situation, give it to the black locust to take care of it. A friend of mine had several of these trees in her yard. A nasty storm blew up with high winds and bolts of lightning, which hit two of these trees and scattered them everywhere. Her property was magickally protected—the locust trees made a sacrifice for the rest of the property. The black locust is poisonous, with a reaction time of one hour. It is found from Georgia, through the Ozark Mountains and into Pennsylvania.

Celandine: Another poisonous plant, used in Pow-Wow magick to break hexes. It is deadly and its reaction time is approximately fourteen hours. Celandine is still used medicinally by herbalists. Check the appropriate herbal books for this information. There are two types, greater and lesser. Greater celandine is associated with the sun and Leo. Lesser celandine is coupled with Mars.

Morning glory: All parts of this plant are poisonous; it carries the nickname Devil's guts.[14] Morning glories come in a variety of colors, and once started,

---

12. *Deadly Doses: A Writer's Guide to Poisons* by Serita Deborah Stevens, Writer's Digest Books, 1990. Page 50.

13. Ibid., page 63.

14. *Garden Flower Folklore* by Laura C. Martin, Globe Pequot, 1987. Page 177.

are fairly drought-resistant. Monks decorated their manuscripts with draw-ings of morning glories. Legend has it, Witches wrapped the morning glory vine around a poppet nine times to banish evil people, which was especially effective if done three days before the new moon. In magick, the morning glory can be used to bind, banish, or promote attraction to something or some-one. Of course, spelling someone against their will is a major Wiccan no-no. My father planted a canopy of morning glories and moonflowers all along my porch to protect our Witches. The idea was to catch any negativity before it could hit where the group does a great deal of their work. (We sit on the porch in the summertime.) Astrological correspondence: moon.

Strawflowers: These plants like sunny dry spots and will hold out until the last frost. Although poisonous, strawflowers are a plant of longevity. Want something to last? Use strawflowers in your magick. At one time, the plant was used medicinally, but it is not suggested for domestic use these days. This is the flower of Samhain, the Witches' flower of the dead, signifying the transition from one type of life to another (the afterlife). Astrological corre-spondence: the sun.

Psychic Self-Defense
(by Lord Merlin)

This little spell was donated to you, my Witch-reader, by Lord Merlin of the Black Forest Clan. I've not met anyone who casts a spell better than he does, especially for protection or money.

When you feel that your shields are down or determine that a little extra protection is in order, try the following:

Moon phase: New, crescent, first quarter.
Moon sign: Aries.
Day: Saturday, Monday, Friday (depending upon what type of protection).
Planetary hour: Saturn, Moon, Venus (again, depending upon what type of protection).
Deity: Vesta.
Colors: Red, white, and black.
Supplies: Incense burner, black candle.
Oil: Sandalwood oil, uncrossing oil, jinx removing oil.
Incense: Sage and cedar smudge stick.

Carry the unlit incense around the room in a clockwise direction and visual-ize a trail of light from the stick. Repeat with the unlit candle. Say:

> *Vesta of the loving light*
> *Guardian of hearth and home*
> *Goddess of fire and purity*

Prepare the way for this sacred rite
Send your loving protection from above.

Vesta of peace and loving charm
Banish any intent of evil or harm
Send protection unto me
As I will, so mote it be!

See your circle fill with white light and allow the helpful angels of this light, especially your guardian angels, to aid in your spell.

Light your dressed candle and place your hands above the flame, high enough so you won't burn yourself (pain is not necessary for this spell). In your mind, see the protecting light from Vesta empower your hands, which in turn, empower the candle. Envision the candle glowing with the white light of Vesta's protection. Say the following:

Elementals of fire
This request of thee I ask
No evil may be bound to me
No ill will or evil intent shall touch me
Banish all negativity
As my will, so mote it be.

Feel the energy from the circle come alive, removing all harm and negativity from within you, draining away from your body. Fill your body with the protective energy of Vesta, drawing your visualization from the candle. When you feel you have collected enough energy, say:

Uriel, Gabriel, Michael, Raphael, please aid me in this spell.
Guardians of the protecting light
Be me with this day and all the night
Guide me away from harmful intent
Return ill will from where it was sent
Aid me in peace and serenity
As I will, so mote it be.

Pull the protective circle around you. Draw anything left into your body. Allow the candle to burn until it is consumed.

Protection Spell
(by Lord Merlin)

Moon phase: New moon, dark moon.
Moon signs: Aries, Pisces, Venus.
Day: Monday, Friday.
Deity: Herne.

Color: Purple.
Supplies: One piece of parchment (3" by 5"); dragon's blood ink.
Oil: Pine or sandalwood.
Incense: Pine or sandalwood.

Write your name nine times with the type of protection needed on the piece of paper.

Dress the purple candle. Place three drops of the same oil on the parchment. Hold the paper in your hands and visualize a vibrant glow of protection.

Light the incense. As the incense fills the room, imagine a circle of smoke. Ask Herne to enter your circle and fill you with protective strength.

Light the candle and place it over the parchment on your altar. Say:

> *Give me loving peace*
> *And protect me from harm.*
> *Aid me in this spell*
> *While I recite this charm.*
> *Cover me with love from the Goddess above*
> *Herne grant me protection, peace, and love.*
> *Return all the ruin addressed to me*
> *As my will, so mote it be.*

(Repeat nine times.)

Pull the smoke circle into your body, transmuting it into positive, healing energy.

Thank Herne for His presence.

Leave the candle burning until it is consumed.

Circle of the Devas

Moon phase: New moon.
Moon signs: Virgo, Leo.
Day: Friday, Sunday.
Planetary hours: Sun, Venus.
Deity: None.
Colors: Green or white.
Supplies: A wind instrument; a pendulum; ten stones, small or large, it is up to you; an aluminum or wooden tent stake (not a steel one).
Oils: Any floral.
Incense: Any floral.

Wash all the stones. Cleanse, consecrate, and empower to pull in Deva energy.

Instruct your pendulum which way you wish it to swing for the perfect spot.

Walk your property until you find the right place for the Circle of Devas. Take the ten stones (each stone representing a path of power) and circle them around the area you found. The area can be as large or as small as you like, though smaller areas are easier to maintain.

Build a small needfire in the center of your Deva circle. Be sure there is water nearby in case you have an accident. (Too many forest fires are caused by poor planning combined with human mishaps.)

Ritually bless the site.

Wait until either dawn or dusk (your choice). Dress a green candle with floral oil. In a pouch, pack the candle, the instrument you wish to cast a protective circle with, a lighter, a candleholder, and your wind instrument. (Note: If you don't want to deal with a candle outside, then you can build a small needfire and throw herbs into the fire for the same purpose.)

Go to the site, and cast the circle inside the Deva circle. Say:

> *I conjure thee, O circle of magick*
> *So that you will be for me*
> *A permanent home for the Devas of this land*
> *A meeting place of positive enchantment*
> *Filled with peace, prosperity, honor, and love.*
> *I stir the Ancient Ones of the East, South, West, and North*
> *To aid me in the erection of this circle.*
> *Thus do I conjure thee, O great circle of the Devas!*
> *As above, so below*
> *This circle is sealed.*

Pound the tent stake in the ground at the North end of the circle.

Invocation

> *Welcome, positive Devas of this land*
> *Only you may enter here*
> *I extend harmony and peace in friendship*
> *Join in celebration of laughter and light*
> *Growth and regeneration*

Sound the instrument now—or if you can, play a tune.

At this point, you can meditate, cast a spell, or simply enjoy the out-of-doors.

Closure

> *Farewell, O positive Devas of this land*
> *You may commune within this magick circle when ere you please*

Find protection, peace, and solace here.
May my love and good thoughts travel with you
Until we meet again.
Blessed be.

If you have a need-fire or candle burning, take care of it now. Do not take down the circle. Simply cut a door, turn, and seal it shut. When you return, simply cut the door to open, then enter. Each time you visit the circle of Devas, you should strengthen the magick circle.

The Traditional Wiccan Flame

This is the last conjuration in this chapter, yet one of the most uplifting practices for you to try. I saved it until the end, a gift of closure to you. Whether we are solitaries, traditionalists, or whatever, there are always times when we feel alone and need the protection and strength of others. If it is midnight, you don't call your Wiccan friend (hopefully) when you need to connect. Here is simple meditation, first inspired by the traditionalists, that you can use within or without ritual. The only props required are two candles, and you don't even need these if your meditation skills are half-decent. The goal is to spiritually connect with the essence of the Wiccan religion.

Place a candle in a candleholder (any color you desire) and in the center of a flat stone (remember your portable altar?). Set the other candle (with holder) off the altar. If you like, put some soft music on the stereo.

Cast a circle (your choice).

Call the quarters (your choice).

Sit in front of your stone. Light the candle. Imagine that the candle is the essence of the Wiccan religion, burning in the darkness of chaos.

Ground and center.

Pick up the unlit candle and imagine that you are the unlit candle.

As you touch your unlit candle to the one on your altar, imagine yourself connected mentally, physically, and spiritually to the essence of the Wiccan religion. Drink in this feeling. You won't forget it.

Place your newly lit candle beside the one on the altar. Take some time to meditate or simply relax. You may wish to do a divination, do a minor magick for self-improvement, etc. It doesn't matter. What is important is your connection to your religious belief.

When you are finished, close in your usual manner. Allow the candles to burn until they extinguish themselves. If necessary, move them to a place where they can burn undisturbed and you are sure they are not a fire hazard.

When the going gets tough, close your eyes and remember your experience with the Wiccan flame. Conjure it in your mind, step by step. This will be a great asset to you in your future challenges.

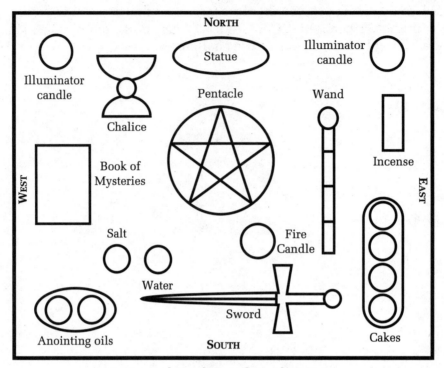

A General Traditionalist Altar Setup

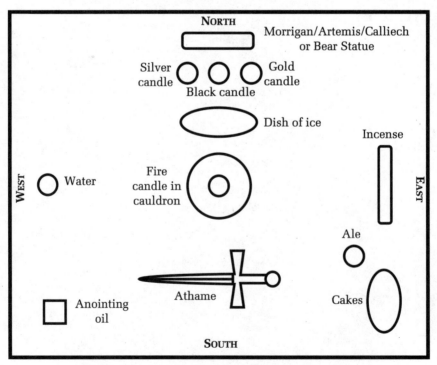

Black Forest Clan Sabbat/Esbat Altar Setup

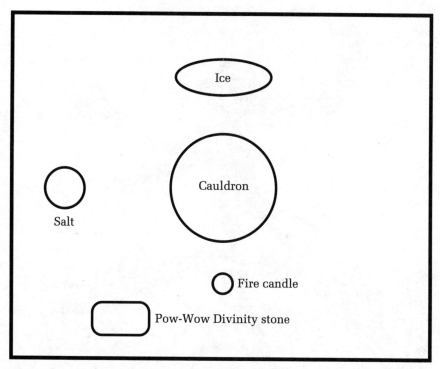

Black Forest Clan Solitary Altar Setup (Second and Third Degree)

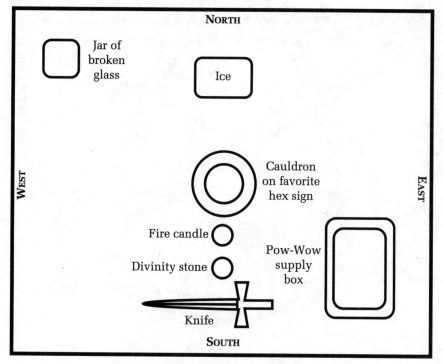

Pow-Wow Altar Setup

Season of the Witch

Conjuring Your Inner Self:
Know the Craft Community, Circa 2000

Once we've learned the basics of Wiccan beliefs and practices,
living our religion is, logically, the next step.
How we allow it to affect our lives is completely up to us.[1]

The Map of the Craft: You are Here

Within every human being is a touch of the Witch! You think I jest? Who has not dreamed of having secret powers beyond society's imagination? Who has not believed in fairies, ghosts, or magick when they were a kid? Who has never asked their mother or father if Dracula was real or if Peter Pan could fly? If you have answered, "Not me," put this book down and find a boring treatise on government today. If you can't be truthful with yourself, you'll never make it in the Craft, and probably won't have success in anything else.

In each person's life, there is a turning point, a time when that person's path lies in communion with the spirit or with the mundane. For some, the path to spirit and magick is shrouded with mist, barely discernible in the personal storms of life. For others, the veil parts, the mist lifts, and for a moment,

---

1. *Living Wicca* by Scott Cunningham, Llewellyn Publications, 1993.

they can see clearly the essence of the Divine. Which path you choose, or even what religion you choose as a vehicle to travel into Divine mystery, is neither right nor wrong. What does count is your positive interaction with the self, Divinity, and those around you.

Witchcraft (or as some prefer, Wicca), is a religion. It is a structure designed for individuals who feel a close affinity to the earth, the sky, and the waters, and energies of life. It is a set of life-affirming beliefs and practices. (Notice how many times I said life here?) Witchcraft is art and science that work interactively. As in any learning process, you can perform sloppily or well. It is your choice to pick up a book, blab a bit, and try to throw energy around. Or, with much perseverance, you can study, practice, and seek to attain perfection. The Craft, a term used by many Witches today, is what you make of it.

The most incredible aspect of the Craft lies in its versatility. There is no one right way to believe in it, nor is there only one set of instructions designed to use its gifts. It is the only religion I know that allows personal tailoring by anyone who practices it. Put it on—I mean, really put it on, and it fits like a glove. It moves with you, grows with you, and leaves you room for error without condemning you to a well-heated place. The Craft teaches you responsibility for your actions. Far too many individuals these days are willing to throw the blame for their transgressions on someone else, whether it is their parents, the school system, or a perverted friend. In the Craft, we say, "We don't buy it. You made the fire; you take the heat." It is as simple as that.

So, you are here, with me. With this book, we broomed into the next phase of your training. Did you have fun? Me, too. Do you think I jest? We all learn new lessons (and repeat some old ones that won't permeate our thick skulls) every day.

Stuff You Need to Know

Through the Wiccan/Pagan Press Alliance and other wonderful contacts over the past ten years, I've managed to pick up much information about the community. I've also discovered what most Witches know, and don't know. Most of the information in this chapter devotes itself to stuff that is good to know if you are a practicing American Witch. I don't feel I'm qualified to speak for Witches in other countries, though Canada has been most supportive to the WPPA. I hope this chapter will broaden your horizons of the current Craft community. It also will help you sort out the dabblers from "the real Craft," should you run into someone with a "Blessed Be" bumper sticker on the back of their Volvo at a fast-food restaurant (it can happen!). Even if you never plan to associate with the outside Craft community, at least you will have the knowledge of what is going on around you. Knowledge always helps the Witch at work to know which way to go.

Much of the solitary and eclectic work done today in modern Craft experienced its birth from traditional Witches. Some of these people are Doreen Valiente, Gerald Gardner, Alex Sanders, Raymond Buckland, Ed Fitch, Laurie Cabot, Scott Cunningham, Z. Budapest, and the Farrars. In the last fifty years, traditional Witches set the magickal and religious trends in our community. If we look at the community, most of its teachings and practices follow traditional flavors at some point. From traditional Craft sprang eclectic groups, churches, and the modern open circle. It is logical, then, that we investigate the environment of the traditional working Witch, without breaking any oaths, of course.

Now, before you roll your eyes and say, "Boring!" let's consider why the following information is important for you to see. I don't know about you, but as I was learning the Craft, I found many conflicting modes of thought. Traditionals didn't agree. Solitaries didn't agree. Eclectics didn't agree. I don't mean that in the good and bad sense, it was simply confusing. For myself, I set out to discover what points agreed with each other the most. I found that traditional Witches use codes of honor to live by. Most of these codes are the same, and some are familiar to most of the community. Solitaries and eclectics followed similar practices, but with sketchy information. Everyone knows, for example, "For the free will of all and with harm to none." That one is fairly straightforward, don't you think? Another is, "Ever mind the rule of three, what you send out comes back to thee." We could all recite this one in our sleep. Other rules, like "fault of the sword," are unknown to most solitaries and eclectic Witches.

Oh, I said the dirty word, didn't I? Rules. Rules, laws, code of conduct, ethics—dear me. Many people don't like authority (possibly because so many authority figures have managed to botch the job in our society). However, traditional Witches follow rules. Some traditions are stricter than others. Some are still following laws that squeak of the archaic, but they do squeak. Others rewrote many of the laws to apply both to their particular groups and modern society. The major stumbling block? They are hard to get. Many codes reveal themselves only in oath-bound Books of Shadows.

The second problem? Few people bother to read the ones they can view. As soon as they see the word "rules," the gray matter somewhere behind their eyes shuts down. Rules imply you are doing something wrong, and now must change to do something right, to satisfy the one who wrote the rules. These rules, old or not, hidden or in plain sight, should be studied by every working Witch, solitary, eclectic, or traditional. In this way, each person can determine which way to go in his or her studies.

My question when an argument arises on this point is this: Why not learn from those who have gone before? In my research I discovered that most Wiccan rules are designed to stop problems before they start, or to keep the seeker from wandering too far off the path of spirituality. These rules were not designed to cramp your personal style. They grew from the needs of those before us. As in any religion, fault often lies with human interpretation of the rules or the lack of creativity to match the right codes to the situation, not the codes themselves.

In this chapter, I will present many of the things I learned about modern Craft functions in the United States. I don't claim to be an expert on every tradition or eclectic group. This is information I've picked up along the way and pieced together from hundreds of eclectic and traditional groups across the country. Before we begin, I ask you to understand that the information here covers a broad spectrum. If you are a traditional Witch reading this material, you may say, "Well, she doesn't know what she is talking about. We don't do that!"—bear with me. I am aware how different both religious and magickal practices can be.

Of Oaths and The Oath

When you take your first step into the Craft, whether by dedication, self-initiation, or through the mechanics of a group initiation, you choose to follow a life of service to humankind. The promise you make is The Oath. The oath does not represent a promise to be a doormat for the world. Consider it honoring the lineage of the Ancients. You promise to do what is within your power to help those who are in need within the boundaries of ethical behavior. The path to Divine mystery is not easy, nor is it straight. At times, it is not even logical. One thing remains constant—Divinity.

Of all the statements and rituals in the Craft, The Oath is by far the most important combination of words you will ever utter in this lifetime. An individual, in my mind, could not attempt to call themselves of the Wicca, if they have not taken a ritual oath of some kind. The Oath is the binding process between you and Divinity. For the traditional Witch, orchestration occurs in a ritual by initiated Witches. Many solitaries take The Oath alone.

Have you ever wondered where the traditional Witches of today come from? Many current traditional groups (not all, mind you) do not accept individuals who have not taken the initiative to study on their own before they seek entrance into a group. Likewise, I personally know of no group that takes individuals under eighteen years of age, unless the parent of that person is already Wiccan. If an adult solitary has performed a self-dedication ritual and studied for three years on his or her own, a traditional group may feel more at ease. The year-and-a-day rule may not be necessary. Keep in mind that every group is different. Many may still hold the solitary to the year-and-a-day rule, despite the student's past study or reputation.

When a traditional Witch refuses to answer a question, saying he or she does not wish to break "The Oath," their statement does not normally mean the information will break the person's commitment to the God and the Goddess. (It depends on who is asking the question.) It does mean that the information will breach the confidence entrusted to him or her by the group, and during The Oath he or she has also promised to keep group information and materials a secret. Various traditions differ on the wording of The Oath, but the basic underlying theme remains the same.

Daily life can infringe on our spirituality. Sometimes we move away from our oath. This is human. The working Witch tries to be ever-mindful of the covenant between him or herself and Divinity and the covenant between him or herself and the group, should the Witch have chosen this type of association. The Oath, regardless of solitary or group work, is a personal committment.

❀ Your Work ✿

Whether you have already taken The Oath or not, spend a little time considering what The Oath entails. It doesn't hurt seasoned Witches to reaffirm the commitment to the Craft and to Divinity. If you had the chance to speak the most important words in your religious life again, or for the first time, what would they be? Once you have rolled this around in your mind a bit, choose a quiet evening, free of disturbances, to write down an oath designed by you. You may wish to burn a dressed silver or gold candle. Whether you have been practicing the Craft for twenty years or only one, there will be times in your life where you wonder where you are heading. No one has high self-esteem all the time. I have found that when these points of pondering occur, it is good to change your daily routine. Get out and about, and look at life from a different perspective. When you have rested, read your oath. Then, during meditation, ask for the information necessary for you to continue your path. If you like, you can reenact your self-dedication or design a new ritual for your current learning period. One note about crises that may be very helpful to you: The psychological period of crises in our lives usually spans six weeks. Think of the first week as the downward swing. The third week is the trough (the absolute pits of the situation). The fourth week begins the upward swing into balance. By the sixth week, you will find yourself back on track and moving ahead through life. Of course, this is the normal pattern. Normal means the average of any set of statistics. Not all life events can rely on statistics, as we know. However, this information is useful when times get tough. Store it in the back of your mind.

A big complaint standard religions wave at Witches is that we do not have large-scale community service programs to meet the needs of humanity.

This is unfair. Many Witches involve themselves in community and humanitarian service projects in place by other organizations. Most contribute to their community without making a big fuss. "Lookie here and pat me on the back" syndrome is not the Wiccan way. Also, there are some areas of the country today that would not tolerate a Pagan Food Bank—and there are individuals who would create all sorts of havoc to ensure its failure. On the other proverbial hand, there are other areas of the country that would accept Pagans with open arms. If you are in an area where Witchcraft is not well received, don't get excited. There are many programs already up and running in which you can participate.

During the next week, consider carefully what type of community service suits your involvement, and arrange to donate some of your time toward that goal. Spend a few hours on a crisis hot-line. Collect food for a local food bank. Help your kids sell candy bars for new band uniforms—anything designed to help others. When someone begins to harass me about my religion or other dumb things, I politely look him or her right in the eye and say, "Go spend time in a soup kitchen. Your energy will be better used there, than standing here with me."

The Oath and Retribution

The Oath and the craft code of honor are much the same. In some traditions, The Oath is the only code given. In others, a long list of rules and regulations are provided. In our tradition, we collect these laws from all over the world and add them to our Books of Shadows as we come across them. Some are downright silly, others do not pertain to our times, but underlying all these rules and regulations is the code of honor, to be followed by all Crafters.

What happens if you break your oath or the code of honor? Some traditions have definite punishments, from banishments for a limited time to banishments forever. Our clan, however, believes in the law of retribution, which is as follows:

Should anyone violate the code of honor or break his or her Oath, the Goddess will know. She knows who belongs to Her, and who does not. She will cast out that part of Her which brings disrespect to either Herself or Her children. The Mother of All condemns those who choose to use others for their own gain. She will eat alive those who hinder others in their learning process, their quest for knowledge, or in their desire to excel. She will tear asunder he or she who feigns secrets over others. She will condemn the oathbreaker for many lives to come.

If one coven fights with another, the Horned Lord will render judgement and exact His judgement. Those powers passed in initiatory ceremony will disintigrate. Anyone who tries to hurt His Lady (for He bows at Her feet and gives power to Her for Her discretionary use) will die a thousand times over before mortal death. Should His Lady be disgraced (or His High Priestess), he will open the doors of the Underworld and call forth His Hounds of Hell.

Should the Horned Lord (or the High Priest) be disgraced, the Lady will strap on Her sword to protect Her Lord and Consort, and slay all who stand in Her way. So be it.

I think that explanation sums it up rather neatly, don't you?

❀ Your Work ✿

In a quiet hour, in a quiet place, outline your idea of the Wiccan mysteries. I'm not talking about the Principles of Belief, that is a modern statement of position. I want you to consider what a Wiccan mystery is. This sounds simple, but I assure you, new revelations will happen, if you let them. You will often hear traditional Witches talk about "the mysteries." It is fine to seek the mysteries, but before you begin, I'd like to give you a word of advice. First, there is no single Witch or group of Witches on this planet who knows and understands all the Wiccan mysteries. Second, don't worry about missing out on something. If you need to know it, the Universe will share it with you. As long as you show through your thoughts and deeds that you both deserve this knowledge and are willing to work for it, the answers will come.

The Rede

"Do as you will, but let it harm none," or "For the free will of all, with harm to none." Some Witches claim the Rede was written around 1937 by Gerald Gardner or one of his cronies. Others say it is as not as old as that, but a product of the stepped-up Witch PR in the 1960s. Still others will tell you that Crowley was the author, pulling the Rede from Golden Dawn and Egyptian traditions. Most elders of the Craft will agree that the Rede is a modern invention for modern practitioners. Most Family Tradition Witches and Euro-ethnic Witches do not believe in the Rede. Remember, it was Aradia, the Queen of Witches, who taught her followers to poison their enemies. German Witches and Pow-Wow practitioners are very familiar with the art of hexing, and believe that if someone comes after the Witch or a member of the Witch's family, he or she is going to stop it. Depending on the circumstances, the Witch may not be too picky about how he or she accomplishes this.

Although the Rede is excellent in most cases, it also manages to paralyze new Craft practitioners, leading them to believe they cannot act in self-defense. Bull-turkey. I am not suggesting you go about cursing and hexing everyone who crosses your path; after all, negative magicks breed negative circumstances and retaliations. However, many traditional Witches still follow the Charge of the Hooded God, wherein He pledges His allegiance to the Goddess, and He is seen as the long arm of the law. His wrath can can be invoked if anyone abuses the rites of the Goddess, Her spells, Her teachings, or Her children (that's us). To call down the Hooded God to avenge the deceitful, the criminal, or the morally disgusting individual is to start something for them that is so horrible that no mortal mind can conceive of it. There is one catch: your personal slate had better be clean, or you are going down, too.

On a more soothing note, take the example of a friend who is sick. You would like to work magick for your friend; however, he or she either doesn't know you are a practitioner or is wary about what you do. Some Witches would turn away, sigh, and say, "That's it. I can't do anything." It is my feeling that these Witches are allowing their own fears to get in the way, and are using the Rede as an excuse. When someone is sick, don't most people say, "Do you mind if I pray for you?" What's the difference if a Witch or a Christian prays in his or her own way? Ethically, there is no difference (although technically, yes, there is a difference in the performance of the prayer).

Another example: Imagine a child is in trouble across the street. Are you the type of person who would rush to aid the child? Let's hope so. That child doesn't care if you are an alien, a race-car driver, or a Witch. What matters is that you are helping. To help others is to fulfill your oath. Therefore, any Witch who has taken The Oath can't possibly be fundamentalist in his or her view of the Rede. Think about it: "for the free will of all, and it harm none" is a wonderful rule, but every rule has its exception. If you are leery about digging your fingers in someone else's business, why not work magick and ask that the "best thing" happen for the individual? In this way, you are petitioning the Universe, and your intention is pure. You aren't naming a particular direction from which the help should come, or indicating how it should manifest. The God and Goddess are quite capable of determinging what is best for the person in question. Humans don't always have to make all the decisions.

Dealing With 'Fraidy Cats: What Will Not Happen

The gates of Hell are not going to open and swallow you during your self-dedication, during any ritual you perform in the realm of positive energies, or when your grandmother finds your pentacle. If you are so frightened that you think one of the above (or worse) is going to happen, the Craft is not for you. It does not mean you are bad, or not qualified, or not special. It simply means that you are not ready to seek the mysteries of the wise. There may be other mysteries for you to explore that are equally important to your life's path. You may come back to the Craft later, or perhaps not.

Now that you have been flying on your own broom for a bit, you may wish to share your work and learning experiences with others. If someone asks for help or asks you to teach them, and fits the above situation, then steer away from sharing the mysteries with them. Who was it that said "teach all who will listen and learn, but do not teach the mysteries to those of little understanding"? They knew what they were talking about. Don't spit in the wind or you are going to get a slobbery face. Such a quotation does not mean the student or friend is stupid, it means he or she is not ready. Sometimes what people learn conflicts with what they know in their hearts. If they cannot find solid ground to draw in and meld the energies of the two, they are not prepared to seek the Craft of the wise.

'Fraidy cats cannot deal with the Wiccan mysteries. They laugh, scoff, or worse—persecute—given the chance. Don't give it to them.

❀ Your Work ❁

Whether you are solitary, eclectic, or a traditional Witch, grab a notebook and a pencil. It's time for you to do some serious thinking. Imagine that the entire magickal community asked you to write a code of honor to be adopted at a huge convention of magickal people. You know there will be disagreements on your code, so you begin working on the most serious issues. Smaller codes, or rules, will be adopted by each group, including their own method of government. Therefore, you won't concern yourself with these now. Before you begin, check your list of mysteries and consider how they will apply to your code. Now, begin writing your community code of honor. This is a serious endeavor and will take more than one day for you to accomplish. You may wish to do a few rituals, some meditational work, and intermingle with other magickal friends before, during, and after you have written your code. Don't be afraid to revise the code. Any famous author knows the best work comes after dozens of revisions.

On Solitaries Studying with Friends

On the same subject of teaching and learning are friends who begin solitary study together. One individual buys a book, likes it, and shares his or her feelings with a friend. The friend buys or borrows the book, and becomes interested. Now they have something unusual in common. They draw closer together. This is wonderful if they are both mature and not carrying around mental baggage that influences their friendship. For example, many friendships become entrenched in the interplay between weak and strong personalities. One individual is the parent model and the other operates more like a teen. This relationship begins with a problem. When discovering a new religion that carries with it an entirely different viewpoint on the world and how it works, difficulties can arise. Typically, one friend moves faster than the other. (Don't think it is always the parent model, either.) Sometimes one becomes more religious. Conversely, the other may become more skilled in magick. If the person lagging is not stable in his or her self-esteem, the other friend may pay dearly.

One woman wrote to me that her best friend tried to "slow her down for her own good." When that didn't work, the friend pulled in the woman's family and other supporters to convince her that she was "unprepared" to go further. The first question in my mind was, How fast is too fast when you are talking about religion? The woman's friend found herself unprepared to seek the mysteries. She was not strong enough to admit her own growth process. Rather than being alone, she tried to hold the letter-writer back. The jealous woman played out her fears on her friend, creating animosity to cover her own inadequacy. The result? Severe damage ensued to both family relationships and the friendship.

I warn you now, it can get deep when you are wading through interpersonal relationships, religion, and mysteries. The jealous friend broke the code of honor. I bet if someone confronted her about her disrespect of another, she wouldn't understand her violation of Wiccan beliefs.

On Finding a Teacher

There is no great teacher holding a golden key elusively drifting in and out of your peripheral vision, nor is there any one group of people or Craft tradition that holds more secrets than another. Yes, they hold different secrets at different levels. However, if someone promises you the moon, whether in the world of magick or the mundane—don't buy it. Only the Goddess can give you access to the moon (it's Her territory). No single person has possession of a mystery that you cannot eventually discover for yourself. Yes, there are wise people, but I hate to break it to you—they are human. Craft elders get wise by wading through a lot of garbage over the parade of years. One important Craft code goes like this: Honor the succession of teachers. This gives the student a clue that not all rests in the mind of one individual or mode of thought. It also tells us, regardless of the outcome of training, the student should respect the teacher for sharing quality time and the Wiccan mysteries. Don't carry this too far and read things into the code that are not there. For example, should there be criminal or moral misconduct (we hope the Goddess not), don't honor the idiot.

If you are a person who needs or likes to work within the boundaries of a structure, like a tradition, then look for a group that will be suitable for to your lifestyle. However, try not to lose sight of your original goal (as sometimes happens) or squelch your personal power and self-development. The group mind is great, but as in a marriage, to give up your personal power is to find divorce at your door. On the other hand, solitaries need to be aware of what is going on the magickal community around them. Traditionalists or eclectic groups won't go away if you ignore them. To become a Witch-turtle is not a step of wisdom.

There are dos and don'ts for both student and teacher in any type of educational setting. For example, if a teacher sexually lures a student in any environment, the teacher is breaking a code of conduct. This also applies to Craft studies. My advice: "Don't mix your meat with your potatoes—you'll miss dessert." In my research of the current Wiccan beliefs across the country, sexual relations between teacher and student (unless, of course, they are currently partners) are considered grounds for expulsion from most Wiccan groups, whether they are traditional or not.

❀ Your Work ❦

Project 1: Rather than waiting for the teacher with the golden aura bright enough for even the mundane to see, sit in a quiet place and close your eyes. Instead of trying to envision the perfect teacher, visualize the type of knowledge you need, and your reasoning for accessing it. See yourself learning and practicing this information. When you are through, write down your experiences and the types of knowledge you envisioned. Look back at your list from time to time during your studies.

Project 2: Look over your codes of conduct. Expand the list to cover the types of behavior you think are important for both teacher and student.

On the Types of Traditions and Legitimacy

In the 1990s, there are five definite kinds of traditions in the Craft. Solitaries often feel like they are less than traditional Witches, and this is not so. Yes, the training and the approach may be different, but in the end, they are all practicing the same religion. Any confusion that a solitary Witch experiences with understanding traditions is going to stop right here. There is nothing more frustrating when you are completely competent in practicing and worshipping alone, then go to a group and not understand the matrix of the situation. There is also a danger in not knowing how the magickal realms are put together—it leaves you open for the con-artist. These people exist everywhere, in every religion, business, or social gathering. They prey on ignorance and I want to make sure you don't get taken in.

Let's make sure we have the correct definition of the word tradition to start. A tradition is a set of repetitive practices, celebrations, or observances handed from person to person, often from generation to generation.

Because the Craft carries the signature of individuality and the importance of growth tailored to personal needs, I found myself in the sea of "I don't understand" many times. It was not the mysteries that I found confusing, but group hierarchy, both traditional and eclectic. For example, I broke rules I didn't know existed from time to time, out of sheer ignorance and stupidity.

In the Craft, the word tradition is like the word love in the mundane world. It means different things to different people. For example, there are old traditions, which often fall under the heading of Fam Trads. These are Craft teachings, handed down generation through generation by the parent or grandparent, and the adult teaches and initiates the child. If the child is not taught and initiated, he or she cannot claim to be a Fam Trad Witch simply on the belief of magick in their blood lines. I bet every single one of us has a magickal person somewhere in the family skeleton closet. I know I do. That doesn't make us Fam Trad Witches. Fam trads do not have to be 700 years old to be legitimate. For example, I cannot consider myself a Fam Trad Witch, but my sons and daughters can, because:

I taught them

I am a lineaged Witch

Our family has rituals and magickal practices that are unique to our family unit

Fam Trad Witches are rare, and more often than not, do not share their lineage or anything about themselves with the general Craft public. On your first meeting with most of them, they will not tell you who they are related to, nor will they even tell you they are a Fam Trad Witch. Con-artists in the Craft often choose to declare themselves Fam Trad Witches because they say they cannot share their lineage information with you; in reality, they are providing a background that cannot be checked. Be careful and use your best judgment.

Once the Fam Trad information leaves the hands of the family member, it is not considered a Fam Trad. For example, historical accounts of Gerald Gardner indicate he was initiated by a relative. Okay, that makes him part of the Family Tradition. When he opened his doors to individuals outside his family line for study and initiation, a new group was born. Why? With the influx of new minds and new hereditary circumstances, the Fam Trad will change to meet the needs of the new group. It is now simply a group, as strong or as weak as the group makes it. It becomes a tradition, named after the Witch who founded it, when that person dies.

Often this type of group, founded in the 1950s and 1960s, carries lineage rolls. With the proper request and credentials, any elder can request to check a specific name. Hence the terms "Alexandrian" and "Gardnerian." Individuals initiated into these groups must memorize the lineage from the elder who does the initiation, degree ceremony, or eldering. If you move in modern Craft circles, you will find elders of these various traditions floating around somewhere. These elders have a set of fail-safe questions memorized in case there is a doubt on what another Witch claims to be. The questions are word of mouth only, oath-bound, and never written. In this way, they protect the entire magickal community, ensuring that the con-artist doesn't get too far. If it makes you feel any better, these elders rarely need to ask the questions. They are wise enough to see deception.

When sharing their lineage with others, they may say something like the following: "I was eldered by Lord Ariel of the Caledonii and Lord Serphant of Serphant Stone, who was eldered by Michael Reagan, who was eldered by Raymond Buckland, who was initiated by Gerald Gardner." This is my lineage, in case anyone really wants to know. You may think anybody could say that and get away with it. Wrong. I knew a fellow once who tried that trick—he didn't last long. The Shining Ones take care of their own as well as the ancestors of any given tradition. The Craft laws should not be toyed with. Built into the code of honor in most old traditions are protective mechanisms to expel those who don't belong.

The third traditional group comes from the lineaged Witches of either a Fam Trad or an old tradition who meld their lineages together in a ritual of friendship. This ceremony relies on the performance of the elders of both traditions. Sometimes they take an new name for the combined group, or keep their group names separate to avoid confusion. For example, a British Traditional Witch is a combination of lineages and groups across the country. Their headquarters (The International Red Garters) keeps the official roles for all the groups. These groups fall into the category of old tradition. An example of the second type of group melding occurred in 1993, when Lord Ariel of the Caledonii Tradition and Lord Serphant of Serphant Stone held a ceremony of brotherhood/sisterhood and combined their traditions. They kept their traditional names separate, and work separately, but remain oath-bound to help each other in need. Craft groups join for strength, political reasons, or spiritual reasons.

The fourth type of tradition can be born of eclectic open circles. This means that a few solitaries really like each other and decided to get together to worship, learn, research, and participate in community service projects. They may be traditional Witches who have separated from their traditions, or who simply no longer practice their tradition. They may be individuals who have no traditional background, but feel they are strong enough to form a group. The first step they take is starting their own coven, thereby closing the door to fair-weather magical people and dabblers. When they grow into a cumbersome group they may split apart and operate within the environs of smaller covens. If they keep a fair percentage of the rituals and magickal applications intact (meaning the groups are relatively practicing the same things), then they become a new tradition without lineage.

The Craft is the fastest-growing religion in the United States today. There are not enough old traditions (like Gardner's) or Fam Trads to go around to meet the needs of the people. A new vehicle of study and worship needed to present itself. This does not mean these original solitaries are using practices that are new, but they are creating a brand-new group mind, will design their own Book of Shadows, make group guidelines, codes of honor, etc., and in time, will function much like the older traditions. Over time, they will develop their own lineage. These groups, like any other Craft group, are as legitimate as they are wise.

The final type of tradition is also a new tradition, but comes from a different background. The best way to explain it is to give you an example.

Jane and Richard are lineaged Witches with completed training in an old tradition. When they reach clergy status, they can leave their training group and begin their new coven under the umbrella of the old tradition. Perhaps all is not well within the old tradition group structure. This could come from a variety of reasons, and they don't have to be bad ones. (Thought I was going to give you a juicy story, didn't you? Too bad!) Anyway, Jane and Richard determine that the wisest course of action for themselves and their coven brothers and sisters is to leave the tradition. If there are no hard feelings to deal with first, they will ask for a separation with honor in writing, followed up by the obligatory phone call or conference. This is part of the Wiccan code of honor.

In Craft law, the separation must be granted. Assuming all has gone well with the separation, Jane and Richard are free to use their clerical training and work with their coven. Should this coven split (often called hiving), as with the example listed in the previous discussion of the solitary growth, they will eventually grow into a tradition of their own, producing their own lineage. The difference here, is that when they speak of their lineage, they will often say: "Of the Whatever Tradition, initiated by so-and-so of the New Tradition name."

❁ Your Work ✿

All Witches, regardless of tradition, work in set patterns. With practice, they find what correspondences work best for a given situation, whether it be planetary hours, herbs, gems, candle magick, or their personal energy fluctuations. They also outline specific rituals for holidays and rites of passage. In a quiet place and in a quiet hour, consider all the types of magicks and religious acts you currently perform. This is your personal tradition. Sit back and relax with your way of doing things. Solitaries often think they are "doing things wrong" simply because they are on their own and using their creative and innovative ideas to practice their religion. This is not so.

On Lineage

Since I've already used this word several times, we need to take a close look at it. Like the word tradition, it too carries several meanings. In brief, lineage means given to you by another, who gave it to them, who gave it to them, etc. Lineage in the Craft makes you part of an energy family. A con-artist can claim lineage out the bazoo, but in the end, it won't help him/her at all. Lineage has to do with the passing of power in a ceremonial environment. Rather than a blood transfusion, think of it as an energy transfusion. Regardless of what other people try to tell you, it cannot be taken away. Karmically, you are connected in that one moment, no matter what passes in the future. Only the Ancient Ones and the Universe can destroy lineage.

There are several codes of honor that apply to lineage. I'd like to cover them briefly.

A Witch never claims to be something that he or she isn't.

A Witch is responsible for learning his or her lineage and understanding its impact on his or her life. For example, if you are given a long lineage list to recite, you should know the history of each individual you are naming.

Every Witch has the right to the privacy of his or her beliefs. Unless challenged by an elder of your tradition, you are not required to reveal your lineage, especially at public events, open circles, in the press, or on a computer bulletin board! Be ever-mindful that a real elder can contact the appropriate individuals to check out lineage without challenging someone in public.

⚙ Your Work ☙

Lineages often carry the representation of the blood/energy line in the shape of a shield. In a quiet hour and in a quiet place, begin to design your shield on a piece of paper. It should represent your strengths, depicting tools, animals, birds, etc. You may want a single image on the shield, or divide the shield into four quadrants, representing the four elements (earth, air, fire, water) or four planetary influences in your astrological chart (sun, moon, ascendant, and midheaven). There are oodles of ideas you can choose from. When you have perfected the design, transfer it to wood, metal, or sew it (like a banner). You can hang it over your altar. If you enjoy going to festivals, you can hang it outside your tent, as this is a common practice.

When you visit a Pagan festival or other function, you may see these banners hung from tents or prominently displayed by other means. In some traditions, these banners are of a specific size and contain a marking or two that is unique to the tradition, with the logo of the coven, clan, or group.

Reveal what you will about yourself, but keep your mouth off other people. This means that if you want to get yourself in hot water, no problem. If you pull someone in with you, you've broken the code of honor. A very easy way to get yourself kicked out of any tradition is if you talk too much. Gossips will be removed from their respective groups. I know of one case where an initiate passed along personal information about another. The Elder Council banned the gossip from group functions for nine moons.

On Degrees

A mystery to most solitary practitioners is the degree system practiced by traditional crafters. The degree structure varies between traditions. The following groupings explain how they may be different. For the sake of clear terminology, I'm going to use the same words throughout the examples. However, many traditions have specific names for degrees other than dedicant, initiate, first, second, third, elder.

The Six-Tier System

1. **Dedicant:** An oath of a-year-and-a-day so the group and the individual can check each other out.
2. **Initiate:** Usually lasts one year, and involves basic Wiccan theology.
3. **First Degree:** Usually lasts one year, and involves basic traditional theology, whatever has been designed for that particular tradition.
4. **Second Degree:** Time period is indeterminate. The individual is very active in tradition training and group function, and substitutes for the third-degree members when necessary.
5. **Third Degree:** Active leaders of the group and responsible to serve as clergy.
6. **Elder:** Serves as clergy and observes ritual and group functions, but does not take the "center stage" unless his or her station requires. Sometimes, these individuals are called "Clan Mothers" or "Clan Fathers," especially if hiving is involved.

The Five-Tier System

1. **Dedicant:** An oath of a-year-and-a-day.
2. **First Degree:** Usually lasts one year, and involves basic Wiccan theology.
3. **Second Degree:** Usually lasts two years, sometimes longer. The first year covers basic traditional theology and the second year is spent training dedicants and first-degree students, as well as learning to substitute for the third-degree members when necessary.

4. **Third Degree:** Active leaders of the group and responsible to serve as clergy, as well as teach second-degree students. Here is where you find the most fluctuation in traditional training. Some traditions feel that second-degree training only revolves around group ritual and religious study. They do not continue magickal training for the second-degree student. Their primary concern is that second-degree students know how to handle group functions. I have met many ceremonial magicians who started in this type of training structure and have eventually left the Craft to hone their magickal skills through ceremonial magick group structures. Other Craft traditions continue magickal training with group training.

5. **Elder:** Regardless of which type of training, when third-degrees in the three-degree system are ready, they may step down from active group service and move into the shadows of group activity, thereby fulfilling the elder portion of their status. Here again is where many traditions vary, especially if the mother coven is a training coven where the leader rarely performs ceremonies but orchestrates all the operations of the students and the tradition. Depending upon the group, elders may be elected for a specific period, for an unspecified period, or is not considered an elected position at all, but one of honor. In the five-tier system, it is seen as a position of honor. Our Black Forest Clan is a five-tier system. Again, some members may be called Clan Mothers/Fathers if hiving is involved.

The Four-Tier System

1. **Dedicant:** An oath of a-year-and-a-day.
2. **First Degree:** Usually lasts two to three years, and involves basic Wiccan theology the first year, tradition theology the second year, and magickal practices the third year.
3. **Second Degree:** May last a full year. The year covers training dedicants and first-degree students, as well as learning to substitute for the third-degree members when necessary. However, second-degree students in this system may choose to hive within a few months and begin what is called a daughter coven, which functions under the supervision of the mother coven until the second-degree student(s) take their third initiation.
4. **Third Degree/Elder:** Active leaders of the group and responsible to serve as clergy, as well as teach second-degree students. Here, third-degree Witches are voted as elders for a specific period of time.

The Three-Tier System

There are two three-tier systems. These systems are not as popular as the Six-, Five- or Four-Tier Systems, for several reasons. First, students do not move as quickly through degrees, and may get stuck somewhere in the training process. This can cause drastic repercussions. Humans appreciate rewards for their hard work. Students often see degrees as levels of accomplishment and not specifically rites of passage where psychic centers open. Several years is a long time to wait, and many people are not so patient. Another reason is the adage, "familiarity breeds contempt." Relationships among people change over the years. If a harmonious balance is not kept, the student will most likely leave with an unhappy heart. Keeping the pace through rewards increases self-esteem and breeds harmony among the group.

1. **Dedicant:** The year-and-a-day timing.
2. **First Degree:** General Wiccan study the first year, traditional theology and practice the second year, possibly magickal training the third year, the training of others the fourth year (or more), and preparation for clerical responsibilities.
3. **Second Degree/Elder:** The same as in the four-tier system.

The second three-tier system goes this way:
1. **First Degree**
2. **Second Degree**
3. **Third Degree**

Notice here, there is no period of a-year-and-a-day; no dedication ceremony. You jump right in and start hauling broomstick. In the three-tier system is where you find the most "forever firsts," a term coined for those Witches who have sought initiation into the first degree, but have gone no further. This can be for a variety of reasons (disagreements within the coven/organization or because the initiate moved from Rhode Island to New Mexico, and cannot find people of his or her own lineage to continue teaching him or her). There are lots of reasons for "forever firsts." Some people do not want to continue into clerical work. There is nothing wrong with that.

In all the systems, dedicants are not considered Witches, but seekers of the correct path for them. Because of this, it is normal for groups to hold back training, materials, or time until the dedicant/seeker/novice determines that the Craft is the religion for him or her. Remember, I'm talking old Craft here, not new traditions or open circle environments, which may have their own rules. A change, though, has come over the Craft community in the last ten years. To the solitary Wiccan, the dedication ceremony performed has become as important a progression in his or her spirituality as the first-degree initiation is to the traditional Witch. Both the traditional Witch and the solitary Witch of the 1990s must learn to make the distinction between the dedication ritual of the traditionalist and the dedication ritual of the solitary. They are not the same.

Well, smartie Witch, say all of you readers, just how do you figure that? You told me. In the thousands of letters I have received, you let the cat out of the bag and into my computer. I have found that fifty percent of the dedicants who come in "cold" (no Craft training) to a tradition do not take the oath; whereas eighty percent of those who take the solitary dedication continue their studies, year after year. This is a statistic to ponder, isn't it?

Now that I've thrown all this information at you, you can understand why the degree system is confusing to both solitaries and traditionalists alike. If someone at a festival tells you he or she is a "second-degree Witch," you have no clue about what this person has been taught, or where he or she stands in his or her traditional training. You also have no clue where you stack up in the scheme of Craft learning and practice. This confusion applies to both solitaries and traditionalists. Such a mystery, then, has a habit of lowering any practitioner's self-esteem.

Although training and status among the groups may differ from tradition to tradition, the degree/tier system also functions for religious benchmarks in an individual's training. It is from these levels of religious intent that the solitary can study and work toward such goals on his or her own. Let's go through the six-tier system again, looking at it from a religious point of view.

The dedicant ceremony is like a small, psychic tap on your shoulder. Enough energies are conferred to help you decide whether or not the Craft is for you. The year-and-a-day is important for both solitaries and group members. This length of time is considered a cycle of gestation. At the end, you may wish to be born into the Craft. Then again, you may not. The freedom of choice is yours.

The first degree ceremony/initiation is the most important ceremony of the Craft. I believe these energies are conferred only once in this lifetime. Of course, there are always exceptions to the rule, but when most perform this ceremony, it is once and done. Here is where the dedicant gives his or her life oath, which says "I vow to hurt no one and help in every way I can to make the world a better place."

This point in your life is also a set of choices. They are:

The decision to walk the path of mysteries with the Wiccan religion.

The decision to meld body, mind, and spirit into raising your level of consciousness.

The decision to work toward balance and harmony in your life.

The decision to set goals and prepare for events you seek to experience.

The decision to act, rather than react.

The decision to set aside a time to study, learn, and experiment.

The choice to help others and yourself.

The choice to work with female/Goddess energy.

After the first-degree initiation, the individual is usually happy, upbeat, full of energy, walking in a sparkling world. As psychic centers open during the ceremony, the student may experience a barrage of positive psychic phenomena. Work and personal study is accomplished during the first-degree cycle. This is the cycle of your birth into the religion of the Craft.

The second degree ceremony represents another set of choices for the individual. This ceremony is designed to help you use both the dark and light sides of yourself. In many traditions, the symbol for this ceremony is the inverted pentagram, as you are moving, or descending, into self. The inverted pentagram here does not represent devil worship. However, second-degree Witches rarely wear the inverted pentagram due to its unfortunate publicity. Instead, they know they are working under the energies of that symbol, which is all that is required.

The choices for the second-degree Witch are:

The decision to deal with both positive and negative sides of self.

The decision to let go of grief and guilt.

The decision to rebuild the self to move closer to Divinity.

The decision to bring balance to the conscious and subconscious self.

The decision to begin teaching others your religion at their request.

The affirmation to consistently work toward helping mankind and repair the damage done to the earth.

The decision to move to a higher, more difficult level of study.

The decision to continue training for clergy and group responsibilities.

The decision to work with God/masculine energy.

After the second-degree ceremony, the elders watch the student very carefully to see if the ceremony "took." There is often a radical shift in personality, where the individual becomes more outspoken and more sure of him or herself as an individual. Psychic centers open, chakra centers align, and the individual takes on the task of becoming one with him or herself and Divinity.

The third-degree ceremony represents the choice of the individual to be responsible for other spiritual lives than his or her own. The set of choices here are:

The decision to live in the most spiritual way possible.

The decision to leave immature and wasteful thoughtforms behind.

The decision to counsel other individuals on their spiritual paths.

The decision to teach individuals inside and outside of the traditional path, at their request.

The decision to perform ministerial functions, such as Wiccanings, Handfastings, Passings, and Rites of Passage.

The decision to be involved in serious religious and philosophical study for the remainder of this incarnation to benefit both the student and humanity.

The decision to work with the unified energies of the God and Goddess.

Another way to see the third-degree energy at work is to watch the student as they progress through their first year after this ceremony. Often an incredible amount of work is done for the good of the self and for the good of the group.

Eldering ceremony alone means that:

Your group trusts you to make the correct decisions when things are bad.

Your magickal and religious skills are a cut above most others—meaning you can pull a student out of the soup if necessary.

You are capable of good government practices for the group.

You strive in every aspect of your life to follow the codes of honor.

The eldering ceremony is in honor of a job well done in the study of the Craft, but also means there is work to be accomplished in the future. You can tell if the ceremony "took" by his or her upbeat, yet reserved manner. He or she walks in authority, but does not laud that authority over others.

❁ Your Work ✿

Determine what goals you want to accomplish and where they fall in the levels of study associated with the degree system. Take some time now and list three-month, six-month, and one-year goals by examining both the levels of training and bench-mark religious experiences that have been listed for you. How many have you accomplished already? How many do you wish to work toward? What aspects of these programs do not interest you? Keep all this information in you notebook and refer to it at a later date.

By understanding the energies of these ceremonies and what they are designed to accomplish, the solitary can better understand the Craft community, and where he or she may fall within it.

Today, traditions face an interesting complication—that of the well-trained solitary. It used to be that when an individual entered dedicant stage or was initiated, he or she knew little about the Craft as a community, or the individual workings as Witches. This is not so today, and presents a conflict between those students who enter with little knowledge and those who enter with several years of personal study under their belts. It is not logically fair to make a well-studied initiate wait the prescribed amount of years and give him or her material the student has already covered alone. Conversely, the years originally required were to make sure everyone got along and work could be done in an expedient manner, rather than working around personal tantrums or misunderstandings.

To solve this dilemma, a few traditions are separating the religious degree ceremonies from leveled training classes, having the two operate separately, then coming together during rituals. In this manner, everyone receives qualified teaching (or has the chance to teach) in a classroom environment and all get to practice and enjoy ritual together. This eliminates someone from telling a well-studied solitary, "Well, you didn't wait your year-and-a-day, so you are not ready to go further in study or degree level." It can happen.

Goals to Work Toward

Let's make believe for a bit. You have been invited to join the Mist Tradition, a collection of solitaries who occasionally work in a group. Your interview has already taken place and you feel comfortable with your choice to join them. They, in turn, feel good about you. Of course, someone will be teaching you. Let's call that person Jamie (since it is both a male and female name, you get to add the gender to it). In this tradition, although you are expected to attend the celebrations and work nights, you are also expected to study on your own.

On your first day of training, Jamie hands you the following set of goals, designed by the tradition, to assist their seekers upon the path of spirituality.

To receive your first degree in the Mist Tradition, you must:

1. Know three types of circle casting by heart.
2. Know three quarter calls by heart.
3. Know an altar devotion and be able to demonstrate it.
4. Pass the testing on all of your lessons.[2]
5. Meet a challenge designed especially for you.
6. Prove you can work as a solitary Witch by demonstrating a solitary ritual that includes raising power.
7. Provide a magickal diary to your instructor that encompasses one full year of your magickal experiences.
8. Show that you are a responsible individual who can be trusted by all members of the Craft and your tradition brothers and sisters.
9. Be able to tell if a magick circle has been erected or not.
10. Be willing to take the oath of initiation and all it includes.
11. Know what a "proper person" is.

To receive the second level of initiation in the Mist Tradition, you must:

1. Be able to perform, in front of the tradition elders, an altar devotion, circle casting, and quarter calls for your own initiation with only two errors.

2. Remember, this is make-believe and anything is possible. Therefore, the lessons and exercises you are to complete are in *To Ride a Silver Broomstick* and *Buckland's Complete Book of Witchcraft*.

2. Have collected all the tools deemed necessary for your use.

3. Write a new moon ritual for both group and solitary use.

4. Write a full moon ritual for both group and solitary use.

5. Write a dark moon ritual for both group and solitary use.

6. Write a lesson to share with your brothers and sisters of the Craft.

7. Complete all lessons given to you by your instructor.[3]

8. Draw down the God or Goddess for a solitary and group ritual.

9. Complete a challenge designed specifically for you.

10. Have joined a community service project and logged at least 10 hours of your personal time.

11. Know a dedication ritual by heart, and have dedicated at least one individual approved by the tradition.

12. Keep a magickal journal for one year.

13. Make an inventory of your Craft supplies and submit it to the instructor.

14. Choose an aspect of the science of the Craft in which you have chosen to specialize.

15. Have investigated the laws of your state and how they relate (or don't) to your religion.

16. Know the history of the Witch and completed a twenty-five page research paper on the history of the Craft.

17. Write four devotionals to be used each day for six full moons.

18. Be able to pass a Wicca 101 test (see Appendix III).

To receive the third level of initiation into the Mist Tradition, you must:

1. Have proven your dedication to the Craft by random acts of service and kindness.

2. Know one type of divinatory tool in which you are qualified to council other individuals and have logged 200 hours of such counseling.

3. Know how to fill out the appropriate paperwork for training, including applications, preparing lesson plans, designing testing procedures, etc.

4. Have kept all holidays in solitary fashion—this means that you have celebrated appropriately on each holiday in a solitary ritual or meditation.

5. Have trained at least two individuals for one full year.

6. Have written and performed at least one funeral ceremony.

7. Have written and performed at least one wiccaning ceremony.

8. Have written and performed all High Holiday rituals.

9. Have written a handfasting ritual.

---

3. Use the exercises in this book to complete this requirement.

10. Have written and tested twenty spells that can be shared with other members of the Craft. The spells must include complete steps, astrological correspondences, etc.

11. Have written ten meditations and have shared them with others.

12. Have chosen your totem animal and have performed at least ten rituals with that totem.

13. Show that you are able to overcome hostile, verbal attacks without losing your temper.

14. Have performed at least thirty rituals alone and ten rituals with a group, not counting those previously listed.

15. Write a ten-page paper explaining why you think you are ready to carry the title of Wiccan clergy.

16. Have logged 100 hours in magickal community service.

17. Have logged 500 additional hours in general community service.

18. Prove you can cast a magickal circle in your head before a panel of elders.

19. Know an initiation ritual by heart.

20. Be able to recite the Charge of the Goddess.

21. Be willing to take the third-degree oath and all it entails.

22. Have become proficient with the specialization you chose at the second level.

23. Meet a challenge designed especially for you.

Now, some of you will say that's too easy. Others will say, that's too hard! Everyone in the Black Forest Clan is expected to do the above, and more. So, if you think no one on the face of the planet does all this stuff—wrong.

Banishment of Someone in a Craft Group

There are times when you will hear that someone was "banished" from such-and-such tradition or group. Christians call it "thrown out of the church"—a term I'm sure many of you have heard around the dinner table when Grandma is relating interesting tidbits from the past, while pushing an extra helping of those cold mashed potatoes onto your plate. This is a sticky subject and depends on the integrity of the group or tradition. Originally, banishment was for bad actions indeed—such as telling the inquisition authorities the names of your coven brothers and sisters, murder, rape, theft, etc. Banishment was the most severe penalty, and often ended with the banished Witch disappearing from the face of the earth, if you get my drift. (You thought those guys buried in the Irish bogs fell asleep there. Fooled you!) Sometimes banishment was equated with fault of the sword, meaning the criminal was going to have an unhappy meeting with a weapon. Now before anyone gets in a tizzy, think seriously for a moment. All traitors and criminals were similarly dealt with in this way (or worse) before and during the Middle Ages. This decree was a product of its times.

Banishment is another word with a multitude of meanings in modern Craft communication. Unfortunately, there are several Craft High Priestesses and High Priests who get a bit overzealous over trivial matters and declare a "banishment of so-and-so." I'm not saying all banishments are not legitimate, but some individuals use it as a quick fix to an interpersonal problem that could be dealt with in a less enthusiastic manner. Today, banishment means "you are not part of the group anymore—go play in somebody else's sandbox."

All individuals should think seriously about the act of banishment. For example, banishment is a human thing, as your karma is a part of you, banishment ceremony or not. The banishment performed (through ritual ceremony only—no blood or guts or goo—we are civilized in this day and age) or proclaimed (in document form) does not carry weight on the other planes of reality if it entails frivolity. Banishment implies that the lineage is broken through ritual by Divinity, and cannot be retrieved by the person banished. In a criminal instance, I believe this is true. If someone has been poisoning the group mind and has seriously damaged someone within the group with unjust or unfair thoughts and actions, this also may hold true. However, if the banishment is performed because someone got their feelings pinched, to whom do you think the banishment will attach itself karmically? Think about it. It's like a banishment spell, which we all know is to get rid of something— permanently. If you are targeting the innocent, the rule of three applies. The rule also holds true for traditional or group banishments.

A working Witch must learn to trust his or her own judgment and intuition. Solitaries get good at this, but sometimes it takes them awhile to get the magickal ball rolling. You can't call your High Priestess on the phone with every little episode of self-doubt if you are a solitary. If you are part of a group, your High Priestess has many responsibilities—getting a call every day when you skin your magickal knee is not going to produce sound relations between you. As with most human difficulties, learning to trust your intuition and judgment is a self-esteem issue. How do you build self-esteem in yourself? Keep working! The more you work, the better you get. The better you get, the more successful you become. The more successful you become, the more your self-esteem rises. It is a chain of personal power. Sometimes we get too infatuated with ourselves, and the chain holds us down. If there are a few links you don't need, learn to discard them with honor. If someone else promises to add to your chain of wisdom, check to make sure the links are shiny, and not tarnished with their own ego. Sometimes well-meaning individuals try to give you broken links in exchange for your complete ones—don't let them.

─────────── ✿ Your Work ✿ ───────────

Consider the serious act of banishment, whether it is that of a person, habit, relationship, or inanimate object. When next you see or hear mention of someone being "banished," remember that there are two sides to every story. If you were responsible for a group, in what circumstances would you consider banishment, and why?

On the Purpose of the Book of Shadows

Many solitary and traditional Witches have a large notebook called their Book of Shadows. Both types of Witches guard them well and hold their contents close to their hearts. Are there pearls of mysticism and magick in them? If opened, will the greatest teacher of all times and realms coalesce slowly from purple mist? If a book like this exists, please write me immediately. I, too, will be waiting in line for that one.

The BOS, or Book of Shadows, is a spiritual testimony of either the solitary Witch or the creative work of a group of Witches who function together in a coven or other traditional environment. To an extent, the words are important and assist in chronicling personal or group growth through the information contained. The BOS also represents the oath you take in the Craft, and therefore carries your energy (or the energy of the group) on every page.

In the past, the BOS was not normally copyrighted as it represents the work of many individuals. For example, as a solitary, you may have several books in your occult library, but like only particular passages or instructions from each. These would be copied into your BOS for quick reference and easy access. If you copy passages from copyrighted books, always put the name of the author and the title of the book after the information. In this way, should you choose to share your book with someone else, he or she will find it helpful to know where the information originally came from. Groups today are tech-smart and many are moving in the direction of the copyright laws to protect their material.

A personal BOS, regardless if you are a solitary or traditional, is valuable due to the amount of effort and energy you used to create it and the positive energy that surrounds it each time the book lies open on the altar or work table when magick and ritual are done.

If you do not have a BOS, begin it now. Choose the binding, decide on what type of paper, etc. Traditionally, the BOS should be in our own handwriting. However, if you are a techno-freak (like me), you can put it on your computer. Don't forget the back-up copies and place the disks in more than one safe place.

❁ Your Work ❧

By now, many of you have begun and are working with your personal BOS. Training materials and experiments are different from work and rituals. Before you continue your path, you may wish to separate these materials into two separate books. Consider what an ultimate BOS would contain. List thirteen such items. Your work is to obtain these thirteen items over the course of the next year.

On Working Indoors

"I always feel I'm not doing it right because I have to do everything indoors," said Elizabeth. It was the Fourth of July, 1994, and while the children and my husband were having a grand time with the "show" he puts on every year in the backyard, Elizabeth and I had some time to catch up on Witchie conversation. Elizabeth is the perfect dinner guest and I have her over often. She is polite, cheerful, gracious and sets a good example for my heathens, who adore her. She brings them gum. (Something I have banned from the house.)

Elizabeth is also very special to me. Unlike many of my students, she walked into our training classes cold. It was hard for her, but she stuck with it and today, is an excellent practitioner of magick and dedicated to the religion of the Craft.

"I live in an apartment and work ten hours a day," she said. "I don't have any property, not even a patch of land to enjoy where I live. In most Craft books I've read, they talk about big, outside group rituals and group magick. I have a hard time understanding how a solitary would do these things." She dropped her eyes and paused. "I also think I'm not as good as the people who work outdoors all the time because I have to do everything inside."

Modern Crafters have done a disservice to their community without realizing it. I'm guilty of it myself. We have created a mythical working Witch. You know the one—the Wise Woman in the forest, complete with her cute little cottage, her glorious beds of herbs and flowers, her midnight walks down paths lined with moonflowers that shimmer in the full moon. Every month, decked in flowing garb of black, she scurries through the beckoning forest, smiling at a gnome or two, to arrive at a huge need-fire, complete with dancing Witches, the Goddess and the God, and little animals sitting around, tapping their paws in unison to the music of the lilting panpipes. It is a Midsummer Night's Dream. And that's all it is folks, a dream. A wish of would be. Yes, it's true. Barbie Witch on Walton's Mountain is a myth. (Don't laugh too hard; the Acquisitions Manager at Llewellyn, Nancy Mostad, looks like Barbie and she's a darn good Witch to boot! So yes, Virginia, there are some gorgeous Witches. Eat your heart out!)

Seriously, though, we've got this myth about what Witches used to do. Well, how the hell do we know what they used to do? Historical accountings are far more fiction than fact. Twisted by politics or simple mistakes, there isn't much to rely on. Today's working Witch needs to trust his or her own instincts, to rely on personal intuition. We are not better or worse than those who came before us. I admire our ancestors, but we live in the here and now. We should not belittle our modern techniques or our courage.

My mother, Goddess rest her soul, ironed all the sheets and pillow cases. She ironed my father's tee shirts, his white hankies, and starched her aprons. Show me a housewife who does that today—show me a housewife who needs to do that today! Ironed sheets did not last longer or smell better. It was a requirement for the housewives of the day, nothing more. As modern working Witches, we need to question everything we do that someone else claims we should be doing. Is it necessary? If the answer is yes, fine. If the answer is no, then have the courage to trash what doesn't fit, and go forward. If you trash it and later realize you made a mistake—no big deal. Have the guts to admit you were wrong and go back and pick it up.

Back to Elizabeth and my husband's terrific fireworks. (They were great; however, he burned his finger, as usual.) Most working Witches of today do their work inside the home. Few of us are lucky enough to have large stretches of property away from prying eyes. Many, like Elizabeth, do not have access to the out-of-doors, unless they go on a day outing or set aside their vacation to go camping. I count myself lucky. I live on a corner property with a good-sized yard for living in town. Thanks to my father, who has thought of nifty ways to keep the neighbors blind with fences of ivy and canopies of morning glories and moonflowers, I have about as much privacy as an in-town person is going to have. I still couldn't prance stark naked in my backyard, but I consider my clothes as important as my skin. I'm not missing anything. From my front porch, I can see the Appalachian mountains. I tell the family, "When they build so I can't see those mountains—then, and only then, will I know it's time to move." I am as connected to my land as I am to my children.

But, I prefer working indoors.

It isn't that I don't like it outside, but it is far more convenient inside. The nature of my life flows with my family and the people who come to see me for help. The most powerful place on my property is my dining room. Here, rituals are held, open circles are conducted, training classes run smoothly (we are closer to the bathroom, for pentacle's sake), healings are done in comfort, readings are conducted with firm support to the back (namely, my dining room chairs), and coffee is drunk by the gallons as Witchie conversation flows faster than my Bunn coffee maker.

The next time someone tries to tell you that you aren't part of the "in-Witchie-crowd" because you don't work outdoors, smile your most intriguing smile and say, "Oh, I thought all Witches worked between the worlds, didn't you?"

When you don't have what it says, work with what you have. This is where your personal study comes in. If you have been solid in your work, then you can build using both logic and intuition in a magickal emergency and in everyday life. We don't all have the money to buy the props, oils, gems, herbs and other things that the books list. I have received countless letters from people who say, "I don't have the money to buy such-in-such," or "There isn't any store near where I live that can supply me with the ingredients you list on page 242 of your book, therefore I can't practice the Craft properly." Wrong. As much as I admire and respect the modern Craft movement, there was magick and ritual before Gerald Gardner, uncrossing oil, or green cat candles.

In the first book of this series, *To Ride a Silver Broomstick,* I showed you how to play with all kinds of neat Craft toys that are part of modern Wicca, then sent you off on your own. In this volume, you learned the advantages of natural magick and ritual and how to make it work for you, without a dime in your pocket.

❀ Your Work ❧

In a quiet place and in a quiet hour, list both your positive and negative traits. Be honest! Pick one negative trait that needs improvement or an overhaul. Consider the ways you can do this from affirmations, study, manual work, check-points in your personal behavior, etc. Map out a plan on how you will remove this trait from your personality and begin to work on it. Choose one positive trait from the list and consider how you can enhance it—continued study, contacting others for advanced information, spending time on a particular talent that you have not used for a long time, etc. How could this positive trait equalize a negative one?

Brooming It

Well, that's it. This installment of life with Silver is done. I'd like to take a moment and thank all the wonderful people who have written to me and thanked me for the help my books have given them. I'd like to say thank you to the men and women of the Black Forest Clan, who read either all or parts of this book and have given suggestions on how to make it better for you. Again, I'd like to thank my family for bearing with me while my face gazed eagerly into the cathode ray tube and my behind became rooted to my old orange typing chair.

Most of all, I'd like to say thank-you to you, dear Witch reader. You, who cuddled under covers past midnight reading this book or who bravely carried it on the subway to catch a paragraph or two. You who balanced a candle in one hand, and the book in another, while trying to conjure harmony in your life. To you, who shoved the book under the sofa when the in-laws came to call, and you who paced the bookstore looking for the right book, and chose this one. Late at night, I wonder what you all are doing, if things are working out for you; if the lessons herein have helped. I too pace the bookstores, thinking of the thousands of writers and the millions of readers, and wonder how the Universe manages to put us together. But it does, and that's another Wiccan mystery I'm thankful for.

Blessings upon you, my dear reader.
Merry meet and merry part,
Until we merry meet again.

The Witches Anti-Discrimination Lobby

26 years and still brooming...

Silver RavenWolf
Black Forest Publishing
P.O. Box 1392
Department WADL
Mechanicsburg, PA 17055-1392

Membership in WADL is granted in recognition of what you have done to fight anti-Craft, anti-alternative religion bias. WADL exists primarily to fight defamation, discrimination, distortion, and dishonest stereotyping of who and what Witches and other magickal community members are. It takes very little time and the cost of one stamp to write a letter of protest.

Membership in WADL is based on deeds. Your positive, non-violent actions in defense of the Craft or any other positive, alternative religion make you a member. To join, write to the above address and request an application form. Be sure to include a stamped self-addressed legal-sized envelope. Processing feel for your application is $5.00. Make a check or money order out to Black Forest Publishing.

What we expect from WADL members:

1. **Be a Media Watcher.** Clip any offensive letters/articles and mail them to WADL Headquarters. Encourage your broom-closet friends to help you

watch for discriminatory information. Be sure to include the name and address of the offending party. For example, if you find a write-up in the daily news, please give us the name of the reporter, editor, and the address and phone number of the newspaper.

2. **WADL staff may contact you for further information or, if they are sponsoring a letter-writing campaign, may ask you for assistance.** If you would like to be a coordinator for your state, please indicate this on your application. When WADL receives a discrimination complaint in your state, the information will be sent to a coordinator. This person will be responsible for conducting any written inquiries and reporting back to Headquarters. If the position of coordinator appeals to you, be advised that we will need your phone number.

How to seek assistance from WADL if you experience discrimination:

1. **Write to Black Forest Publishing, PO Box 1392, Department WADL, Mechanicsburg, PA 17055-1392 and ask for a blank discrimination report.** Include a legal-sized stamped self-addressed envelope. Do not outline the problem in your initial request. Wait for the form. WADL staff will not act without the appropriate documentation.

2. **When you receive the discrimination report, answer every question, including your phone number.** Return to us with a legal-sized stamped self-addressed envelope. Remember, lodging a complaint is not a frivolous endeavor and we must have all the pertinent facts before we move.

What WADL will not handle:

1. Any case involving criminal actions on the part of the Witch or alternative magickal individual.

2. Any case where an individual is fired from their employment due to:
   Theft
   Violence
   Absenteeism
   Alcohol or drug abuse
   Poor performance

3. Any custody case where the magickal individual is accused of abuse, prostitution, violence, alcohol or drug abuse, or neglect, or has been accused of any criminal act.

Please Note: You will not receive a response to your letter unless you remember to enclose a legal-sized stamped, self-addressed envelope.

The International Wiccan/Pagan Press Alliance

Greetings from the International Wiccan/Pagan Press Alliance. We love to hear from anyone interested in the wide array of positive magick and positive alternative religions. *Please remember to supply a legal-sized self-addressed stamped envelope for all future correspondence to us or members.*

The History of the WPPA

Our publishing venture began in 1984. Most newsletters back then were done on home typewriters. Few of us owned computers and only a handful of presses actually dealt with a printer of any sort. Silver saw a need for networking between the various newsletter publishers, a way to communicate with each other, share information, and learn more about the magickal community in general. Since then, the WPPA has grown by leaps and bounds, encompassing all members of the community. The year 1996 marks our twelfth year in publishing and we are proud to have weathered the storm of Pagan publishing.

With the advent of Silver's book *To Ride a Silver Broomstick,* popularity of the WPPA and press members of the WPPA jumped fantastically. We can thank Llewellyn Worldwide enough for promoting the WPPA and allowing the networking section to appear in the book. They also permit this section to be updated with each printing, allowing new press members of the WPPA to be included. Silver has always believed in sharing success and has supported magickal writers, presses, and reporters in their many ventures.

Join the WPPA and we guarantee your money back if you are disappointed in the information you receive. In our monthly newsletter, the *Mid-Night Drive,* you will learn all about the different newsletters and journals available to you, discrimination cases that are important, and news that is interesting to a magickal a person. If you like to write, you will find loads of information on how to approach both small press editors and major publishers. Yearly subscriptions are $18.00 USA, $24.00 Canada, $27.00 Overseas.

The WPPA represents Pagan publishing designed specifically for the magickal person. You don't have to feel out in the cold anymore.

Black Forest Publishing
WPPA
P.O. Box 1392
Mechanicsburg, PA 17055-1392 USA

Guide to Pagan Newsletters and Services

Alternate Perceptions
Eagle Wing Books, Inc.
P.O. Box 9972
Memphis, TN 38190

Azrael Project
Newsletter, The
(Gothic, Macabre)
5219 Magazine St.
New Orleans, LA 70115

Bats 'n Bellfire
P.O. Box 20368
Las Vegas, NV
89112–2368

Calendar of Events for
DC, MD & VA
Vision Weavers
P.O. Box 3653
Farfax, VA 22038–0653

Calendar of Events
(National)
890 Alhambra Rd.
Cleveland, OH
44110–3179

Celtic Connection
P.O. Box 177
Curtain, OR 97428

Church of Iron
Oak/Voice of Anvil
(ATC affiliated)
P.O. Box 060672
Palm Bay, FL 32906

Council of the
Magickal Arts
P.O. Box 6756
Abilene, TX
79608–6756

Connections
1705–14th St., #181
Boulder, CO 80302

Craft/Crafts
P.O. Box 441
Ponderay, ID 83852

Crow's Cause
P.O. Box 8281
Roseville, MI 48066

Dear Brutus Press
Apartado 36 Coban,
Alta Verapaz,
Guatemala

Divine Circle of the
Sacred Grove
(Druid, Wiccan)
16845 N. 29th Ave.,#1346
Phoenix, AZ 85023

Goddess Journal
450 Hibbs Ave.
Glenolden, PA 19036

Green Man, The (Men)
P.O. Box 641
Point Arena, CA 95468

Hawthorne Spinner, The
P.O. Box 706
Monticello, NY 12701

Hermit's Lantern, The
9724–132nd Ave. NE
Kirkland, WA 98033

Hole in the Stone
Journal
3595 W. Union Ave.
Englewood, CO
80110–5215

How About Magick
(HAM)
(For children)
P.O. Box 624
Lakewood, OH 44107

International Red
Garters
c/o N.W.C. (British
traditional)
P.O. Box 162046
Sacramento, CA 95816

Keltria (Druid)
630 N. Sepulveda
Blvd., Suite 909
El Segundo, CA 55433

Leaves (Celtic)
Temple of Danaan
P.O. Box 765
Hanover, IN 47243

Magick Words
3936 S. Semoran Blvd.,
Suite 433
Orlando, Fl 32822

Moonbeams Journal
P.O. Box 6921
Colombia, MO
65205–6921

Moonlight & Memories
4 Spring Lane
Framingham, MA
01701

New Dawn
Publishing Co.
608 Huntington St.
Watertown, NY 13601

New Moon Rising
P.O. Box 1731
Medford, OR
97501–0135

Notes From Taychopera
P.O. Box 8212
Madison, WI 53708

Oak Leaf
P.O. Box 1137
Bryn Mawr, PA 19010

Of a Like Mind
(Womyn centered)
P.O. Box 6530
Madison, WI 53716

Our Pagan Times
P.O. Box 1471
Madison Square Station
New York, NY
10159–1449

OWW—Of Writers and
Witches
c/o WPPA
P.O. Box 1392
Mechanicsburg, PA
17065–1392

Pagan Dawn
BM 7097
London, England WC1
N3XX
United Kingdom

Pagan Educational
Network
P.O. Box 1364
Bloomington, IN
47402–1364

PagaNet News
P.O. Box 61054
Virginia Beach, VA
23466–1054

Pagans For Peace
P.O. Box 2205
Clearbrook, BC V2T
3X8
Canada

Panegyria
(Aquarian Tabernacle
Church)
P.O. Box 57
Index, WA 98256–0409

Phases—Temple of
the Triple Goddess
7625 N. 19th Ave., #121
Phoenix, AZ 85021

Phoenix Publishing
David Brown, Publicist
P.O. Box 10
Custer, WA 98240

Sacred Earth Journal
193 Sugarwood Rd.
Plainfield, VT 05667

Silver Pentagram, The
P.O. Box 9776
Pittsburgh, PA 15229

Unicorn, The
9724 132nd Ave. NE
Kirkland, WA 98033

SageWoman
(Womyn centered)
P.O. Box 641
Point Arena, CA 95468

Terminal Journal
60 E. Chestnut St., #236
Chicago, IL
60611–2012

Upper Group
RR2, Box 2574A
Harrison, ME
04040–9455

Seeker, The
P.O. Box 3326
Ann Arbor, MI 48106

Silver Chalice
P.O. Box 196
Thorofare, NJ 08086

Thoughts
3 The Pines, 100 Bain
Ave.
Riverdale, Toronto,
Ontario M4K 1E8
Canada

Wanderer's Network,
The
P.O. Box 1583
Clovis, NM 88102

Occult Supplies

The Sacred Grove Apothecary
1605 N. 7th Ave.
Phoenix, AZ 85007
(Enclose $5.00 for catalog—great medicinal and magickal selection—DSG is a
member of the Black Forest Family)

Crossroads Metaphysical Bookstore & Coffee House
224 Howard Ave.
Houma, LA 70363
Crossroads serves Wiccan and Santerian customers. Herbs, powders, oils, candles—the staff will burn candles for you or prepare a special candle tailored to
your personal needs. Catalog available for $5.00.

Morganna's Chamber
242 W. 10th St.
New York, NY 10014
Morganna has unique and unusual stock. Be sure to visit her when you tour
the Big Apple! Morganna is a member of the Black Forest Family.

Magus Books
1316 SE 4th St.
Minneapolis, MN 55414
1-800-99MAGUS
They can find any unusual book you are looking for. Also, Magus Books will help
you put up your web page and can host your web page. They are fantastic in
helping you get your own domain name and can answer technical questions.

Mansions of the Moon
1215 S. Main
Old Forge, PA
(717) 457-STAR

Don't miss out on this great store. Vinnie has both Wiccan and Santerian products. He will also burn candles for you or prepare special candles for your personal needs. Vinnie has an event-oriented store and authors visit regularly.

The Electronic Pagan Highway

ADF (Ar nDraiocht Fein): kithoward@delphi.com
AMER: C24884CC@wuvmd. wust1.edu
Aquarian Tabernacle Church: AquaTabCh@aol.com
Charleston Area Pagan Alliance: capaganNet@aol.com
Children of the Moon: Yugal@aol.com
Church of Iron Oak: IronOak@aol.com
Connections: Rwoodsong@aol.com
Covenant of the Goddess: cogfirst@aol.com
Fancifiaraon Church of Wicca: wicans@aol.com
Green Egg: cawnemeton@aol.com
Hecate's Loom: un837@freenet.victoria.bc.ca
Intuitive Explorations: BRST18A@Prodigy.com
Keltria: keltria@aol.com
Military Pagan Network: jmachate@aol.com
Mnemoysne's Scroll: TheScroll@aol.com
OBOD (Order of Bards, Ovates, and Druids): oaktreepress@e-world.com
Pagan Muse and World Report: PMandWR@aol.com
Pan Pacific Pagan Alliance: wyrd@ozemail.com.au
Silver RavenWolf: SilverRwlf@aol.com
Temple of Danann: danann1@aol.com
Witches Brew: witchsbrw@aol.com

A Wicca 101 Test

You are about to embark on a question odyssey. In the Black Forest Clan, you must receive a 97% on this test to obtain your Wicca 101 teaching degree. Be careful; there are several trick questions on this test. Some of the questions are simply designed to make you smile, but you must answer them correctly anyway.

Please do not send Silver RavenWolf your completed test. Look up the answers in this book (and others) and see if your ideas were correct. Hint: You will find many answers in *To Ride a Silver Broomstick.* (Special thanks to MaraKay Rogers who helped me design the original, smaller version of this examination.)

Helpful Hints

1. Read each question carefully.
2. Take your time. If you don't know an answer, skip it and come back to it later.
3. There are a few multiple part questions, where you must answer several parts. Be sure not to miss any parts of a question or they will be marked entirely wrong.
4. Write your answers on a separate sheet of paper.

The Black Forest Wicca 101 Test

Name: _____   Date: _____

1. What is the definition of Witchcraft?
2. What is the definition of magick?
3. What is a traditional Witch?
4. What is an eclectic Witch?
5. What is a solitary Witch?
6. Explain the history of Strega Witchcraft:
7. Explain the history of Gardnerian Witchcraft:
8. Explain the history of Alexandrian Witchcraft:
9. What is a Dianic Witch?
10. What is a kitchen Witch?
11. What is a British Traditional Witch?
12. What is a Black Forest Witch?
13. Who is Raymond Buckland? What is his contribution to modern Witchcraft?
14. Who is Z. Budepest? What is her contribution to the Craft?
15. Who is L. Cabot?
16. Who is Starhawk?
17. Name five books you would use to teach Wicca 101.

True or False
(If the answer is false, give the correct definition)
18. BOS means Bullshit Of Science.
19. Familiar means how close you get to the High Priestess.
20. Skyclad means wearing a blue robe.
21. An elder is a tree.
22. Pentacle means the top of the degree scale.
23. Drawing Down the Moon is the process of using paper magick and illustration.

24. List all the Sabbats and their approximate dates:
    A. _____ celebrated on _____
    B. _____ celebrated on _____
    C. _____ celebrated on _____
    D. _____ celebrated on _____
    E. _____ celebrated on _____

F. _____ celebrated on _____
G. _____ celebrated on _____
H. _____ celebrated on _____

25. Explain "Pantheon."
26. Give the various purposes for a magickal name.
27. What is an affirmation?
28. Write an affirmation.
29. What does "hive" mean?
30. What is the difference between a stang and a staff?
31. What is the purpose of the altar?
32. What is creative visualization?
33. What is the difference between sacred space and a magick circle?
34. Name the five elements, their directions, and their elementals.
35. How do you make holy water AND what is it used for?
36. Outline the steps for a spell AND List all the supplies AND tell when it should be performed (including day, time, phase of moon, etc.) AND give the complete directions.
37. Write a cleansing and consecrating invocation.
38. Define the following AND explain the significance of each to the Craft individual:
    A. Broom
    B. Chalice
    C. Wand
    D. Cauldron
    E. Sword
    F. Bolline
    G. Scourge
39. What is a magickal journal?
40. What is compass point magick?
41. What are minor magicks?
42. List five minor magicks.
43. What can minor magicks be used for?
44. Name ten gems and give a magickal definition of each.
45. Name ten herbs and give a magickal definition of each.
46. Name ten deities (male or female) and explain their archetypical meaning.
47. What is the chakra system?
48. How many chakras are there?
49. Where are the chakras placed? (Show by diagramming)

50. What is graphology?

51. List what goes in a BOS.

52. Name a system of divination AND explain its basic rules and how it operates.

53. Write a self-blessing.

54. How do you dress a candle to bring something toward you? (include diagram)

55. How do you dress a candle to send something away from you? (include diagram)

56. What is the Summerland?

57. Explain reincarnation.

58. Explain karma.

59. Give one example of bending time.

60. Explain the following sentence: The Witch is the magick.

61. Write the Rule of Three.

62. Write the Witches Rede.

63. List each of the cards of the Major Arcana and give their brief meanings.

64. Why do you call the quarters?

65. How do you call the quarters?

66. Why do you cast a circle?

67. How do you cast a circle?

68. How do you draw a circle?

69. How do you Draw Down the Moon?

True or False
(If the answer is false, give the correct definition)

70. A poppet is a flower.

71. A chaplet is a sacred space.

72. Sybil Leek is the founder of Dianic Wicca.

73. The center of any circle is where the Witch is.

74. If you don't know where the directions are, you can pick them by intention.

75. A binding spell should always be done at a handfasting.

76. Only a female can Draw Down the Moon.

77. Only a male can strap on the sword.

78. Every time you have a gripe, you call the High Priestess.

79. A wolverine is a renegade coven.

80. Witches can have rosaries.
81. A cord spell involves musical instruments.
82. Cakes and ale are served at the beginning of a ritual.
83. The eightfold kiss is when you kiss the person next to you every time you fold the altar cloth.
84. Illuminator candles are absolutely necessary in ritual.
85. You must annoint all who come into the magick circle.
86. A Witch must make a Witch for a Witch to be valid.

87. Name the aspects of the Triple Goddess AND explain them.
88. Match the following candle colors to their magickal meanings:

Red _____

A. Good fortune, opening blocked communication, wisdom, protection, spiritual inspiration, calm, reassurance, water, creativity

Orange _____

B. Spirituality, the Goddess, peace, higher self, purity, virginity

Gold _____

C. Influence, friendships, special favors

Blue _____

D. Influencing people in high places, third eyes, psychic ability, spiritual power, self assurance, hidden knowledge

Green _____

E. Energy, strength, passion, courage, element of fire, fast action, lust, driving force, love, survival

Blue _____

F. The sun, intelligence, accelerated learning, memory, breaking mental blocks, selling yourself

Purple _____

G. Earth Mother, physical healing, monetary success, abundance, fertility, growth, personal goals

Silver _____

H. Protection, repelling negativity, binding, shapeshifting

Black _____

I. Business goals, property deals, career, ambition, justice, legal matters, action

Brown _____

J. Telepathy, clairvoyance, clairaudience, psychometry, intuition, dreams, astral energies, female power, communication, the Goddess

White _____

K. Wealth, the God, promote winning, safety, winning, happiness

What candle color do you NEVER use for magick?

89. Who is Doreen Valiente?

90. What is ritual clothing?

91. How does a person "raise energy"?

92. There are eight phases of the moon, which are given below. Explain when they occur AND their magickal applications:
    A. Balsamic (dark moon)
    B. Full moon
    C. First quarter
    D. Disseminating
    E. New moon
    F. Crescent
    G. Gibbous
    H. Last quarter

93. Name the twelve astrological signs and when they occur during the year.

94. What is a medicine bag?

95. Are Witches considered Shamans? Explain your answer.

96. What does the nine of cups stand for in the Tarot deck?

97. What are the Principles of Belief, who wrote them AND in what year?

98. What is meditation used for?

99. Explain the God.

100. Explain the Goddess.

101. Draw two pentagrams, and add arrows to show the invoking and the banishing.

102. What is auric healing?

103. What is an Esbat?

104. What is a Sabbat?

105. What is the descent of the Goddess?

True or False
(If the answer is false, give the correct definition)

106. Totem animals are vegetables.

107. An inverted pentagram is a sign of Satanism.

108. A talisman is the name for a poet.

109. Warding is binding magick.

110. To Know, To Dare, To Will, and To Be Silent are called "The Witches Pyramid."

111. A secret way to tell someone you are in the Craft is to cut an apple in half.

112. Blood of the moon is when the moon is red.

113. A Witch can't heal unless she/he can harm.

114. Runes should be used as a magickal alphabet.

115. Grounding is when you gather earth to put on the altar.

116. What does "ground and center" mean AND when should it be done?

117. What is shapeshifting?

118. What is an OBE?

119. How many Witches does it take to screw in a light bulb?

120. Match the planet to the day AND give the symbol:
    Sunday   _____   A. Mars
    Monday   _____   B. Saturn
    Tuesday   _____   C. Venus
    Wednesday   _____   D. Sun
    Thursday   _____   E. Moon
    Friday   _____   F. Mercury
    Saturday   _____   G. Jupiter

121. Give the Element for each day:
    Sunday
    Monday
    Tuesday
    Wednesday
    Thursday
    Friday
    Saturday

122. Explain invoking and evoking.

123. Explain aspecting.

124. Write a generic ritual outline.

125. Do Witches pray?

126. Write a ritual format to empower a talisman.

127. Write a ritual outline to catch a criminal. Include deity chosen and why.

128. Name the three aspects of the God and what they stand for.

129. What is the magickal reason that Witches do not use an unequal-armed cross in their work?

130. What does the spiral stand for?

131. What is the new chakra vortex? (Hint: its color is pink)

132. Explain how the practice of hypnotherapy may be helpful to a Witch.

133. What are the name of the four types of brainwaves? In which type of wave is meditation begun? In which type of wave do most "visions" occur?

134. What does the six-rayed star stand for in the Lesser Banishing Ritual?

135. What is an altar devotion? Write a short one.

136. Write three brief devotional hour prayers.

137. What is a salute?

138. What is the difference between summoning, stirring, and calling when discussing quarter energies? Who do you summon? Who do you stir? Who do you call?

139. Draw and name the symbols of the elements.

140. Name the four angels and the quarter each represents.

141. Name the colors of the four winds.

142. What is the Lesser Banishing Ritual?

143. Do Witches believe in guardian angels? Why or why not?

144. Why do spells usually rhyme?

145. What is a sigil? List two ways in which it could be used.

146. What is the difference between a charm and a spell?

147. What does moon void of course mean?

148. Name the five major asteroids and their energy associations.

149. Why do we cast a natal chart?

150. What does "As Above, So Below" mean?

151. What is a "thoughtform"?

152. Is Michael a Chaldean prince, predating both Christianity and Judaism, or is he an Archangel?

153. What is the fastest way to break a hex?

154. What does "A Witch cannot heal if he/she cannot hex" mean?

155. Name the four anti-discrimination Craft organizations in the United States today.

156. What is the first thing you should do, should you be faced with discrimination because of your religion? (I'll give you the answer to this one: call an attorney).

157. What is the Key of Solomon the King?

158. What are planetary hours and how are they used?

Bonus Question

What does "fault of the sword" mean?

Magickal Symbols[1]

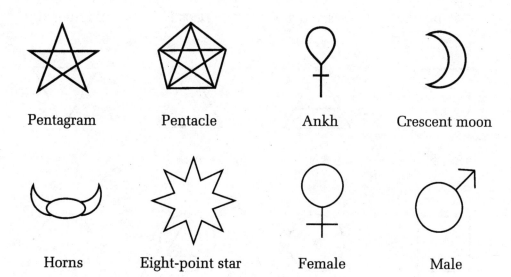

Pentagram	Pentacle	Ankh	Crescent moon
Horns	Eight-point star	Female	Male

---

1. *Living Wicca* by Scott Cunningham, Llewellyn Publications, 1993.

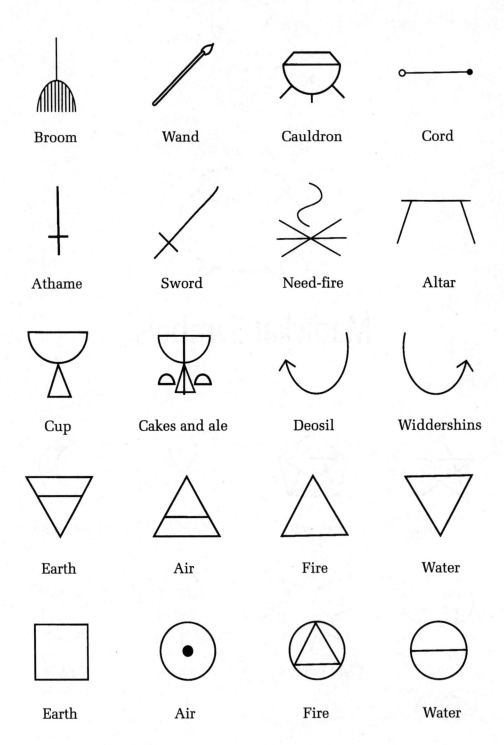

Broom   Wand   Cauldron   Cord

Athame   Sword   Need-fire   Altar

Cup   Cakes and ale   Deosil   Widdershins

Earth   Air   Fire   Water

Earth   Air   Fire   Water

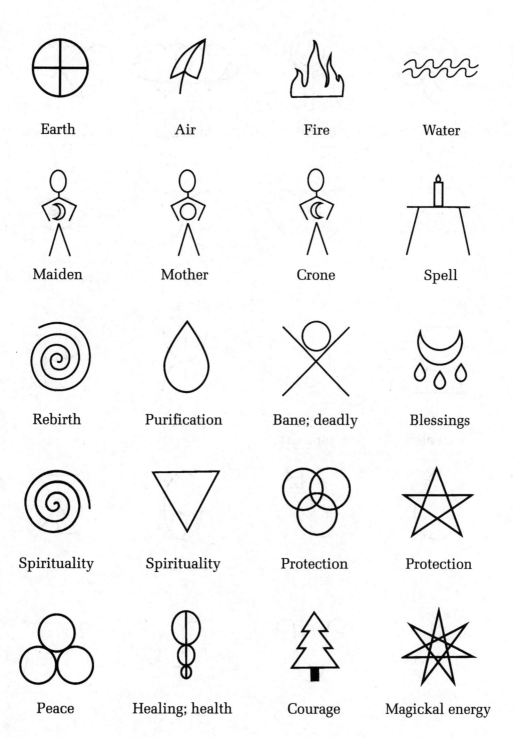

Earth	Air	Fire	Water
Maiden	Mother	Crone	Spell
Rebirth	Purification	Bane; deadly	Blessings
Spirituality	Spirituality	Protection	Protection
Peace	Healing; health	Courage	Magickal energy

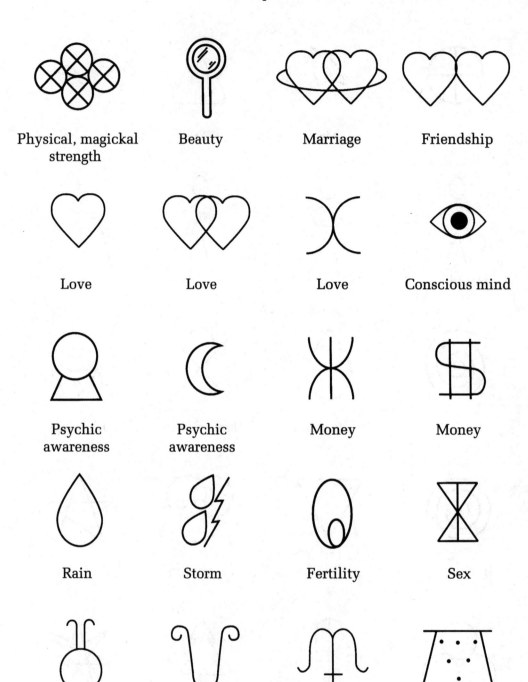

Physical, magickal strength

Beauty

Marriage

Friendship

Love

Love

Love

Conscious mind

Psychic awareness

Psychic awareness

Money

Money

Rain

Storm

Fertility

Sex

Spring

Summer

Autumn

Winter

Suggested Reading List

For the Dedicant

Illusions by Richard Bach

Wicca: A Guide for the Solitary Practitioner by Scott Cunningham (Llewellyn)

To Ride a Silver Broomstick by Silver RavenWolf (Llewellyn)

The Meaning of WitchCraft by Gerald Gardner (Magickal Childe)

The Kybalion by Three Initiates (Yogi Publication Society)

The Rebirth of WitchCraft by Doreen Valiente (Phoenix)

The Truth About WitchCraft Today by Scott Cunningham (Llewellyn)

The Wheel of the Year by Pauline and Dan Campanelli (Llewellyn)

Ancient Ways by Pauline and Dan Campanellis (Llewellyn)

The Spiral Dance by Starhawk (Harper & Row)

What Witches Do by Janet and Stewart Farrar (Phoenix)

The Life and Times of a Modern Witch by Janet and Stewart Farrar

Drawing Down the Moon by Margot Adler (Beacon Press)

Lammas Night (fiction) by Katherine Kurtz

Jude's Herbal Home Remedies by Jude C. Williams, MH (Llewellyn)

Level I Study

Modern Magick by Donald Michael Kraig (Llewellyn)

Practical Celtic Magick by Murray Hope

Earth Magic by Marion Weinstein (Phoenix)

Holy Book of Women's Mysteries by Z. Budapest (Harper & Collier)

The Sea Priestess (fiction) by Dion Fortune

Psychic Self-Defense by Dion Fortune (Weiser)

The Llewellyn Practical Guide to Psychic Self-Defense and Well-Being by Melita Denning and Osborne Phillips (Llewellyn)

Charms, Spells and Formulas by Ray Malbrough (Llewellyn)

Practical Candleburning Rituals by Raymond Buckland (Llewellyn)

A Quiet Strength by Wayne Kritssberg, et. al. (Bantam)

Flying Without a Broom by D.J. Conway (Llewellyn)

The Healing Herbs by Michael Castleman (Rodale Press)

Foundations of Practical Magic by Israel Regardie (Aquarian Press)

Maiden, Mother, Crone by D.J. Conway (Llewellyn)

Level II Study

The Witches' Bible by Janet and Stewart Farrar (Magickal Childe)

The God of the Witches by Margaret Murray

Moon Magic (fiction) by Dione Fortune

The Witches' Goddess by Janet and Stewart Farrar (Phoenix)

The Witches' God by Janet and Stewart Farrar (Phoenix)

The Key of Solomon the King by S. Liddell MacGregor Mathers (Weiser)

Living Wicca by Scott Cunningham (Llewellyn)

Magickal Rites from the Crystal Well by Ed Fitch (Llewellyn)

Spells and How They Work by Janet and Stewart Farrar (Phoenix)

Wild Witches Don't Get the Blues by Ffiona Morgan (Daughters of the Moon)

The Alex Sanders Lectures by Alex Sanders

The Western Mystery Tradition by Christine Hartley

Witchcraft for Tomorrow by Doreen Valiente (Phoenix)

Earth Power by Scott Cunningham (Llewellyn)

A Book of Pagan Rituals by Herman Slater (Weiser)

Casting the Circle by Diane Stein (Crossing Press)

Earth, Air, Fire and Water by Scott Cunningham (Llewellyn)

When God Was a Woman by Merlin Stone

The Goat Foot God (fiction) by Dion Fortune

Magick in Theory and Practice by Aleister Crowley

Seasonal Dance by Janice Broch and Veronica MacLer (Weiser)

Just for Solitaries

Wicca: A Guide for the Solitary Practitioner by Scott Cunningham (Llewellyn)

To Ride a Silver Broomstick by Silver RavenWolf (Llewellyn)

A Witch Alone by Marian Green (Aquarian)

Of Witches by Janet Thompson (Weiser)

Living Wicca by Scott Cunningham (Llewellyn)

Just for Families

The Family Wicca Book by Ashleen O'Gaea (Llewellyn)

The Pagan Family by Ceisiwr Serith (Llewellyn)

WiccaCraft for Families by Margie McArthur (Phoenix)

Bibliography

Leek, Sybil. *The Complete Art of WitchCraft*. Signet, 1971.

Fortune, Dion. *Psychic Self-Defense*. Weiser (1930), 1993.

Budapest, Zsuzsanna. *The Goddess in the Office*. Harper and Row, 1993.

Cabot, Laurie. *Power of the Witch*. Dell Publishing, 1989.

Valiente, Doreen. *An ABC of Witchcraft*. Phoenix, 1973.

Ronner, John. *Know Your Angels*. Mamre Press, 1993.

Fortune, Dion. *Psychic Self-Defense*. Samuel Weiser Publishing, 1930, 1993.

Kraig, Donald Michael. *Modern Magick*. Llewellyn Publications, 1990.

Sanders, Alex. *The Alex Sanders Lectures*. Magickal Childe Publishing, 1989.

Valiente, Doreen. *Witchcraft for Tomorrow*. Phoenix, 1978.

RavenWolf, Silver. *To Ride a Silver Broomstick*. Llewellyn Publications, 1993.

Thompson, Janet. *Of Witches*. Samuel Weiser Publishing, 1993.

Index

☽ LOOK FOR THE CRESCENT MOON

Llewellyn publishes hundreds of books on your favorite subjects! To get these exciting books, including the ones on the following pages, check your local bookstore or order them directly from Llewellyn.

ORDER BY PHONE

- Call toll-free within the U.S. and Canada, 1-800-THE MOON
- In Minnesota, call (651) 291-1970
- We accept VISA, MasterCard, and American Express

ORDER BY MAIL

- Send the full price of your order (MN residents add 7% sales tax) in U.S. funds, plus postage & handling to:

  Llewellyn Worldwide
  P.O. Box 64383, Dept. K424-3
  St. Paul, MN 55164–0383, U.S.A.

POSTAGE & HANDLING

(For the U.S., Canada, and Mexico)

- $4.00 for orders $15.00 and under
- $5.00 for orders over $15.00
- No charge for orders over $100.00

We ship UPS in the continental United States. We ship standard mail to P.O. boxes. Orders shipped to Alaska, Hawaii, The Virgin Islands, and Puerto Rico are sent first-class mail. Orders shipped to Canada and Mexico are sent surface mail.

International orders: Airmail—add freight equal to price of each book to the total price of order, plus $5.00 for each non-book item (audio tapes, etc.).

Surface mail—Add $1.00 per item.

Allow 4–6 weeks for delivery on all orders.
Postage and handling rates subject to change.

DISCOUNTS

We offer a 20% discount to group leaders or agents. You must order a minimum of 5 copies of the same book to get our special quantity price.

FREE CATALOG

Get a free copy of our color catalog, *New Worlds of Mind and Spirit*. Subscribe for just $10.00 in the United States and Canada ($30.00 overseas, airmail). Many bookstores carry *New Worlds*—ask for it!

Visit our web site at www.llewellyn.com for more information.

To Ride a Silver Broomstick
New Generation Witchcraft
Silver RavenWolf

Throughout the world there is a new generation of Witches—people practicing or wishing to practice the craft on their own, without an in-the-flesh magickal support group. *To Ride a Silver Broomstick* speaks to those people, presenting them with both the science and religion of Witchcraft, allowing them to become active participants while growing at their own pace. It is ideal for anyone: male or female, young or old, those familiar with Witchcraft, and those totally new to the subject and unsure of how to get started.

Full of the author's warmth, humor and personal anecdotes, *To Ride a Silver Broomstick* leads you step-by-step through the various lessons with exercises and journal writing assignments. This is the complete Witchcraft 101, teaching you to celebrate the Sabbats, deal with coming out of the broom closet, choose a magickal name, visualize the Goddess and God, meditate, design a sacred space, acquire magickal tools, design and perform rituals, network, spell cast, perform color and candle magick, divination, healing, telepathy, psychometry, astral projection, and much, much more.

0-87542-791-X, 320 pp., 7 x 10, illus., softcover $14.95

To order, call 1-800-THE MOON
All prices subject to change without notice

To Light a Sacred Flame
Practical Witchcraft for the Millenium
Silver RavenWolf

Silver RavenWolf continues to unveil the mysteries of the Craft with *To Light a Sacred Flame*, which follows her best-selling *To Ride a Silver Broomstick* and *To Stir a Magick Cauldron* as the third in the "New Generation Witch-Craft" series, guides to magickal practices based on the personal experiences and successes of a third-degree working Witch.

Written for today's seeker, this book contains techniques that unite divinity with magick, knowledge, and humor. Not structured for any particular tradition, the lessons present unique and insightful material for the solitary as well as the group. Explore the fascinating realms of your inner power, sacred shrines, magickal formularies, spiritual housecleaning, and the intricacies of ritual. This book reveals new information that includes a complete discussion on the laws of the Craft, glamouries, and shamanic Craft rituals, including a handfasting and wiccaning (saining).

ISBN: 1-56718-721-8, 7 x 10, 320 pp.   **$14.95**

To order, call 1-800-THE MOON
All prices subject to change without notice

Teen Witch
Wicca for a New Generation
Silver RavenWolf

Teenagers and young adults comprise a growing market for books on Witchcraft and magick, yet there has never been a book written specifically for the teen seeker. Now, Silver RavenWolf, one of the most well-known Wiccans today and the mother of four young Witches, gives teens their own handbook on what it takes and what it means to be a Witch. Humorous and compassionate, *Teen Witch* gives practical advice for dealing with everyday life in a magickal way. From homework and crabby teachers to parents and dating, this book guides teens through the ups and downs of life as they move into adulthood. Spells are provided that address their specific concerns, such as the "Call Me Spell" and "The Exam Spell."

Parents will also find this book informative and useful as a discussion tool with their children. Discover the beliefs of Witchcraft, Wiccan traditions, symbols, holidays, rituals and more.

1-56718-725-0, 288 pp., 7 x 10, softcover **$12.95**

To order, call 1-800-THE MOON
All prices subject to change without notice

Beneath a Mountain Moon
A Novel by Silver RavenWolf

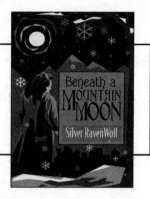

Welcome to Whiskey Springs, Pennsylvania, birthplace of magick, mayhem, and murder! The generations-old battle between two powerful occult families rages anew when young Elizabeyta Belladonna journeys from Oklahoma to the small town of Whiskey Springs—a place her family had left years before to escape the predatory Blackthorn family—to solve the mystery of her grandmother's death.

Endowed with her own magickal heritage of Scotch-Irish Witchcraft, Elizabeyta stands alone against the dark powers and twisted desires of Jason Blackthorn and his gang of Dark Men. But Elizabeyta isn't the only one pursued by unseen forces and the fallout from a past life. As Blackthorn manipulates the town's inhabitants through occult means, a great battle for mastery ensues between the forces of darkness and light—a battle that involves a crackpot preacher, a blue ghost, the town gossip, and an old country healer—and the local funeral parlor begins to overflow with victims. Is there anyone who can end the Blackthorns' reign of terror and right the cosmic balance?

1-56718-722-6, 360 pp., 6 x 9, softcover   **$15.95**

To order, call 1-800-THE MOON
All prices subject to change without notice

Angels
Companions in Magick
Silver RavenWolf

Angels do exist. These powerful forces of the Universe flow through human history, riding the currents of our pain and glory. You can call on these beings of the divine for increased knowledge, love, patience, health, wisdom, happiness and spiritual fulfillment. Always close to those in need, they bring peace and prosperity into our lives.

Here, in this complete text, you will find practical information on how to invite these angelic beings into your life. Build an angelic altar ... meet the archangels in meditation ... contact your guardian angel ... create angel sigils and talismans ... work magick with the Angelic Rosary ... talk to the deceased. You will learn to work with angels to gain personal insights and assist in the healing of the planet as well as yourself.

Angels do not belong to any particular religious structure—they are universal and open their arms to humans of all faiths, bringing love and power into people's lives.

1-56718-724-2, 304 pp., 7 x 10, illus., softcover   **$14.95**

To order, call 1-800-THE MOON
All prices subject to change without notice

Witches Runes
Cards created and illustrated by Nigel Jackson
Rune Mysteries **by Nigel Jackson**
and Silver RavenWolf

The snow-covered peaks, misty heaths, dark woods and storm-wracked seas of the Northern World were the cradle of a remarkable and bold mysticism, whose essence is concentrated in the runes. The runes are a method of communicating with divinity—the god/goddess within each of us who embodies our pure consciousness and inward spirituality.

The Witches Runes cards are rich in beautiful imagery; along with the accompanying book, they are a shortcut to the esoteric rune system. Here, old American Witchcraft and European practices meld into a contemporary evolution of the Northern magickal lore. This system is of immediate and practical use in divination, magick, and self-development. Even a little experience at casting the Witches Runes cards will soon convince you of the uncanny accuracy of their messages.

The card's images were subtly constructed to contain symbolic significance at a number of levels. This visual "unfolding" of each rune's inner mysteries within each card enables you to hear their oracular voices with greater clarity than was ever before possible except at the most advanced degrees of runic knowledge.

1-56718-553-3, Boxed set:
Book: 6 x 9, 256 pp., illus., softcover
Deck: 25 full-color cards   **$29.95**

To order, call 1-800-THE MOON
All prices subject to change without notice

Wicca
A Guide for the Solitary Practitioner
Scott Cunningham

Wicca is a book of life, and how to live magically, spiritually, and wholly attuned with Nature. It is a book of sense and common sense, not only about magick, but about religion and one of the most critical issues of today: how to achieve the much needed and wholesome relationship with our Earth. Cunningham presents Wicca as it is today: a gentle, Earth-oriented religion dedicated to the Goddess and God.

Here is a positive, practical introduction to the religion of Wicca, designed so that any interested person can learn to practice the religion alone, anywhere in the world. It presents Wicca honestly and clearly, without the pseudo-history that permeates other books. It shows that Wicca is a vital, satisfying part of twentieth-century life.

This book presents the theory and practice of Wicca from an individual's perspective. The section on the Standing Stones Book of Shadows contains solitary rituals for the Esbats and Sabbats. This book, based on the author's nearly two decades of Wiccan practice, presents an eclectic picture of various aspects of this religion. Exercises designed to develop magical proficiency, a self-dedication ritual, herb, crystal and rune magic, recipes for Sabbat feasts, are included in this excellent book.

0-87542-118-0, 240 pp., 6 x 9, illus., softcover   **$9.95**

To order, call 1-800-THE MOON
All prices subject to change without notice